ASPHALT & DIRT

Life on Two Wheels

Road Dog Publications was formed in 2010 as an imprint of Lost Classics Book Company and is dedicated to publishing the best in books on motorcycling, motorsports, and adventure travel. Visit us at www.roaddogpub.com.

ISBN 978-1-890623-53-1
Library of Congress Control Number: 2017933657

Road Dog
PUBLICATIONS

An Imprint of Lost Classics Book Company

This book also available in e-book format at online booksellers. ISBN 978-1-890623-54-8

Asphalt & Dirt

Life on Two Wheels

by

Aaron Heinrich

Road Dog Publications

Publisher

Lake Wales, Florida

This book is dedicated to my wife, Lisa, and my daughter, Larissa, whose love and support have carried us down many different roads together.

About the Author

It's no surprise that Aaron created Asphalt & Dirt (www.asphaltanddirt.com). It gratified his perpetual need to answer two of his favorite questions: "I wonder where that road goes, and what's the story here?"

Aaron is a lifelong journalist and storyteller who published his first writing at the age of twelve—a letter to the editor for his local junior high school's clean up project. The power of the written word grabbed him and fueled Aaron's desire to take his writing even further. He went on to obtain an undergraduate degree in journalism from the Walter Cronkite School of Journalism at Arizona State University and an MFA in screenwriting from the University of Southern California.

But a writing career is not where Aaron headed from there. Financial expediency sent him down the path of public relations and marketing. Since making that choice, he's worked with large global companies like Microsoft, FedEx and T-Mobile, and startups to medium-sized companies launching a literal plethora of new devices and services.

Never far away, though, was an innate curiosity for what lie just beyond the next twisty or bend in the road. After a nearly twenty-five-year hiatus, he got back on a motorcycle and proceeded to rack up mile after mile exploring the freeways, highways, and backroads of the West. Several years later, he launched the website Asphalt & Dirt as a platform for telling the stories of individual riders, regardless of what or where they rode. The stories shared in Asphalt & Dirt cover the roads traveled and lives led of interesting people from all walks of life and all parts of the world.

While Aaron continues to help companies of all sizes create and improve their brand stories, he profoundly understands what it means to share the fascinating journey of the human spirit—especially of those who are intimately one with road, wherever it may take them.

Table of Contents

In the Beginning...

Like a lot of guys, I first got started riding on a friend's dirt bike in the '70s. I think it was a Honda 250 something or other. I didn't spend a lot of time on it, but it was enough to get the "I-want-a-motorcycle" bug.

My parents weren't keen on motorcycle ownership as long as I was not a rightful adult. So not long after I turned eighteen, I bought a 1975 Honda CL360 and proceeded to ride that thing anywhere and everywhere I could.

I was living in Colorado, and the motorcycle insurance policies at the time were sold to only cover a nine-month period. They figured no sane person would be riding in December, January, and February. Who were they kidding?! I wasn't sane. I was eighteen! If the roads were dry and I could put on enough clothes, I was on that bike!

Everyone who rides usually wishes for a bigger bike. I couldn't afford one, so I'd get my bigger bike thrills whenever a friend of mine would let me borrow his Kawasaki 650. I had it up to over 100 mph once...with another guy on the back. I thought my little 360 was fun at 70; going even faster was more fun than I had a right to.

A few years later, after leaving college for a time, I enrolled at Arizona State University and moved from Colorado to Arizona. I had bought a Jeep and ended up donating my bike to some charity, and off to the desert I went.

About two years went by...or less...before I found myself on another small Honda. A roommate at the time had a 1974 Honda CJ400 that had been stuffed in his brother's back yard for a couple of years. After a new battery, some air in the tires, and five hundred dollars, the bike was mine. I sold the Jeep to pay for school and then rode that 400 all the way up until I got married five years later.

The 400 went to a charity, too, and I gave up riding. It wasn't that my wife, Lisa, told me to. It just seemed like the right thing to do. She didn't ride; had no interest in it. And we had a daughter a year after we got married. Go figure. But the desire to ride was never that far away.

As my daughter got older, she picked up on this and even made or bought me a few motorcycle items. Once in awhile, I'd go look at bikes, but that's as far as it went. Until about twenty years later...

I could say I finally said, "To hell with it, I'm getting one!" but that would only be part of it. In '07, a friend of mine, José Mallabo, and I started talking about getting bikes. So we got into a motorcycle safety class as the first step. Bam! The bug was back.

José got a bike first. He bought a brand new, bright red Ninja 650. I had Harley envy instead. I looked at some used ones but couldn't justify the price. So he and I happened to go into Arlen Ness's place near where I lived at the time and started looking at Victories. I'd read up on the bikes, knew they had a great reputation, but still wasn't sure I wanted to get back to riding by starting out on a big bike.

I spotted a bad-ass black and red Victory Hammer and asked to take it for a spin. The salesman—a diminutive guy named Chuck who probably stood all of 5'2" and weighed

130 pounds, wet—wheeled it out, put me on it, started it up and said, "Now ride it like you stole it!"

After all of about fifteen minutes, I came back and said, "To hell with it, I'm getting a big bike!"

Meanwhile, José was checking out other bikes on the floor and had spotted a 2003 Victory TC that only had about 7,000 miles on it. For anyone who doesn't know that bike, it was basically Victory's version of a Harley Road King with hard bags, instead of leather. It had everything I wanted—and it was the right color—red!

So that's the bike I bought. I named it "Big Red" and rode that bike for over 25,000 miles in over four years, before trading it in on a brand new 2012 Victory Cross Country.

Since getting back into riding, I've ridden all over California and throughout Arizona, Nevada, Oregon, Washington, and even around Vancouver Island, amounting to probably more than 50,000 miles in a little more than eight years. Not huge numbers by some standards, but more than many people I know who own bikes and barely ride.

But riding alone wasn't enough for me. I wanted to find a way to really immerse myself in the business, the culture, and the people. I didn't have the money or the experience to start a dealership. I didn't want to move to Wisconsin or Minnesota to work for the two big American makers. So one day, I realized that I could combine my writing and PR background with my passion for motorcycles and start an online magazine.

I didn't want to compete with the established motorcycle pubs like *Cycle World* or *Motorcyclist*, or with the custom bike pubs like *Bagger World*. I was more interested in the people who rode, built, and sold bikes and in conveying the idea that most people who ride are regular men and women who would rather ride on two wheels than drive four.

Thus was born *Asphalt & Dirt* which was launched in October 2014.

Initially, I thought publishing once a week wouldn't be too bad, but I quickly realized that was asking too much.

I had seven sections to fill, including the most involved, which was the one profiling the individual riders. So after a few months of that, I changed it to publishing every two weeks, which I did for nearly eighteen months.

During that time, I started to see that I was being introduced to more and more interesting people. Former racers, Hollywood actors, industry insiders, and current land-speed record holders, as well as mostly average people who were doing interesting things on or with motorcycles. One of those people was Mike Fitterling, who owned the publishing company that produced this book.

As he and I got to know one another, I approached him with the idea of turning those profiles into a book, and now you're reading the results of that collaboration.

In hindsight, I could not have foreseen where *Asphalt & Dirt* would lead me. I threw a leg over the idea and let it take me wherever that route would go. I never made a dime directly off of the website, it just never seemed right. But it led to paid writing gigs for *Gizmag* (now *New Atlas*) and Triumph's *For the Ride*. I've ridden a fair share of new bikes, and gone to the Sturgis Rally thanks to Indian. But more importantly, I've met some incredible people, whose lives were far more interesting than mine.

I don't believe this book spells the last of it, though. There's still plenty of gas left in this idea. And as far as what's next? I'm not sure. I'll just have to ride it out and see where it goes. Until then, if you ride, maybe this book will inspire you to create your own adventure. If you don't ride, maybe you'll be inspired to start. After all, there are millions of miles and the stories to go with them. Yours could be one of them.

Some riders have a story or two to tell. Joe Distefano has enough to last a lifetime.

Meet Joe D

Here's what's going to happen when Joe Distefano eventually dies and goes to heaven. (Joe may disagree with me on the destination, but I think he's got a pretty good chance of going up and not down.) The angel Gabriel is going to look at Joe, and Joe's going to stand there, waiting, maybe a little impatiently. He might live in Kansas City, but he grew up in Boston, and Bostonians aren't known for their patience.

Gabriel's going to ask him, "So Joseph, what brings you here and why do you think this is the place for you to spend eternity?"

And Joe's going to say, "How much time ya got?"

See Joe's a talker, a story teller, a man who's lived a few lives in the time most spend barely living one, and he has something to say about each of them. Like the time he spent learning how to work on cars at the local garage in his neighborhood. The years spent as a young teen riding a small dirt bike around the fields near his neighborhood. Barely graduating from high school. His first Harley. College. Teaching. Working for many of the most well-known companies in the motorcycle parts and accessories business.

His initial foray into wrestling. His marriage, divorce, kids… it's a long, list.

So to get to the essence of Joe D let's start at the beginning, or close to it.

"I had a great childhood. Dad was a doctor; my mom was a housewife. We lived in Franklin, Massachusetts, a small town outside Boston, and the first time I rode anything was a mini-bike in 1970. I was thirteen, went to a friend's house, and he let me take it for a spin on this little dirt track he had in his back yard. Man, that was pretty thrilling."

That thrill ride of sorts turned into a passion for dirt bikes. Joe bought any dirt bike magazine he could get his hands on. Then he honed in on trying to figure out how to get a Honda 70—a bike you could literally put into the trunk of a car.

His dad picked up on Joe's newfound interest, so he took him to Bernardi Honda in nearby Natick. They walked in and there were new bikes everywhere. Joe, to this day, not only remembers the name of the dealer, but the smell of all of that new rubber.

"We walk in and my dad, who was one of the hardest working people I know, asks me which one I want. I pointed to the Honda 70. He pays cash for it, puts it in the trunk, and we take it home. I couldn't believe it!"

Home at the time was an apartment, so initially Joe could only ride around the complex. But he had a bike, and to him it was "pretty damned cool."

A few months later, Joe and his family moved into a home with a long driveway and a garage—more room for riding and a place to store the bike. The riding world got even bigger once Joe met up with a few other guys in the neighborhood who showed him the network of nearby trails.

The little Honda 70 lasted about two years then gave way to a Kawasaki 175 and even more possibilities. Joe met other guys with dirt bikes and was soon riding all over that part of the state, sometimes going twenty miles without ever touching the pavement.

"I still keep in touch with some of those guys. We'd be gone for hours and our parents didn't mind or think about it. But most of the places we rode back then are now subdivisions, and I can tell you that as a dad today, I probably wouldn't let my kids be gone like that without me right there with them. That's too bad, because we knew what freedom was like then."

Freedom is an interesting concept defined by a personal point of view. For Joe, like many teenagers then and now, it came in the form of a driver's license—both car and motorcycle. While he'd had the run of the open spaces near his home, the ability to now drive a car and ride a motorcycle on the streets meant that Joe had both freedom and a choice. He chose cars. It probably didn't help that his dad bought him a Camaro Z28—a pretty sweet ride that would make you give up all kinds of stuff, no matter how old you were!

But there is such a thing as a pendulum...and balance. Before you can achieve the latter, that pendulum has to swing for a while. In Joe's case it eventually swung back to motorcycles when a buddy pulled up one night at a local ice cream hang out on a brand new 1976 Harley-Davidson Super Glide.

"The whole town of Franklin had a lot of motorcycles at the time. Hot rods, tough guys, even a motorcycle club called the Living Dead that people were scared to death of. Well, my friend gets this Harley, and then older brothers of friends of mine start showing up on them. And I'm putting it all together thinking, 'I don't want to be an asshole, but I like the mystique of being a biker. I've to get me one of those!'"

That didn't happen right away. But just as his dad had come through for him with the little Honda 70, eventually he helped Joe get his Harley.

But this time there were some strings attached. Joe had to get his high school diploma. Now, it's not that Joe wasn't doing well in school, but working at the local gas station and making his own money felt pretty good, and passing Physics was pretty hard. So the two together were adding up to a high school graduation that might not happen as planned. His dad really wanted Joe to go to college and eventually become a doctor. So the deal was get a diploma, get a Harley.

"I had to retake the Physics final, but I got the diploma, and all I could think of was showing it to my dad. It wasn't about getting the new Harley at that point. It was about showing him that I could finish high school."

So a few months later, Joe and his dad headed over to a Harley dealer in Rhode Island and bought a brand new 1976 Harley-Davidson Super Glide in Champagne Silver—a bike he still owns.

"The ride back from the dealer was one I remember to this day. I'd never been on anything bigger than a Honda 450 until then. I rode back home on a route I'd ridden many times before on smaller bikes, and there was this hill that those smaller bikes had always struggled with. But I'm on this new Harley, and I'm opening up the throttle in fourth gear, and that hill is nothing. I'm smiling from ear-to-ear thinking 'this is the balls!'"

Several months after buying the bike, he did what all new bike owners do—he added stuff—chrome pieces, performance bits, some cool paint. He made it all his. Meanwhile, he was out of high school working as a mechanic. He tried to go to college, but it didn't stick. Then his dad started getting sick, like real sick. Joe decided he couldn't let him down. He went back to college and got serious about it.

He enrolled at Franklin Pierce College—about sixty miles outside of Boston in New Hampshire. He came in with a Harley and a Corvette and he was the "shit on campus." He majored in biology, got on a pre-med track...he was making his dad proud.

But his dad's health continued to get worse, and before he could see his son get his college diploma, and maybe even get into med school...he died.

"I graduated magna cum laude, but it didn't mean much without my dad seeing me finish. My mom became pretty depressed after that and stayed that way until she died. I was depressed, too, but I was younger and masked it by partying."

Joe admits he was pretty angry at this point in his life. So instead of continuing the path to be a doctor like his dad was hoping he would, he went home and pumped gas.

His mom tried to get him to go to medical school. She even tried to call in some favors from friends of the family who were doctors, but Joe wasn't having any of it. The closest he got was teaching some of the lab portions of science classes at a community college. But it wasn't for him.

Joe took the $10,000 his mom gave him from his dad's estate and bought a 1982 H-D FLH Police Special. He went to work as a mechanic for a friend who owned a motorcycle shop and started learning everything he could about Harleys. From that point on, there's no more talk about going back to school or being a doctor. Joe was firmly entrenched in the motorcycle world...and now it was business.

"I worked on panheads, shovelheads and could tear down a bike and rebuild them with no problem. But I knew eventually I had to get out of being a mechanic and get into something that wasn't going to be as hard on me physically. I just didn't know what that was."

The opportunity to make that move came up when he was offered a sales position at New England Motorcycle Parts Company (NEMPCO), now owned by Tucker Rockey. A few years there, and Joe moved on to Custom Chrome, then Global Motorcycle Group, Accel Motorcycle Products, and a few others; basically pulling sales and marketing stints with more responsibility at well-known companies in the business.

By the late '90s, Joe had built a successful career in the motorcycle business, so he decided to scratch another itch—wrestling. That's right, "ARE YOU READY TO RUMBLE!?" wrestling. And the crazy thing is one of the guys he watched wrestle when he was a kid—Killer Kowalski—became his trainer. Funny example of what comes 'round.

"When I was growing up, I used to watch professional wrestling all of the time and thought it looked like fun. So when I got into my early 40s, I was able to get in the ring and wrestle under the name Cadillac Joe D. But the word *professional* implies you make money doing something. I didn't make a dime wrestling and realized that, while I was in good shape, I was too old and I had young kids to raise. But those couple of years in the ring were the thrill of a lifetime."

In case you hadn't picked up on this, when Joe gets interested in something, he goes all in.

Today, Joe readily admits that if he could get back in the ring, he would. But he still remains a promoter at heart and continues to be deeply involved in the motorcycle industry. He now has his own company—ProRiders Marketing—that represents a number of companies like BaggerWerx, Speedway Motorsport Shelters, and Corbin. As a divorced dad, he's also busy helping raise his three daughters—Ashley and twins Kristy and Grace—none of whom have shown any interest in anything having to do with motorcycles.

This doesn't seem to bother Joe. He points out his dad didn't really push him into anything, but was always there to both encourage and reward him. And he instilled in Joe a work ethic he's carried with him his entire life and is instilling in his daughters today.

There are a lot of details to Joe's story that would take a few more articles to cover. It's amazing what he remembers—the people, places, and events that have crossed his path at one point or another. But of all of the people Joe has met, promoted, sold to, hung out with, and rode with—and that's a pretty long list—his dad has clearly made the biggest impact.

So when Joe makes it to heaven, we think his dad will be right there next to Gabriel. And when Joe's said "How long ya got?" his dad will be more than happy to listen.

Most people who know Mark Wilsmore may have the impression that he's had no life outside of the Ace Cafe in London. They would be wrong.

How Mark Wilsmore Aced It

Some people become so attached to a specific thing, or even idea, that it's hard to think of them in any other capacity. Take Mark Wilsmore, Managing Director and revitalizer of the iconic Ace Cafe.

Those who don't know Mark's story may have the mistaken notion that he and the Ace Cafe have always been together, or that Mark has had no other life before the Ace, but both impressions would be wrong...and that's not Mark's doing. Just try searching for much about him that doesn't include his name and the Ace Cafe in the same sentence or paragraph.

But there's much to be learned of the man who still sports the long sideburns and slicked-back hair sported by the Rockers and café racers he associated with when he was younger, and with whom he still does today. They and the lifestyle that went with them are what inspired him to bring back the Ace when most would have been content to let it lie in the worn tread pile of motorcycle history.

Thank the motorcycle gods that the initial imprint made on Mark as a lad was of the two-wheeled kind and that he was a bit of an adrenalin junky early on.

"In the '60s, I was seeing bikes almost everywhere. I was a ten-year-old and thought, 'This is exciting—who's going to be a Rocker or a Mod.' It all seemed fast and dangerous. My best friend at under-elevens school had an older brother who was a Mod. While he wasn't around, we got on his scooters and rode them around."

Here's where a brief history of English biker culture might be in order for the uninitiated or only under-informed. It's important because the Ace Cafe played an early role in that culture, and you'll see why it was important to Mark to make the effort he did to preserve it.

Post World War II saw the rise of a subculture of motorcycle riders on the British Isles called the "Ton-Up Boys"—guys who were able to push their old British bikes to hit 100 mph. They favored early rock and roll music, and café racers became a particular style of bikes that reflected that push for speed.

As the '50s gave way to the '60s, and rock and roll became even more popular, the term *Rockers* took over. These were young men characterized by black leather jackets, motorcycle boots, and pompadour hairstyles.

A few years after the origination of the Ton-Up Boys, an entirely different group of riders came along who were focused on a different style of music and modern fashion. They were termed "modernists" (later abbreviated to Mods), because they not only adopted a modern style—the men often wearing tailored suites—but they also listened to the modern jazz of the time. Rather than ride the larger British bikes and café racers ridden by the Rockers, the Mods rode mostly Italian scooters.

In short, you couldn't have created two more distinctly different types of riders, so it was only a matter of time before they would eventually collide. The most famous conflagration of Rockers and Mods was a spring weekend in 1964, when large numbers of both groups found themselves in close proximity to each other in several seaside coastal towns.

Fights broke out, and the police and others in authority thought the end of society as everyone knew it was near. What's interesting is that the Mods, not the Rockers, were seen as the epitome of moral decay on the British Isles.

Meanwhile, in the US, the Mod look and riding scooters didn't take off the way leather jackets, boots, and big loud Harleys did. To this day, there's a general perception in this country that anyone who dresses like that and rides a Harley, must be bad.

The Ace Cafe was originally built in 1938 and soon began attracting motorcyclists due to its location on a heavily traveled road and the fact it was open 24/7. It was destroyed during World War II, but was later rebuilt at its current site in 1949, where it became a popular gathering place for local teens that liked the early rock and roll music... and motorcycles. It remained open for twenty years before closing in 1969...until Mark Wilsmore got the bright idea to bring it back to life.

This wasn't an idea that sprang from nowhere. It was born of a lifelong love of motorcycles and hot rods, and allowed to simmer in a stew of asphalt and adrenalin.

"I bought my first bike when I was seventeen. The biggest bike you could buy at that age in England was a 250cc because they could mostly do no more than about ninety miles an hour. I bought an RD250 Yamaha, mostly because it was the cheapest and fastest bike I could afford. Had I known there was a Kawasaki dealer not much further away, I would have bought an HD250—a better bike at the time."

About a month after buying that Yamaha, Mark's penchant for speed found himself in the hospital with a broken shoulder, collarbone, and right arm. He was not alone.

"What sticks in my mind is that almost everybody in my ward were all mostly young guys in there for pretty much the same reason: a consequence of riding badly!"

Mark said the crash did nothing to deter his love for bikes or speed, and he's never been without a bike since. In fact, he said he still owns many of the bikes he's bought over the years, except those that he destroyed and didn't replace. His collection of thirteen bikes includes: a Manx Norton, a Rickman Triumph, a Triumph Thunderbird, an early '80s Triumph TSS, a Bonneville Flat Tracker, a BSA Rocket, a BSA Gold Star, and a 1994 Harley-Davidson Electra Glide.

So with his love for unadulterated speed, you'd think Mark would have veered toward the world of racing, taking bikes at high speeds on open roads. Think again.

"When I left school, I wanted to ride a horse. I was quite good with animals and could ride. I decided I wanted to join the Army, but my mother beat that idea out of me. So I worked for quite a while on odd jobs, determined to join the police. I ended up riding horses with the police in London."

That's right, Mark Wilsmore was a mounted policeman in London...and for twenty years. But that came with a bit of a conflict of interest at times.

"My peer group outside of the police was Brit bike owners—riders who still considered themselves Rockers. Then the peer group in the police would be riding Japanese sport bikes. That younger group in the police would make fun of me riding with the old bikes and bikers. While most of those guys were ten years older than me, I liked hearing their ra-ra-stories and riding with them."

Mark said that, while he made sure to avoid being in a position of ticketing or even arresting someone in his Rocker group and vice versa, he did periodically organize multi-day trips with them or his police group to places outside of London, like the Isle of Man or the races at Nurburgring. During those trips away from the familiar is when he saw a switch in how both groups would act.

"The cops would go apeshit away from home, and the Rockers, who weren't afraid of mixing it up at the local bar in London, would become all meek and mild when they got away from home."

Mark could have lived out his time on horseback and continued to organize the occasional motorcycle trip abroad, but he wouldn't have been satisfied and neither would the ghost of the former Ace Cafe.

One of Mark's motorcycle influences is T. E. Lawrence (better known as "Lawrence of Arabia"), and a passage from one of Lawrence's writings best sums up what drove Mark to spend the time and effort to bring the Ace Cafe back to life.

"All men dream, but not equally. Those who dream by night in the dusty recesses of their minds, wake in the day to find that it was vanity: but the dreamers of the day are dangerous men, for they may act on their dreams with open eyes, to make them possible."

Mark's dream was to give the old Rockers back their home and give anyone who wanted to touch history a place to do so. And he did so with both eyes open.

Before the Ace reopened, he said you might ride to one place and have a beer, then ride to an all-night coffee shop for coffee and something to eat. These were places here and there to gather, but nothing that felt like home the way the Ace once had to those who could still remember it that way.

"It really started with the idea of having a twenty-five year anniversary of the closing of the original Ace. So I organized a reunion in 1994, and we had over twelve thousand people show up. Afterward, some friends of mine and I realized we could and should get the Ace Cafe running again."

Over the next several years, Mark and other supporters would continue to hold the reunion, while also working toward re-opening the Ace. He eventually retired from the London police force, and that gave him the time and wherewithal to make his dream a reality.

He formed a limited partnership, began raising money, hired people who knew how to build, run, and design restaurants, and finally re-opened the Ace Cafe in 2001.

Today, there are Ace Cafes in Switzerland and China, with one under construction in the US in Orlando, Florida. Possible sites are being considered in Russia, Spain, and India. Nearly every day, Mark said he gets an email or phone call from someone who thinks they have an ideal place for the next location—quite the accomplishment for someone who had no prior experience doing anything like this before, outside of being, in his own words, "good at organizing."

"I never thought it wouldn't happen. I knew it would be as popular as it's become at the time I wanted to do it because of how many people I knew were showing up at the reunions. I hope I can eventually find someone who can take it even further."

Taking the Ace Cafe further, without the adrenalin and vision of Mark Wilsmore, seems like a tall order. It has to be someone who wouldn't mind becoming synonymous with Ace, who respects its history and stature in the motorcycle world, and who can, as T. E. Lawrence described, "...act on their dreams with open eyes, to make them possible."

Even if such a person comes along, Mark Wilsmore will forever be associated with the Ace Cafe, and that's an association that's well-deserved.

Gard Hollinger is the less famous half of Arch Motorcycle—a custom motorcycle company he founded with Keanu Reeves. Most people know Keanu's story; here's Gard's.

Simple is Hard and We're All Going to Die

It's late spring in the late-'60s, and a group of grade school kids are taking turns whipping their Stingray bicycles with banana seats through their makeshift dirt track somewhere in the Hollywood Hills. Their dreams of speed and catching air on small jumps are interrupted by the familiar braap! of the Honda 50 four-stroke pulling up abruptly, idling noisily, its teenage rider stopping to watch.

One can imagine that kid with little effort—bushy unkempt hair, worn jeans, a multi-colored striped shirt, and dirty white Converse tennis shoes, now mostly the color of the dirt seeping from the surrounding hills.

Time stops. This is the kid who pulls wheelies after school like they were nothing in the cul-de-sac below. Parents probably told the young kids this one was trouble. An eight-year old Gard Hollinger wouldn't have cared. This was the coolest kid in the neighborhood. He was on a motorcycle, and he wanted to ride on their makeshift track!

At least this is the way one might imagine how that first encounter went for Gard as he briefly relays the impetus for his interest in motorcycles.

For those of you who don't know or haven't paid much attention, Gard is now one half of the founding duo that created Arch Motorcycle. Keanu Reeves is the other. And if that motorcycle-riding teenager from Gard's old neighborhood could meet Gard today, the envy would, no doubt, be reversed.

But let's keep things linear here and go back to Gard's past and his motorcycle milieu.

"I didn't get anything resembling a motorcycle until a couple of years later, when I got a new 1967 mini-bike called the 'Purple Taco.' I have an exact version of that bike in my shop now, but my first real motorcycle was a Honda CT70, followed by a succession of dirt bikes that were mostly project bikes I'd buy from friends."

Those dirt bikes propelled Gard into racing. A Suzuki RM125, bought in 1977, was the first new bike he ever owned. Before that, he was racing a 1970-71 Sachs that he bought in 1973. He was, he admitted, always a little behind the other racers.

"I was being raised by a single mom. And while she was always supportive of my riding and never denied me that, she did tell me 'If you can figure out how to do it on your own, I'm not going to stop you.' So I had to find a way to make racing happen on my own."

While Gard was still a young lad, his mom moved the family to the San Juan Islands, off of the coast of Washington. Gard began racing even more frequently through his teens and early twenties—mostly motocross and a few enduros and scrambles.

Racing also got Gard more involved with building and repairing bikes. At first, he said it was mostly just dabbling. But there was a motorcycle club on the island where Gard lived, and an older gentleman who belonged to that club took young Gard under wrench and wing and encouraged him to do more with that interest.

"My involvement with motorcycles meant that fixing them was a necessity. Even with that first Purple Taco mini-bike, I was trying to change that bike. It started with that and went from there."

The Northwest continued to prove to be a training ground for what eventually became Gard's profession as a custom bike builder. During his most successful years racing motorcycles and a stint racing jet skis in the mid-'80s, he and Ted Devol started Devol Racing Equipment, which made and sold some of the first protective parts for motorcycles.

Gard also began what would become a burgeoning friendship with Russ Tom, who owned the Harley-Davidson dealership in Seattle. While Gard said he doesn't have too many people he considers as heroes or mentors, his relationship with Russ would lay the groundwork for Gard's artistic approach to custom builds.

"Russ was building custom bikes from Harleys, but with more of a sportbike approach. I was intrigued by the idea of motorcycles as art. He helped me by allowing me to get involved in these projects, and that gave me the experience I needed to eventually start building on my own."

Gard eventually sold his half of Devol to Ted and found himself back in Los Angeles after also owning a limousine business in Seattle. While he'd been involved in a few restoration projects, including some mid-'70s Harley-Davidsons, he still hadn't fully launched himself into custom building as a business. It took selling his limo business to do that.

"I found myself with the chance to do what I wanted to do. I'd been out of motorcycles for a while, but decided I wanted to really get back into it. I had to decide to commit or walk away altogether. So I answered an ad for a Harley-Davidson shop near LA and took a job there as a fabricator and mechanic. But it wasn't long before the owner and I weren't seeing eye-to-eye, so I quit, and some of his customers asked me to finish their projects for them."

Maybe Gard just needed that kind of "jump-and-see-where-you-land" kind of experience, but not long after quitting that dealer he started his first custom bike shop called "Ziggy Harly" and located it in Canoga Park,

California. A few years later, around 2001, he and another business partner, Gary Seidel, opened an Indian dealership. This was when Indian was based out of Gilroy, California.

"I was trying to mimic what Russ Tom had done in Seattle with his Harley-Davidson customs, so I started doing custom Indians. This is when I started working on what would become Il Pazzo."

The Gilroy Indian plant would file for bankruptcy and stop producing bikes in 2003. This prompted Gard to start LA Choprods, which allowed him to make custom bikes for the rich, famous, and everyone else who began to appreciate his minimalist style and crazy Italian-inspired names.

Let's take a brief intermission for a moment with a quick side trip that could have taken Gard down a completely different path, had he been as passionate about that diversion as he was, and still is, about building motorcycles.

"I spent a few years studying and pursuing acting when I came back to LA in the mid-'90s. I really loved the process and idea of making your living pretending to be someone or something else—kind of like the job a kid has. Ultimately, it was the business side of it, the auditioning, etc., that made me stop."

Gard's foray into acting kind of makes you wonder if he and Keanu wouldn't have eventually met up on the set of a movie somewhere, anyway—like it was all somehow meant to be...

Meanwhile, the custom bike scene in the late '90s and early 2000s was really taking off. Build-offs, reality TV shows like *Orange Country Choppers*, and builders like Jesse James, who were becoming celebrities, were riding the wave. Gard was right there in it, doing the builds, appearing on various shows, and continuing to hone his skills. Then the recession hit.

"I never saw the big giant boom, then bust. It was a bit of maintaining the status quo for me. I kind of tightened my belt, got wily, and hung in there."

Gard came out the other side of that economic bust fairly intact, while many other builders of varying sizes and shapes didn't fare as well. It would still be a few years before he eventually met Keanu Reeves, and even longer before Arch Motorcycle was formed.

"A mutual friend asked if I'd be interested in building a sissybar for Keanu Reeves, and I said no. I've never been that interested in who was behind the name of someone I built a project for. Funny thing is that, when Keanu tells it, it makes me come across as kind of a snob. In this case, I really didn't feel like it was worth spending my time building an expensive sissybar. It wasn't going to benefit me or him."

The mutual friend persisted and later told Gard that Keanu was actually interested in more than just a sissybar. So Gard agreed to meet Keanu at LA Choprods.

"When Keanu came in the shop, he appreciated the bikes that I'd built. He understood the simplicity and organic nature of them. So, instead of doing more work on the bike he already had, he asked me to build a custom bike for him."

That bike became the first KRGT-1 in a process that Gard said took about four years to complete. "He was specific about what he wanted the motorcycle to do. He wasn't just talking about aesthetics, but what he wanted it to *do*. He was also open enough to ideas, so that as the purpose and design started to progress, it became a more collaborative effort."

As the bike began to take shape and the reality of what they were creating set in, Keanu started asking if they could find a way to build more of them. Considering Gard had never taken a production line approach to any of his builds, and he readily admits to conceiving them in his head rather than on paper, there were multiple reasons Gard came up with for why this would not be a good idea.

"No one starts a company planning to fail. You work out the contingencies, the realities first. So when Keanu brought up the idea of going beyond a single build, my initial reaction was to say no. But Keanu was very patient, and when I'd finally gone through all of my questions and objections, he said, 'I've listened to all of the reasons we shouldn't do this. Now can we talk about why we should do it?'"

Gard said he had just one more question, "What's the ultimate reason we should do this?"

And Keanu's response was nothing short of quick and brilliant. "Because we're going to die."

Oh, to be a fly on the wall!

Not only did Keanu's reply help Gard shed all of his objections, but it smartly played into his own philosophy related to life being too short to work on anything you don't want to do. It also reignited a passion that had started to wane.

"I was at a bit of a turning point before Keanu came along. My wife Sharon and I had seriously been thinking of moving to San Miguel de Allende in Mexico, have a shop there, keep a satellite office in LA. It was the idea of furthering an artist's lifestyle. But we weren't so far down that pipeline that we couldn't step away from it. So we did, and Keanu and I started Arch."

One thing Gard is quick to dispel is any notion that Arch is just a vanity project for Keanu. He pointed out that Keanu has an authentic passion for motorcycles that has nothing to do with maintaining some kind of a Hollywood persona. While Gard runs the day-to-day operations of the company and is the lead designer, when Keanu is in town, he's at the shop providing input into the designs and test-riding bikes.

"I sense he's sometimes torn between the two worlds, but he's our number one test-rider. He loves to ride, and he has an uncanny way of breaking things. It's not like he's abusive, it's just that things happen when he gets on a bike that don't happen when someone else does."

Gard said he and Keanu have a clear, unified goal—to make a respected, American-made motorcycle and keep production numbers limited to probably no more than about thirty for the time being. So don't even think about a mass-produced bike with an Arch Motorcycle badge on it.

Considering Gard's love of motorcycles, it's only natural to wonder what's in his garage. The list, unsurprisingly, turns out to be fairly lengthy—ten to fifteen old dirt bikes, some vintage CB450s, a 1967 305 Superhawk, and a rare 1962 CX with twin pipes. The shop also has a new Kawasaki ZX10R and Yamaha R1 for track days. But the bike that he says is mostly his daily rider, if he isn't on one of his own customs or an Arch or any previously listed, is a late-model Moto Guzzi Griso. Of course, it's Italian!

Gard has approached both Arch and all of his builds with a belief that simple is better, but he also admits that approach is hard. Look at his past work and you can see how painstakingly he calls attention to just the right parts and lines, while tucking wires and cables away where they won't interfere with that look.

So his response to what advise he would give someone who wants to become a custom builder is equally simple.

"Run as fast as you can. And if you can't outrun it, then you have to learn it. You can't fake it."

Because at the end of the day, we're all going to die, eventually.

Martin (mar-teen) Chirotarrab is the owner of Spirit Motorcycles in San José, California. They sell Indians, Victories, Slingshots, and CanAm Spyders. He left the corporate world to own a motorcycle business having very little riding or related experience, but he's quickly turned his store into one of the most successful within the whole Polaris family. Here's his story.

From Boardroom to Showroom

The first thing you notice when you enter the showroom for Spirit Motorcycles is not the gleaming new Victory and Indian motorcycles lined up throughout the space or the shiny new wooden floor and fixtures. No, it's two small Yorkshire terriers, Mike and Atti, both sitting patiently, expecting nothing but their share of attention.

Dogs in a showroom? What is this, Silicon Valley? Well, yes it is. San José to be exact, and the dogs are just one sign that Martin Chirotarrab, the owner, is approaching running a dealership a little differently.

"I want this to be a customer-friendly environment, where anyone who comes in immediately feels like this is someplace they want to come back to," explained Martin. "Our focus is to deliver the best experience to our customers. Not to knock other dealers, but like with any business, when you get complacent, you stop caring. That's not happening here."

Martin's foray into the motorcycle world is relatively new. Other than riding a few mopeds and dirt bikes as a kid growing up in Argentina, his real love of two wheels didn't start until about five years ago when he and his wife, Shaye, happened to rent two Harleys while in Vegas. But what happened in Vegas didn't stay in Vegas. They promptly returned to their home in Miami and bought a Fat Boy and a Sportster.

Though that part of the world isn't necessarily known for its diverse riding opportunities—Martin points out it's pretty damn flat—he and Shaye still rode as much as they could. They had the bug.

But the idea of owning a dealership wasn't even an afterthought at this point. Prior to even considering that kind of massive career change, he held some pretty senior positions in finance and sales for Shell Oil and Nokia. That meant a lot of travel and not much time with the family—which eventually included three kids—and even less time to ride.

"At one point, I was on the road for seventeen weeks straight without being at home. It was insane."

His career eventually took him from the UK to Argentina to Miami to Indonesia—Nokia's fourth largest market—where he was allowed to bring absolutely everything he owned into the country, except for the two Harleys. As he explained it, the owner of the Harley dealerships in Indonesia had government connections and forced a law that forbade used Harleys from entering the country. So he sold the Fat Boy and Sportster in the US and rented some while Indonesia. Hey, "when in Rome" (or Indonesia)...

"Riding in Indonesia isn't the same as here. It's made up of over 17,000 islands, bikes are not allowed on the few highways they have, and streets are in really bad shape, so you don't go on overnight trips or even ride more than maybe a hundred miles. But the scenery is incredible everywhere you go."

For some, Indonesia might be the last career stop before eventually heading back state-side or to company headquarters, but in this case, Nokia had other plans and offered to move Martin to Beijing to run their China business—their largest market.

Martin said he looked at his kids, talked with his wife, and realized he was done. No more moving. No more extended business travel. And definitely no Beijing. Time for something else, but what?

He said his father had always owned businesses of his own, so being an entrepreneur wasn't new to him. But he still needed to determine what kind of business would give him some level of freedom and satisfaction, and that other important thing known as income.

"I looked at different business opportunities, and I kept coming back to motorcycles. My grandfather had been a dirt bike racer on an Indian Scout in Argentina, and I remember the stories he'd tell about that experience. Shaye grew up in New Zealand where Burt Munroe [*World's Fastest Indian*] was a national hero. And since we both rode, it wasn't much of a leap to look seriously at owning a motorcycle dealership."

But which brand? Since he owned a Harley, that seemed logical, but getting a dealership in the States was nearly impossible. Very few come available. But owning a Harley meant he was also familiar with V-twins. So he turned to the other American company—Victory.

And here's where you really get a sense for Martin's persistence. After not having much initial luck reaching anyone at Victory to talk about dealership opportunities, he decided to give it one more try and finally got in touch with someone who could help him figure it out. He was living back in Miami at the time, so the person on the other end offered up possibilities in Tallahassee and Ft. Meyers. Martin wasn't having any of it.

"No offense to people who live in those cities, but I wanted something with more potential and diversity in terms of clientele and geography. So I asked about the West Coast. I'd been to San Diego once, but never to San Francisco."

That's right. In all of his travels, Martin had never been to San Francisco, let alone ridden a bike anywhere near there. While that market sounded like a possibility, San Jose was a bigger and better opportunity. There was just one catch. Another group wanted it too, and they were going to be making a presentation in a week at Victory's headquarters in Minnesota. Martin could do the same, but he had to present on the same day.

"I flew to San Jose that weekend and visited sixty-two sites in four days, settled on one, put the presentation together, and delivered the business case. I think all of my sales and finance background kicked in at once. The day after I presented, I got a call that I'd been approved for a dealership."

After some more months of permitting and remodeling, he opened in mid-June of 2014 and cleared out most of his initial inventory of Victories and Indians within less than two months. The day after opening, his service department was booked solid. "Some might call it beginner's luck, I think it goes back to customer service. We have put a lot of attention into [building] our team, recruiting the best of the best in the bay area, starting by our super star General Manager, Kevin King, who previously worked as a GM at Arlen Ness. People already know what to expect, and word gets around. Now we just have to make sure it stays consistent."

So once Martin has some free time, what would he most like to do?

"I've had no time to really get out and ride since we started this process. Here I am surrounded by bikes, great weather, and all of these fantastic places to see. Time to take advantage of it!"

At this point, Mike and Atti get his attention. They seem to agree.

Phil Anderson was an up-and-coming flat track racer in the '70s until his dad made him quit to help him run the family-owned dirt bike park. He works out the regret by teaching others how to handle riding dirt.

It's a Dirty Business

About thirteen miles from where the government tests God-only-knows-what at the Lawrence Livermore Laboratory in Livermore, California, sits fifteen hundred acres of dirt bike and ATV heaven. Much of the terrain at Carnegie State Vehicle Recreation Area is not for the timid or inexperienced rider. In ski or snowboard terms, there are what would appear to be more black diamond runs than green.

But on a hot Saturday afternoon in August, Phil Anderson, a former professional flat track racer, is taking a family of four through their first dirt bike experience in what is decidedly the bunny slope version of the area. In about a one-plus acre oval, the family rides small 125cc dirt bikes around orange cones scattered in one area and over small railroad ties equally spaced out in another. A small four-foot high nub off to the side is about as much hill climbing as they'll see for the day. A smattering of trees gives them some semblance of what it's like to ride around taller and more tightly spaced obstacles. So far, no one has hurt themselves.

"Mostly, there are a few bruised egos and an occasional muscle. I don't let anyone go fast enough to do much more than that. We want them to learn and have fun on the bikes." Phil's no nonsense when it comes to both the safety side and the fun element. I believe him.

Phil and his wife, Renee, own P&R Sports, a certified (by the Motorcycle Safety Foundation) provider of dirt bike instruction. Phil's the instructor; Renee manages the business end. It's an arrangement that seems to suit them both.

It's not what Phil thought he'd be doing when he first started riding dirt bikes at the age of ten in this same area, long before it was designated by the state for doing what he quickly grew to love. By the time he was seventeen, he was the California state flat track racing champion and wore the black plate. He had dreams of taking his racing skills as far as he could possibly take them—nationals and then the world. But his dad had other plans.

The family owned what was then the Sandhill Ranch, an area much like Carnegie, where both dirt and mountain bikers could experience all kinds of terrain. And Phil's dad, who also owned Tom's Cycle Center, saw a chance to take the family's involvement in dirt bikes to a different level. That meant that Phil needed to help tend to business, instead of chase possible glory around a track of mud and dirt.

"I understood it, but it was tough to accept. I didn't have to stop riding. I just couldn't take it to where I knew I could if I would have been able to stay with it."

Eventually, Phil put his racing behind him and began earning a living as a glass glazer. He also took up mountain biking and, of course, mountain bike racing. He still rode dirt bikes when he could, but the mountain bike racing was less expensive and just as thrilling. The odd thing is that, while he got injured more than a few times in his dirt bike career, it wasn't until he started mountain biking and working with glass that he had to go under the knife on more than one occasion.

"I went over the top of my handlebars on my mountain bike once and was injured so bad I don't even remember what happened. And I've had to have three back surgeries from stuff that happened to me as a glass glazer."

Go figure.

Phil doesn't let that pain show during class. It's only after the long six-hour day of teaching is over that you can see he moves carefully and doesn't rush getting his bikes up into his pickup.

Renee helps him and is clearly not afraid to jump in anywhere she's needed. They have the kind of easy relationship that allows them to know what each other needs without having to say much. While they put away the bikes after the class, they talk about how they met.

"It was at a bicycle store. Phil had come in looking for something and asked if I could help him. He thought I was a sales assistant! I asked him if he thought that since I was a woman that I couldn't also be a rider. He didn't know I was a pretty good mountain biker."

"Pretty good? She thought she was pretty hot shit actually."

"Well, I was...actually."

As it turned out, they soon realized they had more than two wheels in common, and soon made the trip down the aisle. Then along comes a daughter, Stephanie, who must have had a bit of gas, rubber, and dirt in her veins. It wasn't long before she was following in her dads' footsteps and racing—first beating all of the girls then most of the boys. She's now in college and doesn't race anymore, but she still rides when she can.

"It doesn't bother me that she didn't take it any further. She and I will ride together once in awhile, and if we're running through a course, she'll beat me. That competitive spirit is still there."

This is definitely a family with many layers. Besides running the business side of P&R Sports, Renee is a professional harpist, and she and Phil raise guide dogs. Not what one might immediately associate with dirt biking. But as Phil was going through a post ride debrief with the family, it's evident that this is a family that is just as happy keeping things in low gear now as they may have once done when it was easier and more desirable to go faster.

When asked about any bad experiences with students during the course of teaching, they're quick to point out that they aren't bad experiences as much as they are either frustrating or surprising ones.

"I had an actor out here once who had to learn how to ride a dirt bike for a short scene that required him to ride all of a hundred yards, stop, and say a line. That was it. He was out here for five hours and couldn't get that bike to go ten feet, let alone ten yards."

He and Renee both say they've seen a few parents get impatient with kids who may not be getting the hang of riding the way they expect. That's probably tougher for them to watch. But when they get a kid who comes out and has a grin that Phil said, "will lift the helmet off his head," or an eighty-two-year-old man who has learning to ride on his bucket list, they agree it makes up for the occasional frustration.

As Phil and Renee put the last bike up in their pickup and get ready to leave, I can't help but notice that there are a lot of kids at this park riding everything from four wheel ATVs to dirt bikes of every size imaginable. I ask Phil about what he sees with kids that take his course.

"There are a lot more kids who come out here thinking they can just get on and ride a bike because they've done it in a video game. They come out here and learn otherwise, and their parents wonder what's going on. I don't care if it's here or somewhere else, but those kids need to get out more."

Well, the video-game playing thing kind of worked for Tom Cruise in *Days of Thunder*, but that was a movie. Maybe there's a place for those kids at the lab up the road.

Lilly Gonzalez is a retired nurse who decided to prove that Mexico wasn't all drugs and killings. And she did it on the back of a motorcycle...by herself.

It's Better the Faster You Go

Mexico, speed, and women on bikes. Where's Hunter S. Thompson when you need him? Well, he's dead, and this story is about Lilly Gonzalez (aka Tiger Lilly) and what led her to take a 2,500-mile trek by herself through Mexico that proved that "F(uck) T(he) W(orld)" doesn't mean giving up on life.

But first let's step back about eleven years.

Lilly didn't grow up on bikes or even near them. She vaguely remembers getting on the back end of one or two when she was a kid, but that's about it. Then in '03 she happened to be visiting her brother, Ray, in Texas and asked him to give her a ride on his Harley. And that's all she wrote.

"He took off so fast that I screamed like a little girl in a horror movie. When he stopped, he asked me if I was okay. I told him to DO IT AGAIN AND GO FASTER!"

So she promptly went home and told her husband, Burl, to go buy a Harley...or else. Burl didn't care about the "or else" part, nor did he ask if she was serious. He was going to buy a Harley. In the meantime, Lilly left it at that.

But in his search for the perfect Hog, Burl found himself buying a Victory, instead, and there was Lilly riding on the back. It seems, though, that Lilly was a fidgety passenger and sometimes got a little playful with Burl's crotch, which didn't sit too well with Burl's riding sensibilities. After all, he'd just gotten into riding himself, and "keep your hands to yourself" was a policy that he needed Lilly to follow. So one day her fidgeting and playfulness got the best of him. He pulled over into a casino parking lot, dropped Lilly off, and rode away.

"That pissed me off, so I got determined to walk the eight miles home. Meanwhile, Burl was trying to call me on my cell, but I was ignoring it. He ended up looking for me back at the casino, found me walking, and we made up. But it convinced us both that I should get my own bike."

So Lilly enrolled in a riders' course at a Harley dealer in Las Vegas and passed with flying colors. Then came her first bike—an all-chromed out, pearl-white 1200 Sportster. Six months later, she found herself riding with a girlfriend throughout England on a much bigger—and faster—Harley-Davidson Heritage Classic.

"We had an incredible time riding through London, the countryside, seeing all of these historical places. The thrill of riding in a foreign country through fog, hail, sleet, rain, and the occasional sunny spots was great. It also made me realize that when I got back to the United States, I needed a bigger bike!"

The barely broken-in Sportster got traded for a new 2005 Fiftieth Anniversary Victory Kingpin. Since Burl had already started modifying his Vic, they did the same to Lilly's—all with the intent of making it go faster.

In the meantime, Lilly was working as an operating room nurse. She'd been in the Marine Corps, where she and Burl met, and when she got out, she wanted to "help people." So at forty, she went back to school, got her degree, became licensed as a nurse in eleven states, and did what she calls "everything from birth to death" nursing.

"I became a real strong advocate for the patients, once I saw how doctors, in particular, treated them...or not. That didn't make me very popular, but at least I knew I was doing the right thing."

Eventually, she said she had to get out of nursing or else... There's that "else" again.

A few years later, it's May 2014, and Lilly's on her way to Mexico from Utah, by herself, on her motorcycle. Which by now has racked up over 120,000 miles.

"I couldn't get Burl to go, but I needed this ride. Riding is the biggest cure for depression that I know of. Once I'm on my bike, everything just goes away. I also didn't want to wait much longer to do a ride like this. Old age doesn't run in my family, and I have rheumatoid arthritis. I said, 'FTW, I only have so much time, and I'm going to keep living it!'"

So a combination of boredom, curiosity, and ticking clock found Lilly riding by herself, heading south to Mexico. She speaks Spanish fluently, and she figured as a woman she was actually less of a target to the narco traficantes than if she was a guy, or even riding with guys.

Her route took her down the Baja coast, through Guaymas, Sinaloa, Mazatlan, and eventually east from Sayulita to Dolores Hidalgo. From there, she rode north to Saltillo, then over to Monterrey and the Mexican-Texas border at Tamaulipas.

"I had originally intended to go all the way to the tip of Mexico, then head north from there to Mexico City and San Miguel de Allende. But the heat and humidity was starting to get the best of me, so I cut the trip short. I got really depressed as a result, but my sister talked me through it and convinced me to head north so I could see my grandson in Texas and few other friends in Mexico along the way."

Lilly said she had no real route planned out and just enough gear, money, and a credit card to get her as far as she initially had planned. She alternately stayed in campgrounds, small motels, and an occasionally nicer place to rest and clean up.

Did she ever feel unsafe? After all, she was a woman, traveling by herself in a place the media portrays as a lawless country being over taken by drug cartels.

"Only once, well, maybe twice. The first was a night I spent in a motel in Puerto Vallarta. I was covered in mosquito bites and had heat rash, so I was really uncomfortable. I'd finally drifted off to sleep, when I suddenly woke up to some old fart with one eye stroking my arm. I slept with a knife under my pillow, so I pulled it out and told him to get the hell out before I cut him open. Keep in mind, as a nurse I knew exactly where to cut for the most effect. He left pretty fast after that. Turns out, he was the owner and gave me a full refund the next day."

Lilly describes the second time as actually being one that, on gut feeling alone, made her keep going. She'd pulled into a small town near Mazatlan to avoid a toll road. It had recently rained, so the road was damp and the potholes were nearly invisible, since they were filled with water. It was night, and nothing was open, except for a couple of bars that were filled with mostly drunken men.

As Lilly pulled into the town, she said, "I got the creeps so bad I kept going and didn't stop until I got to the next town about fifty kilometers (thirty-one miles) up the road. I never had another problem after that, until I got back to the Mexico-US border."

There are two things Lilly insisted on bringing with her, besides the knife—coconut oil and Adderall.

"Coconut oil is a great hair and body conditioner, and it doesn't attract bugs. I took Adderall, because I knew that keeping my concentration on long distance travel could be a problem. I'm not suggesting it for everyone, but I knew for me it would help."

"My bike broke down right on the Mexican side of the border on the way back into the US. The US Border Patrol must have thought I looked like a terrorist or something. Once we all started talking about bikes and where I'd been, though, it was fine. But initially they were acting like a bunch of Nazis."

Lilly made it safely home to Utah from there, but before you think Lilly has returned from Mexico satisfied, think again. Like any good Hunter S. Thompson tale, there's more to do and tell—helmet laws to poke a finger at, loss of freedoms to write about, and more rides to go on before Lilly can ride no more. But all of that is best saved for another day.

A software programmer by day and a motorcycle racer and rider on weekends, Curtis is proof there's still plenty of life after fifty.

50-Plus at 150 mph

It's 9:30AM on a hot August day, the temperature has already hit close to eighty, and Curtis Zeeb has worked up a sweat. He's done two laps during a scheduled track day at Thunderhill Raceway near Willows, California, about three hours northwest of San Francisco. And the day's just getting started.

At fifty-plus, Curtis is one of the older guys out here, but he's so focused on having fun and making sure his bike is set up right that he doesn't care. Most guys stop riding sportbikes in their late thirties and forties and move to something with a more upright position. Instead, Curtis turned back the clock, leaned way forward, and went to the track.

But it wasn't a single straight line to get there. In fact, the motorcycle gremlins threw him a big curve a few years back, but one that led him to this eighty-degree morning, stuffed inside a one-piece leather suit and ready to rocket down the straightaways at over a 150 mph.

"I like big bikes, so in 2006 I bought a Hayabusa and just loved its power and speed. But I high-sided it on a ride soon after I bought it, broke some ribs, and had to be life-flighted to a local hospital. That gave me a few months to recover and think about what kind of riding I wanted to do. So I started reading up on everything I could related to track days and sportbikes."

That was over four years ago, and notice he didn't say whether or not he wanted to keep riding. That, my friends, never entered his mind. After all, he'd been riding since he was eighteen, and the accident pointed out just how unpredictable street riding can be. What he saw in track riding was a more controlled and, ultimately, safer environment.

He blames it on his brother who let him ride his 1970-something Kawasaki 900 that Curtis said, "Was fast as hell and just beautiful." So brothers being what brothers are, Curtis promptly went out and bought a newer and faster Kawasaki 1000.

"After that, I got to be friends with the dealer, so every year or more, I'd trade in a bike and get a new one for about a thousand dollars out of my pocket. This went on for about six years, so I got used to having the next bigger, faster bike."

Several years and bikes, and nearly as many moves from Michigan to Florida to California, eventually brought Curtis face-to-face with one of the biggest bikes on the market at the time—a 1998 Honda Valkyrie. For anyone too young to remember or too into a single manufacturer to know, this bike had a ninety-three cubic inch, liquid-cooled, flat six-cylinder engine, with each cylinder having its own carburetor. It was a beast to the more refined Gold Wing, and Curtis was determined to own one.

"I had taken my wife with me to look at them, and just as I was about to sign off on a black one, she pointed out a green Valkyrie Interstate, which was their fully-faired and bagged touring version. She said, 'If you're going to get a big bike, then get one I'm going to be comfortable on.' So I did."

That began Curtis's long-term relationship with big Honda bikes and major touring. After buying the Valkyrie, he and his wife, Charng-Huey (Chung-Way), started taking overnight trips that grew into long weekends that eventually became trips of a couple weeks or more. They ended up traveling so much they bought a travel trailer they could pull with one of their big bikes.

And that big bike collection was never static for long. Eventually, Curtis moved from the Valkyrie to a Gold Wing to a Harley-Davidson Ultra Glide. Each of them all dressed up with lots of places to go. He said some of their most favorite rides have been in California—up to Mt. Lassen, along the coast, and through Gold Country in the Sierra foothills. They also have property in Oregon, so they rode up there a lot, exploring different routes with friends who also rode, or on their own.

But just when he thought he'd seen big enough, he found himself in Laughlin, Nevada in '04, staring down a herd of behemoths—mastodon-sized bikes—aptly named "Boss Hoss." Two years later, he owned one of those, too.

"I couldn't believe they could fit a small-block V-8 onto a frame and two wheels and have it look like it fit, and which could ride as well as it did. That bike was the epitome of *big*, and it was just a helluva lot of fun to blast around on!"

A few more years of touring went by until one day Charng-Huey decided she'd had enough with being a passenger. She was ready to ride on her own. Rather than following the big theme Curtis had laid out, she went with small and nimble—a 2009 Kawasaki 650 Ninja. And that's what got Curtis onto a Hayabusa. As long as his wife was going to have a sport bike, he might as well have one, too!

After the accident with the Hayabusa, Curtis decided to dial it back a notch if he was going to give sportbikes a try. So he bought a used Yamaha 600R but quickly realized that one of the reasons he always liked big was that his 6'2" frame needed the room. So he got rid of the Yamaha and bought a Kawasaki ZX10R and turned that into a dedicated track bike with about two thousand dollars' worth of faring, fork, and other adjustments. Charng-

Huey followed suit and turned her original Ninja into a track bike as well.

"People don't realize what kind of shape you have to be in to come out here and throw a 400-500 pound bike around a two-and-a-half mile track at speeds up to 150 or more. One of the best ways to get faster on the track is to get stronger. This has helped us both be better riders, and it's forced me back into shape."

So what does Curtis do when he's not riding? He's bombing through code as a technical lead for Kaiser Permanente for their recruiting and Human Resources systems. He's in charge of all of the technical integration of everything from job codes for the entire staff to salary info for new employees.

As he walks me through the mods he's done on his Kawasaki track bike before he heads out for another round of laps, it all starts to fall into place. This isn't just about Curtis taking up a new form of motorcycling because circumstances led him to it. He's rewriting his own code every time he goes around the track...and having a blast doing it.

Jack Stevenson has led a life pursuing what he loved and making it work for him, rather than having to work for it. An accomplished chef, avid biker, and loyal friend, Jack's life has included many different paths.

Of Golf, Cooking, and Riding

Jack Stevenson is a chef. We're not talking short order cook at some diner. We're talking the kind of guy who knows that a reduction sauce has nothing to do with speed and that you can never have enough tongs in the kitchen. So what makes him *Asphalt & Dirt* profile material?

Well, Jack also rides a motorcycle and has for nearly eighteen years.

While being a chef is interesting on its own because it doesn't fit the stereotypical biker image, how Jack came into riding and cooking make for a better story. It's one where fate seems to have been a constant.

The cooking part started when Jack was around eight years old. He said his mother loved to cook, he liked to cook with her, and he used to watch *The Galloping Gourmet* on television after school.

"I never knew then that Graham Kerr [host of the show] was drunk half the time. He just looked like he was having a good time," explained Jack. "So my mom encouraged me to stick with it, and one of the first books I remember ever getting as a present was *The Galloping Gourmet* by Graham Kerr."

Jack said that as he got older golf eventually took the place of cooking. He grew up living on a golf course, and his dad was a golfer, so that wasn't much of a leap. But there are a lot of guys who grow up in similar circumstances, and not all of them get good enough to be a scratch golfer or qualify for the California State Amateur Tournament. That's what Jack did by his senior year in high school. While most guys in that situation would be considering what college to play for, Jack wasn't so lucky.

"No one told me I needed to actually apply to colleges to get in. So there I was at the end of my senior year in high school with no idea of what to do next. So I joined the Air Force, and guess what? Instead of making me work on planes, they let me do the two things I knew best—cook and play golf!"

This was the late '70s and the only significant war at the time was the cold one. So when he wasn't in an Air Force base kitchen, Jack traveled around Europe playing golf. That four-year tour quickly passed, so he re-upped and found himself out of the kitchen and into top secret work, basically telling surveillance pilots where to fly to get the best photographs. Another tour of duty went by, and when it looked like the next step after the military might be the CIA or NSA, he decided it was time to get out.

"I couldn't see myself being an analyst for spies, so I came home to California and decided that maybe the best place for me was back in the kitchen. So I enrolled in the California Culinary Academy and have been cooking for a living ever since."

Jack points out that while people may think being a professional chef is easy, it's one of the hardest jobs he's ever had.

"Think about it—kitchens are a mad house. You've got boiling liquid, flying knives, glass containers everywhere.

The slightest slip up and you're going to hurt yourself or someone else. Add in all of the waiters and other chefs running around the kitchen giving and taking orders...it's pure adrenalin and definitely not for the weak and timid."

His worst experience as a chef?

"The guy responsible for making clam chowder at this restaurant I was working at in San Francisco was out, so I had a temp taking his place. We were also having a special spicy bean soup that night, and I told this guy to make a batch of both. I leave him to it, come back an hour later, and he's mixed them both together into something like a spicy bean clam chowder. We let out a collective 'Oh, Shit,' but eventually put it on the menu and called it Brazilian spicy bean chowder. We were sweating it for awhile because nearly everyone who comes to that restaurant expects to order real clam chowder. But, guess what? We sold out of the Brazilian made up soup!"

Maybe fate played a hand there, too. Which is an awkward segue back to motorcycles...and an entirely different story.

Unlike a lot of people who ride, Jack didn't start out riding some friend's dirt bike as a kid. And he didn't find himself in a mid-life crisis thinking two wheels was some form of intervention. In fact, it was his wife at the time, Susan, who got him on to two wheels. Funny, considering more often than not it's the better half that tries to keep their husbands off of anything that can't sit upright on its own.

"It was a few months from her birthday, and she asked me if I'd like to know what she wanted. What guy wouldn't like that kind of insight! Turns out, she wanted me to take motorcycle lessons then rent a Harley so she and I could take a trip together down to the Florida Keys. We were both working in the high-end hotel business at the time, and all of these guys who were managing the properties rode Harleys. She's never admitted it, but I think that's what prompted it for her."

So Jack took a motorcycle safety course and somehow managed to get his 6'5" frame onto a little Japanese-made bike for two days worth of slow-and-go. He then rented a Harley Road King for a day of riding on his own, before finally renting another for a three-day birthday trip with Susan. For the next nearly fifteen years, that's how Jack rode—rent a Harley (mostly Road Kings) for a few days and go for a ride, mostly with Susan, sometimes by himself, sometimes for two- or three-day rides, sometimes less. He said he never really had the time to ride enough to justify buying one. But that all changed in 2010.

Having ridden nothing but Harleys, Jack didn't think of buying anything else. But one of the guys he worked with had a Victory and told him he should go down to the nearby Victory dealer—Arlen Ness—and check them out. The whole time the guy is talking about Victory, Jack said he was just thinking to himself, "Harley, Harley, Harley."

"Eventually, I heard the words *Victory* and *Ness*, so I went to Arlen's and spent almost two hours there looking at a bunch of Victorys. I never realized that there were bikes that didn't vibrate and that a motorcycle could be that comfortable."

Jack left the dealer, did a bunch of research about Victorys, then found one online that he couldn't live without—a 2011, white-pearl and silver, totally dressed up Victory Cross Country. He figured if this was going to be the first bike he was going to buy, it might as well be the one he really wanted...and he really wanted that bike!

It showed up for sale at Arlen Ness's a few days later, and after about a week, Jack took home a slightly used, fully loaded touring bike for $16,000 that the former owner had dropped $28,000 on less than a year earlier.

"I've taken that bike all over California, up into Canada, and through the deserts of Arizona. There was a point in time about a year ago that I almost thought I'd have to sell it, but some guys I ride with convinced me to keep it. I'm glad they did because that bike and I were meant to be together."

For the uninitiated, lots of guys name their bikes. So what does Jack call his? Fate. Something he's known since he was a kid watching the *Galloping Gourmet* drunkenly make his way through one dish after another.

[Note: Jack now owns his own restaurant, The Bistro, in Cannon Beach, Oregon. He's also learned to like riding in the rain.]

Some people only dream of traveling in foreign countries by motorcycle. Jose Mallabo—a public relations and marketing professional—made that dream come true with an epic ride in India and Nepal.

Blame It on Ewan and Charley

We're trying a different format here. Not being lazy, just seeing how this plays out. Besides this guy we're writing about—Jose Mallabo—well, he's a friend of ours, and a pretty good storyteller in his own right. So we decided to let him tell it...with some editing on our part.

What got you interested in riding?

"I actually can't remember if it was watching the Ewan McGregor/Charley Boorman movie *Long Way Round*, but I suppose watching that got me interested in riding. And that tied to my interest in travel and doing visceral things. I always feel a bit neutered by day-to-day life and have a sense of restlessness after spending most of my day sitting. I drive to work, then sit in front of a computer and answer emails and calls. I've been doing that for twenty years. Riding gives me an outlet that is the exact opposite of that...which is closer to what I did as a kid and teenager. Just go out and play for the sake of it!"

What was your first bike?

"A red 2008 Ninja 650R. Loved that bike. There are days I wish I still had it.

Who taught you to ride?

"I took a motorcycle safety class through the Motorcycle Safety Foundation—highly recommended for anyone just getting into riding. Then I just went about dropping that Ninja all over the Oakland Hills until I figured it out."

What do you ride now?

"I own a BMW R1200R and an Aprilia 1000R. I ride them both but prefer the rawness of my Aprilia, so I tend to be on that more often than the Beemer."

In 2013, you went on a Himalaya bike trip that took you through northern India, Nepal, and Tibet; what prompted that?

"I didn't think I was skilled enough for a ride like that. I did it to prove to myself I could. So it was definitely for the challenge of it. Until that trip, I didn't have a huge interest in Nepal and Tibet until *after* I signed up for the ride. The more I read and prepared, the more I realized this was probably the most daunting and special overland trek of any I could have chosen. That only made me want to do it more."

Lots of people probably told you not to do it—too dangerous, it's freakin' Nepal. What made you go—"Screw that, I'm going anyway?"

"Funny thing is I knew people would say that, so I limited the people I told to those who knew me really well and knew I'd only be more resolute to go, or were people who ride bikes and knew they'd do it if they could.

"What was interesting was to hear the feedback people gave me after they knew what I did. It's a strange thing, *fear*. It keeps us from doing stuff, but it's what people rally around when someone gets past it."

What was your most uncomfortable moment during the trip?

"I was uncomfortable pretty much the whole time. The terrain was brutal at times—hardscrabble roads, potholed cobblestones in small villages, and single-lane hard-packed dirt. And I'm not a dirt bike rider by any stretch of the imagination. But hour one of day one was by far the most uncomfortable and frightening.

"The bikes [Royal Enfields] were like nothing most Westerners would ever ride post 1970, and the kind of traffic we set off in was completely foreign to anything I'd ever driven or ridden in before. No rhyme or reason to any of it. Bicycles, motorcycles, cars, and trucks all mashed together with pedestrians and animals taking up the rest of the space. And by animals, I'm not talking just your domestic dogs and cats—no, throw a few cows in the mix. You could see there was a rhythm to it that the locals had somehow figured out. But I walked around the first day in Katmandu, and thought 'how the hell am I going to even get out of this city without running into something?!'

"By day two I felt like I at least had the clutching and gearing on the bike figured out and all that was left was to avoid the animals, people, trucks, bikes, and sheer cliff falls for another two weeks."

Did you ever feel unsafe—even for a brief moment?

"Not really. You kind of assimilated into the dance that was the chaos of it all fairly quickly. I felt most unsafe when I stopped and looked at what we were going to be riding through or down or up. But once I was on the bike I was entirely in the moment. I wasn't as concerned about crashing as I was about what the hell happens if I get a cut as a result of the crash."

What were you most concerned with before you went?

"Other than being in a completely foreign country, my real concern was being at altitude. I'm not used to being above a few hundred feet above sea level let alone 10,000 or more. I knew that everyone reacts differently to altitude, so I did some altitude work to help prepare for that."

So did you take any major spills during the trip?

"Yeah, I dumped a bike a few days in. Hard enough to crack a few ribs, but didn't know it at the time. I thought the heavy breathing was from the altitude. That probably didn't help. But I stayed with it. Hell, I came all that way. I wasn't going back until I finished that trip! The bike barely had a scratch. Those Royal Enfields are like little tanks."

What did you absolutely make sure you took with you and glad you did?

"Wash and dry boxers. Those are proof that you can pretty much go anywhere in the world with just two pair of butt huggers."

How long did you plan for the trip?

"From start to finish, probably five months. The last three months was where I put in the real prep work—from learning how to ride a dirt bike to doing cardiovascular work and living at altitude."

What route did you take?

"I was living in Philadelphia at the time so I started there. Then I went to Lake Tahoe where I could work out at some elevation. I started the trip with a flight from LA to Tokyo. Then I went from Tokyo to Burma, then Burma to Kathmandu. Word of advice—don't use the men's room at the Kathmandu airport. Get that taken care of before you deplane."

It's pretty hard to top that ride. Any others that stand out?

"I rode to Americade in upstate New York from Philadelphia in 2012. That doesn't sound nearly as adventurous, does it? But a big chunk of that ride up and back was in the rain, and at one point I was riding at night. I had a Triumph Sprint at the time. Great bike, but I had water running down parts of me where there shouldn't have been. Having newer tires was the key."

When you're not riding, what do you do?

"I run marketing and communications at the Savannah College of Art and Design (SCAD) in Savannah, Georgia. It's often a six-day-a-week job, so I try to get out on one of my bikes any chance I get. [Since publication of this article, José has gone on to found C'reer, an app that let's high school students plot their way from interests to college to careers.]

Any other family members ride?

"My wife, Jen, rides. She's on a Honda Shadow right now, but she keeps saying she wants a bigger bike. My father-in-law also rides. He has an older Gold Wing he had converted into a trike."

If you could ride anywhere tomorrow, where would it be?

"Without getting on a plane, I'd ride the Florida Keys and stop when I got to Key West to pull up to a vodka gimlet."

[Note: Jose has since left his position at SCAD and is now the CEO of Vireo Labs.]

Sheila McQueen is proof that the experiences in our youth do have a habit of influencing us on into adulthood—no matter where they might come from.

Making An Impression

Anyone who thinks media—print or otherwise—has no influence on young minds hasn't met Sheila McQueen. See, in 1985, she was an impressionable fifteen-year-old reading a UK-based magazine called *Looks*, probably not unlike other female lifestyle magazines popular in the US at the time.

A particular issue of that magazine captured Sheila's attention when she saw a makeover reveal of a young twenty-something, glammed up and sitting on a motorcycle. It was a look that not only appealed to the "wannabe" sophisticated side of her, but also the adventurous one. And that was the defining moment when Sheila heard the call of two wheels.

In case that wasn't enough to drive the point firmly into high gear, the impression was solidified with continuous viewing of two particular kids' programs about biking that were also popular in the UK at the time—*KickStart*, for trials and off-road riders, and *Sorry Mate, I Didn't See You*, which covered basic riding rules and road safety.

"I read the *Looks* article and thought 'I too want to wear big boots, have spiky hair, and ride to interesting places on my extremely large motorcycle.' I also was telling my mum that I was watching something much more suitable to young ladies at that time, but sent off for an information pack from Kawasaki."

Sheila plays down the parental influence in the mix. Seems her dad was a "scooter boy" in his youth and occasionally regaled his daughter with stories of riding two-up through Switzerland in the 1950s on a 250cc Lambretta with a double bass player in the Scottish Youth Orchestra. Sounds like a story we'll have to pursue at a later time.

Meanwhile, the Kawasaki information pack arrived, and Sheila thought her two-wheeled journey was on its way. In 1985, she said she could have ridden the Kawasaki AR125 with the equivalent of a learner's permit, and that bike was a mini-version of the bike she had seen in that *Looks* photoshoot. It was not quite the "big bike" she had envisioned, but it was a motorcycle. But given her job, working in what was the equivalent of a newsstand, she still couldn't afford it...or anything else that burned fossil fuel.

The years ticked by. She got a car license, instead. Then she got a job in Oxford and proceeded to join hundreds of thousands of cagers sitting grid-locked while watching bikers lane-split (*filtering* in the UK) their way to work. And that sealed it for her.

"I didn't know any bikers and didn't sit on a bike until the morning I went for CBT [compulsory basic training]. I got on the bike, and the first thing I did was drop it. I thought it was a good idea to get that out of the way early!"

That experience made clear to her two things: one, she was a slow learner and two, she needed to get her own bike and ride it slowly around parking lots before she would get out on the open road.

This was in the '90s, when a lot of online forums had sprung up on the web. Her husband at the time had introduced her to one called "CIX," which was populated almost entirely by tech geeks, many of whom she points out were also bikers.

"I started spending a lot of time on there asking questions. They'd argue, swap fettling tips, and organize track days and rideouts under the banner of "Team Waste." They welcomed wannabes like me with warm insults and open hearts."

Sheila said she never knew anyone's real name in the group, but they sold her her first bike—a 125cc two-stroke Kawasaki that had been passed around among new Team Waste members until it was her turn. She said she wasn't brave enough to get it and ride it back herself, so they delivered it to her door.

"For a few hundred quid, I finally had a bike. But keep in mind, I'm about six feet tall. So when I rode that little bike it was like a frog on a matchbook."

She kept the little bike-that-could long enough to finally get comfortable riding in more than a parking lot, retook her CBT, passed it without dropping anything, and turned around and bought a bigger bike—a Yamaha 600cc Diversion.

As she got more comfortable riding, she began taking longer rides and buying larger bikes. Today, she owns a 2000 Triumph Adventurer.

She eventually joined a group of riders that periodically participated in the annual Round Britain Rally—a navigational scatter rally that takes riders to different places around the UK between Easter and the end of October.

She also did the End-to-End Run three times. You ride the length of the British mainland—starting at Land's End at the furthest point south then go 870+ miles north to John O'Groats in Scotland. (For anyone who saw the movie *Long Way Down*, you'll know this is where Ewan McGregor and Charley Boorman started their trip.)

"These aren't just road trips for me; they're therapy. Each one related to a relationship I was ending or starting at the time. But each trip tied to the next, and if I hadn't done the third one, I wouldn't have ended up riding with the Blue Knights in Australia."

It's not surprising that Sheila would end up flying halfway around the world to ride nearly two thousand miles around the southern part of Australia—mostly by herself. Besides the long rides previously mentioned, she said she's also fond of riding the A4, which takes you from London and out into what she refers to as the West Country.

She said these are trips that could take at least a week and go past some of Britain's most ancient and interesting sites—like Sibury Hill and Avebury. Typically, she'll camp along parts of it—mostly because she said it's less expensive. Plus, she's not averse to being by herself.

"While I planned the trip to Australia to see my brother and some friends, I also wanted the time to explore on my own. The funny thing is that people were so open there, I was rarely by myself."

Some of those open types were members of the Blue Knights of Australia. This is an international group of law enforcement men and women who enjoy riding motorcycles. Their website points out that this is the oldest law enforcement motorcycle club in Australia. For Sheila, they became her best friends.

"They welcomed me as if I was one of them. Different members would escort me around scenic places, have me join them on group rides, and eventually gave me the highest honor possible—a Blue Knights patch and a personal escort out of Perth."

I asked her what else she did on her Australian venture, and she sent me this list:

Koalas photographed—11
Days on the road—8
Dolphins seen—7
Bikes ridden—4
Swedish barmaids met—2
Lighthouses climbed—2
Emus spotted—1
Lookout trees climbed—1/2

When asked what the trip had taught her, she said it was more about being reminded of something she had learned earlier on. "If I want to be an adventurous solo traveling person who has conversations that make for interesting anecdotes, then I need to start acting like one."

In other words, don't just talk about it, do it.

And so she has. Although she's been a freelance contributor to motorcycle travel magazines for a few years, she's now left her job in public relations for the University of Cambridge to make travel journalism her full-time career. Perhaps not a big stretch, but one that curiously brings her back to writing about the thing that got her to this point nearly thirty years ago.

Sounds like it's now her turn to make an impression.

By all accounts, the car accident should have taken the life of Michael Althouse, but he survived... and he credits riding motorcycles with helping him recover from that and much more.

Crossing the Line

There are lines we sometimes cross in life—both real and symbolic—that can define who we are or who we become. For Michael Althouse, the center line of a mountain road somewhere in the Sierra Nevadas became the one that would do both.

It was fall of 2000 and Michael was driving his then thirteen-year old son to school. As he drifted off to sleep behind the wheel, his Jeep Cherokee drifted with him. Before his son could get his attention, the Jeep plowed head on into an oncoming big rig loaded with freshly cut logs. Both vehicles were doing over fifty miles per hour. The Jeep was totaled.

Five weeks later, Michael woke up from a medically -induced coma. His left leg had nearly been separated from his body; he had multiple fractures to his femur, a lacerated kidney and liver, and had nearly died several times. At the scene of the accident, his severed femoral artery had bled out as much blood as the paramedics could put in. No one then thought he'd live, let alone fully recover.

Meanwhile, his son had escaped with only some cuts and bruises. Someone was looking out for both of them.

As a young boy, Michael and his family used to take vacations in Southern California. That was before Interstate 5 was completed, so they'd find themselves tooling down US 99 headed for sun and warm beaches. It was during one of those summer road trips that the rumble and dull roar of twenty or more motorcycles going past the family car in a staggered formation got Michael's attention. As they went past; all noise, long hair, and beards; Michael swore to himself that's what he wanted to do some day.

"It looked like freedom. There was something about that group, that sound, just everything about it that appealed to me."

The line had been crossed. Michael had the motorcycle bug, and all bets were off as to whether or not he'd eventually find himself on one. The only thing standing in the way, as it is with many of us, was his mother.

So when he turned eighteen, he bought a very used 1973 Honda 500 Four, which he promptly beat up and rode the hell out of. That was followed by an old Kawasaki KZ 550—the predecessor to the Ninja—which he also rode until it could be ridden no more. Then he got married, hung up his helmet, and did his best at being a husband and father to three sons.

"I really didn't have much direction then. I was in and out of jobs. Made money, lost money. Got into some occasional trouble. I wasn't paying attention to where I was at or where I needed to go. I lived like that for nearly twenty years."

Then came the wreck. That line that nearly brought him over to the other side. The white light. The end of the line that became almost permanent.

"It didn't happen right away, but within a few years after the wreck, I realized that I needed to start doing things different. It was a big wake-up call."

A used 2000 Harley-Davidson 883 Sportster welcomed him back to riding. He rode, wrecked, fixed up, and rode that bike until the need and ability to get a bigger bike presented itself. That bigger bike was a new 2007 Road King that he then rode even more. This included a 4,500-mile cross-country trip over an eleven-day period in 2010.

"Even though I didn't have Harleys when I first started riding, I was drawn to that iconic image. Maybe it goes back to seeing those guys riding past us during that summer vacation. Like anyone, I thought it was kind of bad-ass to own one, and that appealed to me."

Like so much of Michael's life, that 4,500-mile trip up through Wyoming, the Dakotas, and into the Pacific Northwest was without a plan. No defining parameters or lines to follow. But it wasn't without a destination.

The idea was hatched among a group of friends, all determined to make the trip. But as the day of departure approached, the well-intended group slowly dwindled to just him and a buddy. The two of them left with an idea of where they wanted to go, a Harley-Davidson road atlas, and all the gear necessary to get them through fair weather and foul.

"We had to take some detours along the way, and a few times we got lost. But the lack of planning also led to some welcome surprises. Scenery, new roads, and even a hotel room in Jackson during the time of year we probably wouldn't have gotten one. There were times when we said, 'What the hell are we doing.' But then we reminded ourselves that if the two sons we had in Afghanistan at the time could do that, we could do this."

When Michael returned from that trip, he'd already gotten his bachelor's degree in journalism as a forty-something magna cum laude graduate from Sacramento State. He was finishing up his master's degree at the same university and doing well at it. Anyone who had known the younger Michael might have been surprised.

He admits to being a lousy student when he first tried college right out of high school. In fact, he was thrown out of San Diego State after his sophomore year when he earned a less than D average. His dad was a chemistry professor at Stanford University at the time, so it's not as if there wasn't some impetus to do better. But he didn't. Timing is everything.

The years, money, and marriage went by, and it was only after taking some aptitude tests at American River College in the mid-2000s that the education spark was lit...and another line crossed. Michael was on his way to higher ed, but as a much older and wiser student.

"I went back to school because I knew it was the right thing for me to do, and I had people in my corner, encouraging me to do it. I hadn't planned on going beyond a bachelor's degree, but the few dollars I made after graduation, writing for some small newspapers in northern California, just wasn't enough. One of my professors encouraged me to go back to school and teach. So I did."

Two years later, with a master's degree in hand, Michael was further encouraged to take his writing ability and love of rhetoric and music to the next level. He applied to PhD programs at multiple universities while still managing to rack up the miles on his Road King. Eventually, Louisiana State University would be one of the few schools that were attracted to his story and ability.

Today, Michael's nearly one hundred percent recovered physically from that wreck and is in Baton Rouge, Louisiana, teaching public speaking to undergrads and working on his PhD and a thesis that in the simplest of terms can be described as examining how the many different faces of Bob Dylan have impacted the world. Heady stuff for a guy who just a decade earlier wasn't quite sure where he was going to end up.

After over fifty-thousand miles, Michael traded the Road King in on a brand new 2014 Street Glide that he's already put over eleven-thousand miles on, with rides mostly throughout the South. For him, riding is no longer about the image of it, but the feeling of it—the freedom, the ability to clear everything away, and just be focused on where you are in the moment.

"The wreck got me to this point. I had my life before it, and a different life after it. It created a line between the two. I'm determined to stay on this side of it."

Some lines are eventually meant to not be crossed. For Michael Althouse, this is now such a line. Ride safe, brother, Wherever you may go from here.

Zoë Cano is no stranger to adventure and big dreams, but the idea of a solo ride on a Triumph across the US was one that she wouldn't let go unfulfilled. Here's how she got to that point and made it happen.

Roads Less Traveled

Sometimes we deny our parents' influence. We think we've constructed ourselves, as if godlike we created something from nothing. Perfectly imperfect but failing to acknowledge the part the parental units played in the process.

Zoë Cano is not such a person. She admits to being adventurous and independent, but readily acknowledges the influence her father played in both helping further and give credence to those characteristics.

"My father, Alan Matthews, was an amazing influence on me in terms of finding freedom and exploring. Although he didn't have a bike when I was growing up, I did see the old black-and-white little photos in his albums of him on one. He instilled in me the passion to explore and to be inquisitive of all things new and different."

That independence showed itself early on and played out in a string of events that eventually led Zoë to a long distance solo ride across America and a subsequent book about that journey. But the two-wheeled element first came into play when, as a seventeen-year old Brit living and working in Paris, she had scooter-riding friends who were able to get her hooked up with a bright new Peugeot 50cc scooter.

We think traffic is bad in the US, but a common theme between everyone who has commuted in major cities in Europe is that it's absolutely brutal in Paris. Such brutality and the cost of keeping a car, eventually drives one to something cheaper and more nimble. Zoë was no exception and, despite having three scooters stolen in a nine-year period while living in Paris, she continued to make two small wheels her primary mode of transportation.

Zoë eventually made the move from scooters to motorcycles, but not without a slight detour via endurance horse riding. For the uninitiated, that means you get on the back of a horse and ride fifty or more miles in a day. And we're not talking a nice casual trot through the park. This is the equivalent of riding an Iron Butt on dirt roads! And in Zoë's case, over some serious mountains.

"I guess it's that spirit of independence and wanting to go where a car can't. I've ridden and trekked in some incredible places—the Andes, through Kenya, and the Atlas Mountains in Morocco. Going from horses to motorcycles didn't seem like that big of a stretch."

And when she said trekked the Andes, she means a several hundred mile journey lasting a few weeks atop a native Peruvian Paso Fino.

But about eight years ago, wanting to get on something bigger than a scooter and less finicky than a horse, Zoë bought herself a 2001 Triumph Bonneville T100 and proceeded to ride throughout England, Wales, and parts of Europe. Some of her favorite routes have taken her through France into Normandy and through mid-Wales, including the Elan Valley, the Brecon Beacons, and the Black Mountains. All the while, she's making a living in the film industry and planning major sporting events around the world—including equestrian and rugby. That work eventually brought her to the United States.

"I lived on the East Coast for about four years and knew that when I left I wanted to get back and see as much of the country as I could. I didn't know for sure how or when other than I had this idea that it would be on a motorcycle."

Before you get the impression that Zoë's love of freedom and exploration makes her impulsive, impetuous, or a big risk taker, think again. This is a woman who pursues adventure with a plan. Reminder—most of the greatest explorers throughout history were the same way. None of them got in a boat, on a sled, or a horse without some semblance of a plan.

In Zoë's case, this was a plan four years in the making—beginning with a conversation about bucket list items between her and a girlfriend in the venerable Ace Cafe in London. This then led to a full-blown effort to see this item all the way through, with one of the considerations being able to eat well and sleep comfortably.

"I could have roughed it a bit more and spent less money, but I really didn't want to travel that way. To be honest, I grew up in a home where my mother was a professional chef, so when I travel, I always make sure to eat well and healthy."

What Zoë was willing to forego were some of the technical gadgets that are standard fare anymore for most long distance riders—like a GPS and a big dual-sport bike. Instead, she used old *National Geographic* maps to plot her routes and give her an idea of the different sites she wanted to see along the way, again with the idea of exploring something out of the ordinary. And she wanted to make the trip on her Triumph.

"I love that bike, and it just seemed like the right thing to do. But I quickly found out how expensive it was to ship it to the States. So I set about trying to find one in the US that would be as close to mine as I could get."

She lucked out when a couple of degrees of separation put her in contact with the folks at EagleRider in Los Angeles, who were just beginning to add Triumphs to their livery of mostly Harleys at the time. They eventually agreed to ship a newer Bonneville from Los Angeles to Boston, where Zoë started her cross-country trip.

By spring of 2012, between paychecks, selling her wedding dress, renting out rooms in her home, and auctioning off odds and ends, she had enough money to be on her way. She got on a plane in England, landed many hours later in Boston, Massachusetts, and was on the road the next day. Two months later, she found herself on the other side of the United States, having fulfilled her dream and having done it her way.

"People have asked me if I had any favorite parts of the trip, but I tell them the entire trip was my favorite. I got to see parts of the country most people who live in the States don't see, and I met some wonderful people along the way."

While there was never any doubt that she would finish the trip, there were times she said when it did get dicey for her. Heavy continuous rains on roads shared with big trucks, and roads like the Dragon's Tail and Highway 1 in California with hairpin after hairpin turns are two examples.

"There was one point that I had just about had enough. I was heading into Salt Lake City and had been riding in the mountains in freezing rain for hours. I pulled into a gas station, cold, wet, and miserable. I actually started crying. Then a guy on a Beemer pulls up, sees me, and starts talking to me. He reminded me that it's times like these that help you remember trips like this. So I got back on the bike and finished what I started."

Would she do anything differently? She quickly rattles off a short list: more waterproof gear, taken a better look at the long-term weather forecasts, and used some sort of navigation...besides old maps.

Zoë returned to London and decided to turn this particular adventure into a book. She wrote *Bonneville Go or Bust: On the Roads Less Travelled*, chronicling in detail the entire trip. That book got the attention of Triumph USA, who earlier this year brought Zoë back to the States to ride

2,000 miles through Alabama, Georgia, and Florida and on a new Triumph Bonneville, no less.

"I'm looking for every opportunity I can to return, since I feel I've really only scratched the surface. I don't think people understand just how incredibly diverse the geography and scenery is in the United States, or how open the people are. I want to experience more of both."

Whatever or wherever Zoë's next adventure might be, we think her dad would be proud.

Alex Crookes is a motorcycle rider, entrepreneur, and code writer. He put all three together to come up with an app that not only solved a problem, but helped create an online community.

Bits, Bytes, Eat, Sleep, Ride...Repeat

If bits and bytes could be turned into a street or trail, Alex Crookes would be one happy rider. A serial entrepreneur as comfortable writing code for his EatSleepRIDE app as he is riding hard and fast on two wheels, he's the epitome of someone who's turned his passion into a business.

But getting to this point wasn't ever the plan, and it certainly wasn't much of a direct path. His passion for two wheels started at the age of eighteen, when a friend gave him a very used Honda CB 125T. And while you'd think that would have meant riding through wooded trails or along country lanes of England, where he grew up, think again. Alex honed his skills riding where he worked while in college—a water treatment plant.

"It covered acres of ground. There were plenty of roads and no one on them. It gave me an ideal learning environment, and I didn't have to think much about what could get in my way."

Hmm, might be a business idea there—water treatment plants as motorcycle training centers. But I digress.

Once Alex had fully abused the little Honda, he traded it in on a Yamaha XJ900F that he rode throughout college. After some off-again and on-again bike ownership due to college, career, and moves from England to New Zealand to Canada, he now finds himself in Toronto and the owner of three bikes—a KTM 450 EXC, a Triumph 1200 Tiger Explorer, and a Triumph Speed Triple. And like most riders, he can easily tick off the reasons for buying each one.

"I recently got into dirt riding and just loved the KTM ethos. Plus, I was in my 'need a big bike' phase. The 1200 Explorer was me getting old. I wanted something a bit sporty, but also capable of covering distance in comfort. I was drawn to the Ducati Multistrada, but the reviews [in the UK] had just been published for the Triumph and that was it for me. I got the first one in Canada."

He said his wife was the influence behind the Street Triple. It seems she had just learned to ride and for some reason did not want to ride the Daytona 675 he had at the time. They tried the Ducati Monster and a few others, but the Street Triple was it for both of them.

"I didn't have the heart to tell her it was essentially a Daytona without the fairing!"

Riding also involves Alex's thirteen-year old son on a Suzuki DR125 and his eleven-year old daughter on the back of whatever Mom or Dad is riding. Isn't there a saying about the family that rides together stays together?

Before we go further, Alex wants to point out that, despite what may seem like a personal and possible family obsession with Triumph, it's more a case of good reviews coming out right when he's in the market to buy. He does, however, own several Triumph T-shirts.

But riding, for Alex, isn't just about having different bikes for different purposes.

At this point in his life, it's both a stress reliever and an open lab of sorts for EatSleepRIDE.

"Running a business is hard. It takes a lot of work and a huge amount of responsibility. But all of that goes away when you fire up the bike. You get on, head down the road or into the hills, and all of the stress just disappears. And what better test lab for a riding app than being outdoors on two wheels!"

Alex didn't plan on being a serial entrepreneur. Not many people do. In his case, it happened by coincidence when he left a company that he said wasn't terribly well managed. A friend came to him with the idea to offer personalized ringtones for cell phones at a time when cell phones were gaining popularity as more than a business device. The idea took off and so did the company.

That company was eventually sold, and Alex moved on to another called Sharp Robot. That one also became highly successful then merged with a Boston-based company called m-Qube. Alex became that company's CTO, but two years later, it was sold to Verisign—one of the largest Internet security and domain registration companies in the country.

By this point, Alex and his business partner, Nick Dunlop, decided they'd had enough of the merger and acquisition treadmill. So they decided to get on two wheels and just ride.

"We spent every day for six or seven months riding everywhere we could and on many different bikes. We were frustrated with an inability to really share the routes we were riding or the experience of meeting different people we came across."

He said they were also trying to figure out an easier way to let people know where they were without having to stop frequently and call or text them.

"We've all been on rides where you run late because you're just getting lost in the experience. But someone is getting worried because you're not home when they thought you would be. We wanted to solve that problem, too."

EatSleepRIDE didn't start out as a rider app. It was initially a blog where riders could share information about their rides with other riders. But Alex said they really didn't put the effort into it, so it never really took off. It was the combination of a simple mobile game and a chance encounter with a group of riders in the Blue Ridge Mountains that put EatSleepRIDE on a different course.

"We'd been working out some elements of the app, and I was playing Super Monkey Ball on my phone during a break. I realized how sensitive that device was in terms of picking up on the motion of the game. I thought, 'What if you could do that with a bike—read the bike's motion and put that information on a phone?'"

So there it was—create an app that would give you more information about the motion of the bike that you could also share with others. Other apps do something similar—at least the sharing part, thanks to GPS. But Alex and Nick were aiming for something more, and that would come with a chance encounter in the Blue Ridge Mountains.

"We happened to be riding in Blue Ridge Park, and we met some other riders gathered at the park station. We noticed they had these particular memorial patches, so we asked about them. As it turns out, that same group had been riding the same route a year earlier, but one of their members had gone missing.

"They waited and they waited. Still not there. So they backtracked to look for him; to see if there were any signs he'd run off the road. Nothing. Even the police couldn't find him. It turns out that three or four months later, a bunch of hunters came upon a motorcycle and a skeleton down off the road. That guy had gone over the road, broken his leg and collar bone, and died of dehydration—alone."

And that led Alex and Nick to add one more piece of functionality to the app that could be both a lifesaver and a stress reliever. Called "Crashlight," it's a separate element of the EatSleepRIDE app that automatically notifies selected contacts with emergency information and your location via voice, text, and email when you go down.

If the crash is just you accidentally dumping the bike in the parking lot, you have three minutes to let your emergency contacts know you're okay, then the rest of the day to come up with a better story.

"Riding has taught me that I'm not a risky rider, and consequently, I'm not a risky businessman. It also reminds me that you need to be passionate about what you do, and in my case, this business gives me an opportunity to do that every day."

So what's in store for Alex and EatSleepRIDE?

"I'd like to see us offer more tools and services that make riders lives easier and empower them to want to ride further and more often. And secretly, I'd like to see me get more seat time, whether it's on asphalt or dirt."

Well said, and well-played, Alex. One happy rider coming up.

Gary France is a self-made man who's management company oversaw the construction of some of the largest projects on multiple continents. He finally allowed himself a Harley as a reward for decades of hard work. Then he rode it on a 12,000 mile journey across the US.

Screw Impulse Control

When you're a sixteen-year old kid faced with having to bear the responsibility of providing for your family, the future doesn't look like anything but the end of the day you started. A motorcycle becomes nothing more than a cheap way to get from home to work and back again because the alternative is an over twenty-six-mile ride by bicycle.

That's where Gary France found himself a few decades ago. And any impulse to do much more was one to be controlled and channeled into building something, anything that would be more than the day he found himself in.

"My father was a watchmaker, who died suddenly when I was twelve. My mother tried to keep things going, but it got harder and harder. So when I was sixteen, I left school to help her support my brothers and me. I got into construction because it was a fairly easy thing to do at the time."

Gary's first motorcycle was a little Honda Cub that took him to different jobs as a beginning draftsman. Then, like so many of us, at the age of twenty-five he started a family, sold the bike he had at the time, and gave up riding. But the idea of owning another bike and one day riding more than a few miles here and there never left him.

As he watched his friends finish high school, go to college, travel, and then start their careers, Gary continued to work in the construction business. Eventually, he and a partner started a construction management firm, but he said he made himself a promise that one day he would make up for all of the things he missed and eventually go on a real adventure.

"When I was younger, I worked hard, and I never gave myself much time to do anything but work. But I also never gave up knowing that one day I would fulfill the dream of getting on a motorcycle and just taking off. I just didn't know when that would be or how long it would take before I could make that happen."

His construction management business eventually led Gary to oversee projects in nine countries, including: England, France, Holland, Ireland, Spain, Qatar, Russia, UAE, and the United States. These weren't small projects. These were multi-million dollar affairs like Terminal Five at Heathrow Airport, the 2014 Winter Olympic Games in Sochi, and the entire Olympic Park in London for the 2012 Summer Olympics.

All of these massive projects and the supervision of the tens of thousands of people and the materials involved, gave Gary an eye for logistics and planning, both of which would prove to be particularly useful later. But there was still that nagging sense of wanting to get on a bike and ride.

"In 2006, I was early to a meeting in London and had some time to kill. So I wandered into Warr's, a nearby Harley-Davidson dealer, and I knew the minute I laid eyes on those bikes that I had to have one. No question about it."

Before Gary was going to buy a Harley outright, he decided to rent one and try it for a few days...just in case. Keep in mind, this was the largest bike he'd ever ridden, and he hadn't ridden for about twenty-five years. It didn't matter. As he got more comfortable with the bike over the three-day rental period, the grin on his face became more permanent.

So as soon as he returned the rental, he bought a brand new 2006 Harley Road King.

Eventually, he rode that bike all over England, bought a couple of other Harleys, and rode to a Harley rally in Austria. But it was a custom bike show that pushed him even further into multi-bike ownership.

"I just loved what guys were doing with different bikes. The stretched frames, the custom exhaust...all of it. So I worked with a custom builder in Ireland to build a low rider I eventually named 'Tradewinds.' Then I had a '70s-style chopper built that I named 'Amelia' and have ridden all over Europe. People look at me like I'm crazy—they think it looks uncomfortable—but it's one of the most comfortable bikes I've ever been on."

So 2009 comes around and Gary decides it's time to retire. He was only fifty, but he'd been working for thirty-four years, and for the first time in his life he wasn't anxious to get back to work after Christmas break. He'd made his mark and considered himself lucky enough to be able to even consider an early retirement, let alone take one. The dream of a long motorcycle adventure was about to become a reality.

"I thought it was time to pay myself back for all of those early years I missed out. It was time to go west, clear my head, and ride across America."

Gary's years of preparation and attention to detail on large projects kicked in. He started poring over maps, reading different books, and contacting motorcycle bloggers. He researched equipment, GPS and sat nav devices, and points of interest. He wanted to get it all right, so he wouldn't miss seeing anything.

It also helped that his wife, Jackie, was from the United States, and they'd taken occasional trips to see her family in Seattle, Washington. But Gary was determined to see much more than just that.

"I had a couple of key criteria for this trip—I wanted to go north-to-south, so I'd get to the West Coast before the weather got bad. I wanted to go east-to-west so I'd never start with the sun in my eyes. And I had to see New York City, the Rockies, the Grand Canyon, Las Vegas, California, and Sturgis!"

All of the planning culminated in late June 2010 when he shipped his Road King to the United States, complete with a new custom paint job featuring portraits of leading actresses from the '40s and '50s. Gary joined his bike (now called "The Leading Ladies") a few days later in New York and began what originally was supposed to be a 13,500-mile odyssey to one that evolved into more than four months, covering over 21,000 miles, across twenty-seven states.

If you look at Gary's route, you'll know why. It's as if you gave a marker and a map of the United States and told a four-year old to draw a line through every state at a diagonal between Maine and California. There's some backtracking in places—like the ride up to Maine from New York and back—and some interesting loops, where he either got side tracked with a specific point of interest or nature forced a change in plans. But just try finding a straight line. Not gonna happen.

Gary saw all of what he had hoped for, and he had riding companions at different points along the way—some planned, some impromptu. But as he consistently discovered, the biking community is a friendly bunch, particularly in America.

"One of the best parts of the trip was just meeting all of these friendly people, many of whom would offer to put me up or buy me a meal, even though they'd just met me. This is also a nation that has just about every kind of scenery and geography you can imagine. I never got tired of it."

The only point where Gary said he felt any regret was riding down the Ventura Highway in California, headed to Los Angeles. This was where his trip would end, and he would be putting 'The Leading Ladies' on a plane back to London. He teared up because he knew it was over. He had the same feeling in the taxi ride to the airport when it really sunk in that he was heading home.

"I couldn't wait to get home to see my wife, my sons, and my dog. But at the same time, there was still a part of me out on the road, and I was a bit sad to leave it there."

Gary later recaptured much of what he saw and experienced in a coffee table book called *France in America*. Neither a travelogue nor an adventure diary, the book manages to convey both the diversity of the United States and Gary's impressions about his trip in a very personal way.

Many might think that the trip and the resulting book would be the culmination of Gary's riding experience. After all, he had fulfilled his dream. But given Gary's past oversight of big construction projects, he's really now moved into reconstructing his own life built on his passion for motorcycles.

He's since started a small motorcycle tour company that takes Harley-Davidson owners to rallies in different locations in Europe. There are still another twenty-three states for him to plan to see, and he's begun building a flat tracker to race on the Bonneville Salt Flats in 2015 or 2016.

"The first time I went on the salt at Bonneville in my car, the hairs stood up on the back of my neck. I knew I had to come back and be a part of that...but on a motorcycle."

For someone who had to curb, if not downright squash, the impulses of youth, if the desire to ride wherever two wheels might go strikes you, Gary, have at it. You deserve it.

Some people only dream and never act on them. Some act on them, but are forced to cut them short. Ran Zilca dreamed, acted, and went all the way.

Keepin' The Dream Alive

Dreams matter. Just ask Ran Zilca. As a kid growing up in Tel Aviv, Israel, he played with toy motorcycles and dreamed of riding free across the open spaces of America. That's a pretty big dream when you're living in a country where a motorcycle is considered a luxury that only the rich can afford, and good luck finding any bike over 500cc. It also didn't help that it was a dream imagined alone—no one in Ran's family rode, thought of riding, or had even been on a motorcycle. But somehow, in this desert of motorcycle nothingness, Ran's dream managed to survive and would eventually find its way to reality.

"By the time I was in my late 30s, I had achieved a good deal of professional success. I was a veteran of an elite technology unit in the Israeli army. I had worked for the world's largest private research lab. I had become a hi-tech startup entrepreneur. And I'd even learned to play the guitar and drums and had a band on the side. But something was seriously missing. So after months and months of reflection, I said, 'That's it, I'm buying a motorcycle.'"

Quite the decision for a guy who'd never even been on a bike. And at that point he's then living the suburban life in New York, was married, and a father of three. Typical mid-life crisis is what his friends and family thought. More than likely, they also thought it would pass. But it didn't.

Because his decision to buy a motorcycle wasn't the impulsiveness of a guy looking at the shorter end of a long life. Granted, turning a certain age makes one think about what you didn't do as much as what you should. But here's something else you need to know about Ran. He's a smart guy. Wicked smart. He's the CEO of a company called Intrinsic Mobile—they develop digital products that help people improve their lives. He holds eleven patents. He's written numerous publications on topics as diverse as pursuing happiness and speech analysis. So while the decision to buy a bike and eventually ride across America may have seemed to come out of the blue, in fact, it was fairly well thought out...and there was some science involved.

"In 2009, I was working with all of these different people like Deepak Chopra and Stephen Covey to develop personal growth programs that you could access on a mobile device. But I was paying more attention to the programs from a business standpoint, not how they could apply to me personally. Then I decided to try them for myself, and that led me to remember that dream of riding a motorcycle as a kid. The problem was, I had no idea where to start. But I knew it was a start that I couldn't turn away from."

So Ran took his then seven-year old son to a Harley dealer. Why not? A dad brings his kid to look at motorcycles. But he said the salesman barely gave him the time of day, but he did give him a brochure.

"After I spent a few minutes drooling over all of these great looking bikes, I made my way over to this guy who literally rolled his eyes when I asked him about what I should be looking for. He handed me a brochure and said, 'everything you need to know is in there.'"

Inside the brochure was information about the motorcycle safety course. So Ran took the course soon after...and failed it. He dropped the bike a couple of times during the final test and started to wonder if maybe this wasn't for him. But he went back, tried again, passed the course, and got his license. But a big bike was out of the question. The last thing he wanted to do was spend a lot of money only to drop it, or worse. As a novice, he said he just wasn't comfortable getting on a big bike.

This wasn't a delay, just a reminder that some things take more time.

Getting his license didn't automatically translate into getting a bike. For Ran, this was going to be a step-by-step, well-considered process. So he got the gear first—a helmet, followed by a jacket. So, there he is, all decked out with no place to go and no bike to go on, until one day he happened to go by a Yamaha dealer near where he lived and bought a Yamaha V Star 250. While it wasn't going to get him out on the open plains, it was a bike.

The only problem is that Ran's a big guy—tops out at around 240 and is well over six feet. That's not much of a bike for a guy that size. But he was determined...and realistic. This was the first of a few steps that would finally allow him to fulfill that boyhood dream. And it was a step in the right direction.

"It helped that I joined a group of Yamaha riders. They welcomed me; no questions asked. They didn't make fun of me or the bike or being a new rider...none of that. If they hadn't been so welcoming, I might not have become as comfortable with the whole idea of riding. But they did, and it made the decision to continue much easier."

As Ran got more comfortable, he decided to go bigger. He traded in his little 250 and got a Yamaha V Star 950. Then he started racking up some miles and preparing for his long distance journey that would take him from New York to California in 2010 by way of the South—thirty-four days and over 6,000 miles.

While physical points of interest were inherent in his trip, what made it much more than just a cross-country solo ride was his decision to meet with and interview people, very specific people. They would make this as much a spiritual journey as a physical one.

"I felt that if I went on the road alone, with no purpose or a 'project,' it could be depressing. So I decided to turn it into a project by interviewing the authors and scientists I work with. I realized that I have a unique opportunity to learn deep insights about life by combining the reflection and meditation of the riding experience with the answers the experts would give me, and with the random conversations I knew I would have with people. So I decided to video the trip and to write about the experience later so I could share it with the world."

There probably isn't a biker alive who wouldn't agree with the idea that there is something meditative and at times even spiritual about riding. The necessity to focus intently on your surroundings or risk getting maimed or killed heightens the senses, even to the point where you do feel more alive. Yet, as with anything where repetition takes over, that somewhat altered state can eventually be taken for granted. Ran's desire to capture every element of his trip assured that wasn't going to happen...at least not for him.

But the trip was not without its problems. He dropped the bike the first day. He had stopped on a hill to take a picture, didn't realize that the kickstand wasn't down, and the bike dropped to its side. Given all of the gear and equipment he had packed, there was no way Ran could get that bike back upright. So day one meant asking for help. Luckily, it came a short time later with the heft of a heavily tattooed guy at a nearby gas station. There was no major damage to the bike other than a loose mirror, and Ran was back on the road.

"There was a certain ignorance or naïveté that probably helped more than hindered me. Not knowing the effects of weather or the road conditions made me less likely to think about them and probably made me less apprehensive until I was right up on them. And by that point, I just had to deal with it."

I ask him about how his wife got behind this trip. After all, most wives would either come along, send you on your way, or possibly put their foot down. He said that his wife saw that he was a different, better person after each short ride. So, while it was difficult for her to see him off, he said she admitted it was something that could be good for him. But despite that support, Ran said guilt was a fairly significant element of the trip.

"I don't think there was ever a time when I didn't feel guilty about taking this trip and leaving my wife and kids on their own. There were times when I'd call my wife and think that her response on the phone was her being upset I was on the trip, leaving her by herself. In reality, she told me later, she was just plain scared for me. No one wants their wife and family to feel that way, but at the same time she knew how important this trip was to me."

Ran and his family now live in Israel. They moved there two years ago after he and his wife took a hard look at what they wanted for the rest of their lives and where they wanted to spend them—another offshoot of that motorcycle trip and what Ran learned along the way. The only problem is that it's still tough to own a big bike in Israel, so he sold his Yamaha and manages to keep his motorcycle dream alive by renting a bike—mostly Harley Road Kings—whenever he travels outside of the country.

He also published a book about his trip—*The Ride of Your Life*. In it, he lists key takeaways from each of the interviews he conducted with people like Deepak Chopra, Phil Zimbardo, and Byron Katie. He also has his own personal list taken from the trip itself.

While that list is not a long one, it is a worthy one, with references to service to others, the inherent goodness of people, and the importance of family. But there's a bulleted point at the end of one of the chapters that best sums up Ran and the pursuit and eventual realization of his childhood dream: "Your dreams don't have to be earth-shattering to others, but they have to be earth-shattering to you."

Want proof? Just ask Ran Zilca.

Jeff Hesseltine has found a way to mix his passion for motorcycles, a good cup of joe, and a tasty breakfast. In the process, he's created a bit of a haven for bikers in the northwestern corner of California.

Nails, Caffeine, and Bikes

Sometimes you have to make adjustments. You get your heart and mind set on something you really want then BAM! the reality hammer slams down and breaks the fingers of desire. And you're left flailing about, reaching for a straw that doesn't quite fit into your now well-mangled hands.

Well, that's probably a bit too dramatic of an explanation for how Jeff Hesseltine got into the motorcycle-themed restaurant business, but it's not entirely inaccurate. Hammers were involved at one point. So were adjustments. Let's just chalk the other verbiage up to my well-caffeinated brain and lack of sleep.

See, Jeff is now the owner of a fine and growing establishment called "Black Lightning Motorcycle Café" (BLMC, as they like to shorten it) located in picturesque Eureka, California. His path to get there started on a mini-bike, wound itself through a short-lived life as a weekend AFM racer, then through the hallowed halls of Humboldt State University, eventual ownership of a construction business, and finally the kitchen of the BLMC.

"I always wanted to own a motorcycle shop, but once I decided to make that happen, I realized there were already enough of those in this area. The original idea was to have a place you could grab something to eat, then either watch a custom build take place or go work on your own bike. The city had some rules in place to prevent me from doing that, so I had to go with the next best thing."

Like we said, adjustments. So that meant a café that serves breakfast and lunch, some of the best coffee this end of Seattle, and motorcycle apparel and some bits and parts for bikes. That's right, you can get an espresso, breakfast sandwich, and a new helmet to start your day. Sounds a bit like heaven.

Who among us didn't have a go on a mini-bike as a kid? As Jeff tells it, he was around ten and would take his Uncle's as fast as he could up and down his grandmother's driveway in central California. At the time, that probably felt like 100 mph, and it didn't matter if it wasn't. It was two wheels and a taste of freedom.

Of course, at some point, a mini only takes you so far. So that same uncle had an actual bike—a YZ100—that Jeff decided should be his. After he pestered his uncle more times than his uncle could probably stand, Jeff got the bike.

That little YZ gave way to a 1970s' RD200 and a bunch of other bikes of varying small to mid-size that would let Jeff scratch his itch to go just fast enough to feel it.

About the time he was riding that little mini-bike he was also getting collector cards sent to him of various racers. One of the big names then was multi-time world champion Giacomo Agostini, or Ago as he was called. And Jeff kept Ago's card pinned next to his bed and began dreaming of racing, which eventually he made good on.

"I went with a friend out to what is now Infineon Raceway in Sonoma, California, and saw these guys racing, and they were all amateurs. I didn't know you could do that, so I got hold of an old bike, fixed it up, and joined a club and raced in AFM sanctioned events."

Jeff raced for about five years, during which he said he never finished higher than second and never finished a season higher than fifth. He started on a 1985 FZ600 then got some smaller bikes from the junkyard, so he could fix them up. Those included a batch of Ninja 250s that were given a second life at tracks, mostly around northern California. He said money became a factor, and it was a long way from where he was going to college at Humboldt State.

Even though he gave up racing, he didn't give up riding. He said he went through a lot of bikes that were, again, mostly saved from the junkyard. One of his favorites was a Honda XL600.

"That bike was just bulletproof. It never broke down. You could do wheelies all day on it. You hosed it off when you were done. Then take it out the next day and do it all over again."

Jeff considers himself a gearhead as much as he does a rider. So he doesn't mind taking what is literally another man's junk and turning it into a bit of a treasure. That's probably why he went into construction after graduating from college, a path that eventually led him to start his own company (Carpe Diem Construction) he had for ten years. All of that banging things around, putting things together... the whole being the sum of the parts kind of thing.

While two-by-fours and sixteen-penny nails are a long way from two wheels and four-stroke engines, they paid the bills for most of his adult life. But they didn't get him close to what he really wanted to do, which was to own some type of motorcycle shop. There's that adjustment thing again.

"The construction business is pretty hard on you physically. I'm only in my forties, and I was already feeling it. So I figured if I was going to make a change, now was the time to do it."

So his first thought was to open up a shop. Bad experiences at different places and his own knack for taking old bikes and making them whole again, led him to believe that could be an opportunity. But when he saw how many shops there already were in his end of Northern California, he decided to go a different route.

He and his wife had owned a sandwich shop about a decade past, so it's not as if he didn't know what he was getting himself into when he decided to try to mix a place to eat with some type of moto maintenance. What he didn't count on is that the city of Eureka, where he was going to put his business, was going to nix the idea of eating and working on bikes in the same building.

"I had this idea that people could come and grab a quick something to eat—basically, donuts and coffee—and either watch a build take place or have a couple of spots where they could work on their own bikes. The city wasn't having it, so I had to do away with the shop idea and go a different direction."

While Jeff made the menu of the BLMC simple—breakfast and lunch only—he also made it healthy, with a focus on using locally grown produce and other items. And then there's the coffee. After all, it isn't really that far from Eureka to he coffee mecca of Seattle.

"I used to not really care about where I got coffee or how it tasted, mostly because I was usually getting it for free every time I went to a lumberyard. But then I had a really good cup of well-made coffee and had to make sure that was one thing we would do really well at BLMC."

So Jeff went to coffee school. That's right, coffee school. There was a long-standing school in Bend, Oregon, and Jeff was one of its graduates. The school recently closed down, but Jeff said he's now about as close to being a coffee snob as you can get.

And of course there's the motorcycle theme at BLMC. It's evident in everything from the logo, to the names of some of the lunch menu items to the apparel and parts being sold there. That's right. You can literally go and try on a leather jacket while your Bultaco Panini is being made. That's Chipotle chicken, Monterey jack, and guacamole, in case you were wondering. Leave well-fed and caffeinated, and with some new gear in hand.

On the road to get there, Jeff had more than a few scrapes with disaster. One of the worst, in particular, was on a Ducati when the brake locked up and he low-sided the bike on a busy highway. Luckily, there was very little traffic, he slid into the bushes, and walked away with nothing more than a cracked thumb.

"It could have definitely been worse, but it wasn't. I suppose that was when I started thinking that I needed to do something different with my life."

While, like most small business owners, particularly restaurant owners, Jeff spends a lot of time at work, he still makes time to ride. He said his current stable has a few bikes that need some work—like the Aprilia Shiver he bought with the money the insurance company gave him from that wrecked Ducati. It needs a new battery. Then there's the Norton 750 Commando, a barn bike he got in trade several years ago in exchange for some construction equipment he didn't need anymore.

A Norton Commando...we're drooling and it's not because we're hungry.

"I got it to where I could at least start it and ride it, and just fell in love with it. I don't want to necessarily fully restore it. But I do want to get it running well enough to where it's my daily ride."

His working bikes include two motocross numbers—a KX125 he traded for some coffee, cash, and a leather jacket and a 1980 Honda 250XL—both of which he shares with his ten-year old son and sixteen-year old daughter.

Clearly, Jeff isn't opposed to bartering if there's a good bike involved.

With so much riding experience and a varied career that has taken him from home building to sandwich creation, I asked Jeff what riding has taught him. His response, while somewhat typical, also surprised me because he knew the answer right away, and he said it was something he had thought of early on.

"It's helped me with everything. You have to be Zen on a bike. You have to pay attention to all kinds of details. Like what's happening at intersections. What's going on with the cars around you. It teaches you not to panic. And you can't ride angry. You have to be calm. You have to be patient."

If I didn't know better, I'd swear Jeff read *Zen and the Art of Motorcycle Maintenance*.

But unlike *Zen* author Robert Pirsig, Jeff's riding experience does not include a long road trip. The longest one he could think of was a few days spent riding down to Calistoga to watch a flat track race. He said if he could take a long trip it would be through Canada or Alaska. He just needs to find the time. Until then, he's okay with riding the asphalt and dirt on and along the California coast.

Maybe an adjustment there is forthcoming.

Motorcycles have been chopped, lowered, raised, raced, and beaten up, but only a few guys from the South would think of creating a race featuring one-wheeled dragsters. Welcome to the world of unimotorcycle racing.

One-Wheeled Racing Wonders

Back in 1988, two friends, William Nassau (aka "Sidecar Willy") and Bubba Banks, were throwing back some beers at Daytona Bike Week. After more than a few Buds, they started thinking about what fun it might be to make a one-wheeled motorcycle then race it and see how fast you could go. They wrote up some designs on a napkin...and went off to build one.

Sidecar Willie got another buddy, Bob "Shit 'N' Get" Sheskie, involved, and the two of them built the very first one-wheeled drag racer, dubbing it a unimotorcycle. From there, they developed some rules, created a sanctioning body called the "American National Unimotorcyclists Society" (now the International Unimotorcyclists Society) and began promoting the fledgling sport.

As Sidecar Willie has been quoted as saying elsewhere, "This is basically a junkyard sport. People use old parts and good old American ingenuity to build something that can go one hundred feet on one wheel without killing them in the process."

It would take another three years before there was an official race and recognized time. That happened in 1991, when Shit 'N' Get made what would become the first successful run on his "Beast" (the term that is now synonymous with the one-wheeled racers) at what is now considered a painfully slow 5.2 seconds.

On the downside, Shit 'N' Get passed away in 1999, unable to see how far a sport has come that originated on a napkin and was influenced by a few Budweisers.

Unimotorcycle racing now includes nearly twenty chapters in Europe, Russia, India, New Zealand, Australia, and Indonesia, and another nearly half dozen in the US. In fact, the recognized world record is held by a Russian. Yes, a Russian by the name of Roman Koltakov—not anywhere close to Florida. And he did it on ice—with a "beast" of a machine going across a hundred feet of frozen H_2O in 2.38 seconds, powered by a 600cc Yamaha engine. Go figure.

It's highly unlikely that Sidecar Willy, Bubba, and Shit 'N' Get had this in mind when they first thought up the idea and built those first beasts. But who said a couple of guys and a few Buds can't make something happen?

To get a better idea of what's really involved in this sport, we spoke to its current president, Tiny Knuth, the head of the Indiana chapter; Brad "Chaos" Songer; and the California chapter president, Katlyn "Kat" Holsman.

"I'd known Sidecar for many years. We first met when I was eighteen, and I was raising hell in some bar in Albany, New York. He rode up on a BMW with a sidecar, asked if I wanted to go for a ride; I said yes, and we've been friends since."

Tiny later went on to college, got a business degree, worked for a US Senator, but kept herself as involved as she could in the motorcycle community. About the time Shit 'N' Get established the first race and world record, Sidecar came to Tiny and asked if she'd help organize the sport. He recognized that, while he might be the showman (he came from a family of entertainers), he also didn't have the business experience to organize this idea into something more than a backyard sport.

But Tiny wasn't sold...at least not right away. Sidecar wasn't deterred. He kept asking, until Tiny finally said yes about two years later and not only took on the role of heading up the organization, but also became part owner... and a world record holder.

"The first time I saw a race, I knew I had to give it a try. So I built a bike that runs in the rocket class. That's a bike that can be propelled by anything other than gas or electricity. Mine runs on compressed air."

Make no mistake; this is not a sport for the faint of heart. Steering brakes are optional. There are no shocks. An out-of-control unimotorcycle tends to pinwheel. And you're laying or sitting behind a bike that has to go as fast as you can get it to go in a hundred feet. It's like riding a wheelie but with all of the power up front.

Most US-based and European races are conducted on dirt. All you need is a hundred feet for the race itself and a few hundred feet after that to give you plenty of room to slow down your "beast." Race organizers might be thoughtful enough to have some hay bales at the end to slow you down. Spectators stand off to the side, barricaded away from the track, although a runaway beast has been known to go into the crowd.

The Russians and some of the other European chapters prefer ice. Now *there's* a soft surface.

"People can get hurt, but not like other sports. Mostly scrapes, cuts, and bruises. Mostly, people are just having too much fun to get hurt very seriously."

Tiny points out that there are rules—ten of them, in fact. (Hey, NFL, why don't you try that!) They mostly dictate the length of the drag strip (one hundred feet of unpaved surface), the age restrictions of the power plant (five years or older, and it has to be stock), dimensions of the beast (four feet wide by eight feet in length), and that your body can't touch the ground forward of the axle during a run.

With multiple classes, there's no shortage of opportunities for backyard builders to show off their building and mechanical skills. Here's how they break down:

Electric
Rocket (compressed air or rocket)
0-199cc
200-399cc
400-749cc
750cc to unlimited

What's interesting is just how popular this sport is in Europe versus the US. They have more chapters, more races, and more racers. But Tiny wants to change that.

"This was and will always be a low budget way for the average person to get into racing and have a blast doing it. I want a chapter in every state, and there's no reason we can't make that happen."

Tiny can't do it alone. The growth of unimotorcycle racing is going to take the dedication of people like Brad "Chaos" Songer. He shares Tiny's vision for growing the sport. As head of the Indiana chapter, one of the first in the US, he's passionate about his involvement, and how the sport has opened up opportunities for anyone with even a little mechanical ability to get into racing.

"I like to tear bikes apart and have been riding most of my life—dirt bikes, Harleys, Japanese bikes. I always wanted to do something more with them, but wasn't sure what that meant. Unimotorcycle racing gives me a chance to race, without having to put much money into it."

Brad said he can build a beast for as little as five hundred dollars. Most of the time he doesn't spend a dime. He goes to junkyards, finds the base engine he wants for the class he wants to race in, then gets the other parts he thinks he needs and starts the build. That process can take a few weeks or longer, depending on the frame and engine set up.

He's got a couple of beasts he's building now; one of which he's keeping under wraps until he's ready to run it later this spring once the weather warms up. When he's not working on or building a bike, he's also a family man with young children—something that sometimes doesn't go with racing of any sort.

I asked him what his wife thinks of all of this.

"She's a hundred-and-fifty percent behind it. It helps that she likes to ride. But she also sees how much freakin' fun this sport is and how much it means to me to continue to help grow it."

While there's no height or weight requirement for riders in this sport, it seems more than a coincidence that two of the women most involved are small. Kat said she's just over five feet. Tiny is probably there or not far behind. Yet Kat was the first woman to run in the sport's largest class with a beast powered by a former KZ1000 Police Special. (That bike new put out a claimed 85-90 hp and nearly 60 ft lbs of torque, but that engine was pushing more weight in a regular motorcycle.)

Just like Tiny and Brad, Kat's also a dedicated rider. She credits her dad with getting her interested in riding and said she could ride a motorcycle before she learned to ride a bike.

Today, she has a newer GXR 1000 and said she was riding up to just a few days before her daughter was born. Now seven years old, her daughter has her own gear and rides a little 50cc bike. Kat also has a two-year old son who she says likes the sound of the bikes. Both come to watch her race.

But how do you go from riding motorcycles to racing unimotorcycles?

"My dad has been riding his whole life. He and my uncle went over to Holland several years ago to visit a club there, and they happened to see a unimotorcycle race. They came back and were just really excited to get into the sport. They built a bike, and once I saw it and a race, I asked them to build one for me."

Kat's been racing for about seven years now, and most recently, became head of the California chapter. She ran a race last year in which she ended up running on only three of four cylinders. But even at that, she was still timed at 63 mph. Damn fast for one hundred feet.

"This is a sport where you can be competitive but have a lot of fun doing it. I really want more people to see it. Once they do, they'll get that it's not like any racing they'll ever see."

While unimotorcycle drag racing is still in a nascent stage, there's a willingness to support it coming from some interesting places. Later this year, at the seventy-fifth anniversary of the Sturgis Rally, organizers are working to put together a USA versus Russia series of races. Tiny is driving that, but Brad, Kat, and many other IUS members are working to make that happen. It may not eclipse the audience of former Olympic hockey matches, but if the passion of these three people is any indication of what's in store, such a contest could definitely match the intensity—with a few cubic inches of fun thrown in for good measure.

Most of us sleep through our dreams and barely remember them when we wake. Alisa Clickenger paid attention to one in particular, and she's made good on it ever since.

Transformation on Two Wheels

Alisa Clickenger is running. It's World War II, she's in France, and someone is chasing her. She comes upon a lake. Breathing hard, she looks around. There's a motorcycle. A way out. She runs to the motorcycle, and before she reaches it...she wakes up. It's the mid-'90s, and Alisa is living in Connecticut, caught in the middle of a divorce, about to be single, and she's just had a dream. And the only thing the dream made clear to her is that she has to get a motorcycle!

That's how Alisa describes what got her started on motorcycles. It wasn't a friend when she was a teen or younger growing up back East. It wasn't a brother or her dad, although she said her dad did give her a ride once when she was a kid, but it scared the crap out of her. Plus, her mother thought they were "evil."

"That dream and learning to ride was really transformative for me. I'd never done anything like that before, and now I can't think of doing anything else."

"Anything else but ride" was still a long way off after that initial dream. A chance encounter with a bank customer at the teller window she was staffing two days later gave her some impetus and information. A short time later, she found herself with a bike, all of the gear, but no license. At least the transformation was underway.

"I found an old Kawasaki 440 LTD that had Air Force base stickers all over it. I paid more for my Shoei helmet than I did for that bike. I had a friend take me for a ride on it first—he's pushing six foot six, and I'm almost six feet. So we must have looked pretty funny on that little bike."

Alisa bought the bike, took the first of what would be many motorcycle training courses, and then proceeded to ride. But for the first year, that wasn't very far or fast. Transformation isn't the same for everyone. She said she was a pretty timid rider and never went over thirty-five miles per hour. She'd been a shy housewife, was pretty depressed following her divorce, but riding started giving her a level of confidence she hadn't had before.

"As I broadened my comfort zone on my bike, I broadened that to my life as well. Some things you're both attracted to and scared of. That was the way it was for me when I first started riding."

That older Kawasaki eventually was replaced by a Harley-Davidson 883 Sportster. It was the first year of the Evolution engine, and Alisa said this was the bike that triggered the biggest leap in both confidence and change. It got her riding a lot and with a group of people who were entirely accepting of her and where she was at with her riding.

She later realized it wasn't the best bike for long rides, so she got rid of the Sportster and bought an older Honda Gold Wing Aspencade. On that she was able to go three to four hundred miles a day—quite a change from the 35 mph rides she started with. But she wasn't riding daily, so the bike sat a lot. That wasn't what she wanted, so she bought a Yamaha Seca 2—something lighter and faster. You can see how this transformation thing works.

"About this time, I was about to turn forty. I'd been working as director of operations for an IT company up until then and still felt like I hadn't fully reinvented myself yet. So I quit my job and walked the Camino Santiago, or Way of Saint James. I met a German motojournalist on the way who taught me the difference between living to work rather than working to live. I realized that's what I wanted."

So when she got back to the US, she sold both the Honda and the Yamaha and bought a BMW GS1150 Adventure. She looked for one furthest from where she lived so she'd be forced to ride it back across the country to get it home.

The GS forced her to start riding off-road—more pushing her limits. That led to going to dual-sport events... and discovering that she really liked off-road riding.

"That Beemer was a little too big for some of the riding I wanted to do. I kept it but bought a Suzuki DR350 and joined a local trailriding club. One day, a guy named Edward shows up on a DRZ 400, and we both started riding together. Now he's my partner."

At this point, Alisa has gotten more comfortable riding long distances, and has thoroughly embraced the idea of working to live. So she started planning to ride to South America. But before doing so she needed to get even less encumbered and get some more long distance riding in.

She rented out her home. She and Edward took the summer of 2009 to ride the Trans-America Trail and the Divide Trail. By the following year she was ready to head south—by herself.

"By now, I'd also been leading demo rides for BMW—this is how embedded in the motorcycle world I'd become. I was hoping they could get me a bike for this trip, but that didn't happen. So I sold my 1150 and the little Suzuki to pay for the trip and bought a Suzuki DR650 that I rode the whole way."

Twisted Throttle ended up sponsoring the ride and kitting out the bike for her. She'd been doing some product reviews and testing for them. They took the bike from her, did all the work, and then delivered it back to her ready to roll.

And how did her mother deal with this big adventure and the evils of riding...?

"My mom wasn't keen on the idea of the trip and still didn't care for me riding. But by this time I think she'd resigned herself to the fact this is what I loved. So before I left for South America, I bought a bunch of maps and a spot tracker so she could keep up on where I was."

When Alisa got home, her mom proudly showed her all of the maps and all of the points where Alisa had stopped.

"I'm the wrong daughter for my mother. I test all of her expectations. But she knows that I treat riding professionally, and she knows how much I value being prepared."

But despite all of the preparation and the transformation over several years to get to this long, solo ride; there was a time along the way that Alisa said she came the closest to quitting.

"I'd been seven months on the road by myself riding through South America. I was just worn out. So I said, 'That's it, I'm going home.'"

She made it most of the way, but didn't reach the most southern end of the continent. She said she's okay with that. But she also didn't give up riding. She got back to the States, and Edward convinced her to ride with him to Alaska. So without much of a breather, she said yes, but on one condition—they wouldn't ride more than two hundred miles a day. Edward agreed, and they left Idaho for Alaska... and hit eleven straight days of rain.

"It wasn't fun, and I was glad to get back home from that trip. The two trips taught me I could live without a lot of stuff. I don't know if you can ever come back from selling all of your stuff and go back to accumulation. I certainly didn't."

Since riding in South America, Alisa has also ridden in Europe, the Middle East, Africa, and Asia. Her Asia trip included a ride up the Khardung La—at over 17,000 feet it's the highest motorable road in the world. She's done so without any life threatening falls or crashes, mostly due to a focus she's had on continuous rider improvement since buying her first bike.

Every time she's gotten a different bike, she's taken the Experienced Rider Course (ERC) offered by the Motorcycle Safety Foundation. Once a year, she takes some kind of training to keep her reflexes and skills as good as they can be.

"I'm a training junkie. I believe a safe ride is a fun ride. If you're always on the edge of your comfort zone, you're probably not having much fun. Besides, my ego won't let me be a bad rider. I want to be as good as I can possibly be."

That concentration on safety and skills is probably what also keeps her in demand as a demo rider for group rides and as an occasional leader of rides for women.

Several months ago, Alisa returned from a four-month stint in Namibia with Biosphere Expeditions to help count wildlife. While she didn't go there to ride, she was able to do a short ride with Renedian Adventures.

Now back in the United States, she's resumed writing for different motorcycle magazines, and doing a variety of PR and marketing work. She also continues to contribute to her own blog—one she initially started to chronicle her South America trip. Her transformation, however, is still ongoing.

"Riding a motorcycle has changed my life, and while this is going to sound cliché, it has taught me that life is about the journey, not the destination. It's also about the people you meet—they're usually the best part of any trip. And personal horizons are only as limited as you make them."

Words to live by. And to think it all started with a dream where she was running.

[Note: since this article first appeared, Alisa went on to organize the Sisters Ride to commemorate the 100th anniversary of the ride the Van Buren sisters took in 1916 that made them the first women to cross the United States on separate motorcycles.]

There are a lot of casual riders out there—people who might be lucky to put a few thousand miles a year on a bike. Will Pizzolato isn't one of them, and he's found a way to rack up the miles, no matter what he's owned.

Sometimes It's Just About the Ride

You know when you go on a site like Craigslist and just start looking at bikes for the hell of it, and you typically see bikes with really low mileage? Say 1,500 miles for a five-year old bike? And you wonder, why did this guy…or gal…bother buying a bike if they weren't going to ride it? Then you come across one that has 50,000 or more and you go, "That's what I'm talking about! That person was a serious rider."

Will Pizzolato is that guy. You know the type. He rides whenever and wherever he can. Even if his job means he has to "dress professionally" on the days when it's more casual, he rides. It isn't about proving anything or putting any demons to rest. It's just about riding. He said it's been that way since he first got on a bike at the age of nineteen.

"I was in college in upstate New York, and I started riding out of necessity. I couldn't afford a car, and it was a cheap way to get around. I rode as far into winter as I could get away with. Now I can't imagine not having a bike."

That first cheap mode of transport was a 1974 Honda CB450 he bought for six-hundred dollars. And not to date him, but insurance was $39...a year, and gas was way under three dollars a gallon. Yes, my friends, those were the days!

So for Will there was no "friend with a dirt bike" or a dad who rode to get him started. It was just Will and necessity. And by necessity Will continued to ride a bike through college. The little Honda lasted about a year, but he said one of his most memorable trips was on that bike.

"I used to take these long trips from New York down to Florida and back. So one year my brother, who had a Honda CB750, rode down with me. When we got to Florida, I noticed the bike wasn't running that well, so I started taking the spark plugs out and ended up stripping the threads on them. I had to put a helicoil in, but that ended up being a temporary fix. The bike kept getting worse on the way back up to New York, until it finally just stopped. So we hooked up a rope on my brother's bike and mine, and he ended up pulling me thirty miles until we finally found a shop that could fix it permanently."

A few months after the 450 spark plug incident, Will got a bigger bike—a Honda 650—thanks to his grandmother who gave him the money when he graduated from college.

"I know that's not what she wanted me to spend the money on, but I really wanted a bigger bike. I think I told her that if I bought a newer, bigger bike, I'd be able to see her more often."

Will tried to see his grandmother when he could. But life after graduation meant less riding and more working. After a short but unfulfilling internship at IBM, he took his brother's advice and moved to Silicon Valley. Rather than using his engineering degree to be an engineer, he realized he was better at sales, instead. He's been in semi-conductor sales ever since.

So there was a big stretch of time until around 2000 when Will didn't ride. But it wasn't about being married or having a family, and he wasn't short on cash. The need just wasn't there. Then something happened that reawakened that two-wheeled beast and said, "Necessity be damned."

"A friend of mine at the time had a Harley—a retired cop bike. I took it for a short ride and realized I not only needed to get back on a bike. I wanted that bike to be a Harley!"

So Will bought a brand new 2001 Dyna Super Glide and managed to put 80,000 miles on it in about eleven years. That included trips all around California, out to Utah, and down to Mexico. This from a guy who admits that when he first started riding he barely rode more than fifty miles at a time.

But Harleys don't last forever—no bike does—but when Harleys go, they do have a tendency to go out in style. Will happened to be returning to San Francisco from a trip to the Grand Canyon when the entire air cleaner came loose after he gunned the bike to ninety to pass a semi. He said the only thing that kept that part from flying off was the vacuum tube.

The closest dealer happened to be Arlen Ness in Dublin, California, where they not only kick out cool customs and parts for them but also work on just about any V-twin you can pull in the service bay. Will got them working on his bike, then started wandering around the showroom looking at Victorys. Well, the look turned into a buy, and he ended up riding out on a new 2012 Victory Cross Roads.

"Even after I bought my Dyna, I was never that big of a Harley fan. Mine got me where I needed to go for many years, but it had its faults. I've since made my Vic the bike I want to keep for a long time and satisfy my desire to keep riding on long trips."

Those long trips mean that on any given weekend Will might find himself leading either all day or multi-day trips to places like Death Valley, Las Vegas, or up the California coast. He didn't intend to be the one leading them, but more often than not he is.

"I found that if I wasn't leading, I wasn't riding. So I started putting rides together with just my buddies and me.

Now I mostly organize rides via a Meet-Up group, which allows me to lead rides with just a handful of good riders."

He said he likes to keep the group to no more than eight riders so everyone gets a chance to get to know each other. Plus, it's easier to keep track of everyone. Besides, ride management isn't really his thing.

"I'm not really interested in the kind of ride management required when there are dozens of riders. That's just more opportunity for something to go wrong and less opportunity for the kind of camaraderie you get with a smaller group. I also prefer to ride with seasoned riders, because I'm not the guy to look to for teaching newbies. There are plenty of groups that welcome new riders, and that's a better group for them to be in."

Will said he also makes sure that the riding styles of the people who ride with him are similar—i.e. fast and in control. Which means his Vic will haul ass on the sweepers and straightaways but won't be the bike to keep up with crotch rockets in the twisties. And he's okay with that.

"Look, I ride any chance I get. It's a cliché to say it's about the freedom, but that's the truth. I get to go places where a car sometimes can't, and I get to do it with people who share the same love of riding as I do."

And where would his ultimate ride be?

"I'd like to ride around Latin America, in particular, parts of Argentina and Chile. I have travelled through almost all of Latin America as a backpacker, and to ride over the Andes and through the deserts would be quite an adventure."

Yes, it would, Will. And for a guy who just likes to ride, that adventure is probably not too far off.

Circumstances put Peter Thomas into situations and careers most guys would die for. Which means he's got more than his share of stories to tell.

Stuntman, Weapons Expert, Biker, Writer—the Life of Peter T.

Peter A. Thomas (Pete) may just be one of the most interesting men in the motorcycle world. He's been a stuntman, martial arts expert, junior Olympian, weapons and explosives expert, racecar driver, precious metals trader, author, and a biker. You could pick any one of those and probably have more than enough to write about...and maybe even enough to make a movie. But that would be unfair to Pete and probably not as interesting.

See, he kind of downplays a lot of this. He'll tell you the movies he worked on weren't that big. (Hello, *The Untouchables*!) The directors were mostly not that well-known. (Michael Mann anyone?) And the majority of the actors were, well, just B-level guys and gals. (James Woods probably wouldn't consider himself in that category.)

But his path to Hollywood was purely by circumstance, and he credits a bad day at the racetrack for the change in career.

"I was a silver trader by day and racing cars in the Group C-class series on weekends in the early '90s. I happened to be racing at Elkhart [Wisconsin], hit a patch of anti-freeze, spun out, and slammed into a wall. I was fine, but the car was completely destroyed. Between the wreck and my slamming the car with my helmet, I caught the attention of this guy who gave me his card. Turns out he was a professional stuntman. I guess he liked the fact I survived and the car didn't."

Pete said the cars kept getting smaller to shave weight, and at six four, it wasn't getting any easier for him to squeeze into them. So the decision to head to Hollywood wasn't that difficult. Once he got there, he started making a name for himself as a stunt driver and fight coordinator, where bashing cars and surviving wasn't a bad way to make a living. If you've seen *The Blues Brothers*, where car after car and a shopping mall are destroyed, that's an example of Pete's handiwork.

But he was also good at something else and that was weapons and explosives. Believe it or not, before Pete came along, most of the explosions in movies were improvised guesswork based purely on past experience, or as Pete refers to it, powder mass analytics that had been passed on from father to son.

What Pete brought to the set was a science background from his college days as a pre-med major, which meant he knew something about physics and chemistry—both important elements of explosives. And he'd been around guns since he was five, including a place on the US Junior Olympics shooting team. So by the time he became an adult, he'd become pretty expert in a multitude of firearms, which meant he could go from being a stunt car driver to becoming a weapons and explosives expert.

"I had already developed a reputation for being very analytical. So I took that to the next level and wrote a book that any director, stunt master/coordinator, production company, or insurance company could use to safely plan just about any explosion you could think of. I put my name on it and gave it away."

From explosives to guns.

As he worked on more movies, he said he noticed something no one else seemed to: "They had all of these high-paid action heroes running around with 50-60 million dollars into the picture. Even though they were using blanks, the guns could still pack a punch and hurt someone if they didn't know what they were doing."

So Pete convinced Paramount to start a certification process for actors to handle weapons. The idea was to bring a star into the gun shop, start them with a little B-B gun, then move them to a .22, then a .38, and keep getting them comfortable with bigger guns until the training culminated in the use of an automatic weapon. Once they successfully completed the course, they'd get a certificate.

"The studio loved it because it meant far less possibility of an accident happening on the set, and the actors looked far more comfortable with a gun when they had to be."

He said he didn't really have a favorite actor while he worked in Hollywood, and he declined to say who might be on a list of least favorites. But one of the things he didn't mind sharing was how he worked around situations where a director might have the wrong-sized gun for the size of the actor.

"When I worked on *Richie Rich* with McCauley Culkin, the director wanted to give him a gun that was just way too big, so I found an alternative. The same for Bruce Willis. He has pretty small hands, and he looked ridiculous holding the gun the director wanted him to use, so I found a different gun that still looked big on screen but didn't make Bruce look silly holding it."

He said most people don't fully understand the role of the stunt coordinator. They see the explosions and car crashes and might be inclined to think it's all up to the director. But there's more to it than that.

"There are three guys who can stop a camera roll on a set—the director, the safety coordinator, and the stunt coordinator. I was one of those guys. I hated to leave that business, but my knees gave out. All of the standing around on cement and hard surfaces just took its toll, so I gave it up and went back to trading precious metals."

As it turns out, he credits his dad with getting him into riding. His father not only got him into his eventual long-term career as a trader, but for all intents and purposes told Pete to get a motorcycle, instead of a car.

"This was about forty-five years ago, and at the time when I was growing up in Chicago you had to get your parents written approval to drive a car, but not a motorcycle. So my dad told me to get a motorcycle so I could go ride on my own."

Pete said his first bike was literally a piece of crap 1947 Harley Flathead, complete with hand shifter, that he bought from an old coal miner because "it was shiny." He taught himself to ride it, rode it down to the local DMV, and a simple straight line ride and stop test in the parking lot was all it took to be fully licensed.

Eventually, Pete would own an eclectic combination of bikes that has included a blue 1968 Bonneville TT that caught fire and burned to the ground, an Atlas twin, two black Norton commandos (one was a parts bike to keep the other running), and a Norton P11. But he said his favorite bike of all of them was a Kawasaki Z900.

"I bought the bike from a buddy of mine. You could bring the front end of that thing up in third gear. At the time, it was just freakin' fast and so much fun."

But it's been nearly eight years since Pete's been on a motorcycle. Four surgeries—knees and feet mostly—from his Hollywood days means getting on and off a bike is damn near impossible. That doesn't take away from his fondness for talking about them and the kind of riding he liked to do when he could.

"The thing is I was kind of an old-school rider. I didn't really care what I was on and didn't really care where I was riding...as long as I was riding. Most of the places I rode were the back roads of southern Illinois, Tennessee, Kentucky. At the time, it was inexpensive and not many people around."

Pete said even if he could ride, none of his three kids do, and all of the guys he used to ride with are now dead—age-related or car versus motorcycle accidents. So today he trades in precious metals and writes.

While much of his writing is work-related, last year he wrote his first novel, *The Darkness Below*, a late-'60s era crime drama featuring drugs, guns, disenchanted Vietnam vets...and motorcycles.

"I wanted to write something that would give people an escape from how mundane life can be today. It's about guys who live in the moment, look out for each other, and who share a love for two of my favorite things—riding motorcycles and shooting."

Could *The Darkness Below* find Pete back in Hollywood? He said there's interest, and that's as much as he's willing to reveal for now. But if Pete's life is any indication, he could one day be adding screenwriter to that long list of accomplishments.

Not all motorcycle clubs are created equal or even similar. Sons of Thunder doesn't necessarily defy description, it defies expectations.

Sons of Thunder—A Different Kind of MC

Motorcycle Club—two words that can strike fear or at least anxiety into the hearts and minds of non-bikers everywhere. "Quick, Marge. Get the kids in the house. That motorcycle club is coming!"

But those of us who ride know better. We don't all belong to clubs and every MC isn't an outlaw club. In fact, some clubs are decidedly as far from the one-percent as you can get. We're talking the Christian biker clubs or motorcycle ministries. You might have seen them at biker rallies or even riding en-masse. When one of them, Sons of Thunder, reached out to us, we decided a story was in order.

While it's hard to say who was the first self-identifying Christian biker, the first person to create a club or organization around Christianity and motorcycles was probably Herb Shreve. Turns out, Herb was pretty progressive for a Southern-based minister in the '70s.

Blame it on his rebellious teenage son. As the story goes, Herb thought getting them both on motorcycles might be a way to close the widening generation gap. As they rode to different biker events together, though, it became clear there was no one engaged in actively evangelizing to bikers.

So Herb left his church and started the Christian Motorcyclists Association (CMA) in 1975. This is an organization that, according to Wikipedia, now has over 125,000 members around the world with 1,200 chapters in all fifty states and thirty-one countries.

Now the CMA line is that it is not a club but a ministry…and therein lies the rub for other bikers who also consider themselves Christians, but may have a different interpretation or purpose. Here's where Texas-based Sons of Thunder comes in.

Formed in 2009, Sons of Thunder (SOT) considers themselves a motorcycle ministry and a motorcycle club. One look at their patch and you'll see they also fully embrace the edginess typical of more hard-core clubs that may be completely opposite of what Sons of Thunder does or stands for. Ken "Thunderman" Stiles, president and cofounder of Sons of Thunder, said that was done on purpose.

"When I got the idea to form the club, it was based on my personal desire to be more intentional about bringing people to the Lord and to do so through motorcycles. But to be more effective, I thought we needed to be sure we didn't look like a typical Christian club."

"Thunderman" explained the religious symbolism of their patch. The two Js on either end of the handle of the sword stand for James and John, the two disciples Jesus evidently referred to as the Sons of Thunder. The dragon is the devil, and the word *invictus* is Latin for unconquered or undefeated.

Now what gets a bit confusing is that there are other Sons of Thunder motorcycle clubs. "Thunderman" said he's met some who took the name because they like the sound of it and have no religious base whatsoever. Others formed for the same reason "Thunderman" and his cofounding members had, but did so more specifically through an individual church. In fact, a quick search of a few different patches shows you that most of those depict the more obviously recognizable Christian cross.

"We've had guys from one-percent clubs and other motorcycle clubs come to our meetings and rides. The first thing they'll say is that they can't believe how accepting we are of everyone who shows up. And that's regardless of the color of their skin, what they ride, or whether or not they belong to a church."

"Thunderman" said they've even had a couple of guys from those clubs join SOT, and they said they did so because there was no real brotherhood in their other clubs.

"As one guy from another club told me, I had a lot of buddies, but not a lot of friends."

Today, Sons of Thunder has about eighty members in nearly half a dozen chapters, with another five to six chapters ready to come on board in several different states. There are really only a couple of requirements for membership: get a sponsor and actively participate for sixty days.

Prospects are called "Rounders," because they hang around before becoming members, and monthly meetings are called "Thunder Alley," which is more of a name to define the place than the meeting itself. Once a Rounder becomes a member, they are required to attend every monthly meeting and some defined events. In the past, events have been everything from a motorcycle run to a local casino to prison visitations to helping at charity concerts. The only time a specific religious requirement is enforced is when a member wants to be in chapter leadership—they have to be committed to evangelizing.

"Our biggest challenge is to keep the current culture alive and thriving as we continue to grow. I don't want to lose that feeling of complete acceptance new potential members feel when they come to a chapter meeting or ride."

When you talk to "Thunderman," there's no hard sell religious thing going on. But you can tell he's committed to growing the SOT into a national, maybe even an international organization. As a successful business owner who helps other business owners do exactly that, he's got the experience to make that happen.

It also doesn't hurt that he's been riding for almost forty-five years, going back to being a teen in Texas when you could get a license when you were fifteen, when he bought a basket case Honda 90 Scrambler just to get back and forth to his job at the local Dairy Queen. Through most of his teen and early adult years he never owned anything bigger than a Honda 360.

Since then, he's owned an American Iron Horse, a Honda Gold Wing, and a Suzuki Boulevard that was his wife's for a time. Today, he rides a 2012 Harley-Davidson Electra Glide.

But the story of SOT doesn't begin and end with "Thunderman." He's had help getting here.

"Face" is one of the original thirteen members who, along with "Thunderman," have helped take SOT from an idea to a reality. His motivation to do so is pretty simple.

"I love riding. I love being a Christian. They are two things I'm passionate about, and Sons of Thunder gives me a way to express that and help others in the process."

A fellow Harley rider (2010 Ultra Classic), "Face" is the club treasurer with his own wealth of riding experience. Growing up on a farm, he started riding when he was five, then eventually moved to street bikes about twenty-five years ago. Though he took a brief hiatus from riding at one point, he's never been without a bike since. In fact, his fiancé also rides—a bubblegum-pink 883 Sportster.

"While Sons of Thunder is a men's club, we wanted it to be family-friendly and encourage women to participate as Son's Angels. These are women who may have their own bikes or like to be passengers on others."

When "Face" isn't riding and meeting with Sons of Thunder, he spends his workdays as a branding artist for the Army/Air Force Exchange Service. This includes flying around the world to different bases—including a volunteer stint he did in Iraq and Afghanistan.

As for where he sees the SOT going in the future...

"It took us a year or two to really get ourselves organized, but with the chapters we have on board and those that are joining soon, our ability to grow is unlimited. The key will be to make sure we continue to make everyone who shows up feel included."

"Dino" is not one of the original thirteen members, but he did quickly move from being a member to joining the board and is now the club secretary. He's been with the club for four years.

"I'd been riding with other groups, mostly ones I'd find on Meet-Up, but always felt like I was riding with strangers. Everyone rode together then left. No one made an attempt to get to know anyone. But the first time I rode with Sons of Thunder, I felt like I was included right away. And that's never wavered."

Like many others, he started riding young and then quit after getting married and having kids. The closest he got to riding during that time was an occasional ride on an in-law's bike. As a long-haul truck driver at the time, he said there wasn't much time to ride or the energy.

"When you've been on the road for days and sleeping in the truck, the last thing you want to do is get back on the road."

He said he had always considered himself a Christian, but then, in 1999, he and his wife at the time split up. That forced a bit of re-examination. A year later, he was baptized and he admits that changed his life and outlook.

"Dino" has since remarried a woman who loves riding as much as he does. In fact, he said she sold her Mustang before they got married to help him buy the bike he now owns—a Yamaha Warrior with custom paint and pipes. He's since made riding a bit of a family affair.

"She rides with me, and my grandkids like to get on and ride when they can. The youngest even has her own vest."

Yes, he did say *grandkids*!

Today, "Dino" still drives a truck, but only locally. He's not interested in getting into the long-haul business again. Besides, like "Thunderman" and "Face," he sees the opportunity for Sons of Thunder to be something bigger and is committed to helping make that happen.

"I'd like to see us expand nationally, but we need to make sure we have the right leadership and members. Even though we accept everyone, some guys just find that they can't make the commitment. And that's okay."

So regardless of your belief or lack thereof, Sons of Thunder seems to be a club that truly embodies the idea of brotherhood. This line from their website probably sums it up best: "Our strongest allegiance and loyalty is to our Brothers who ride the highways and byways with us daily."

Brotherhood, allegiance, and loyalty—something we could all use a dose of. "Quick Marge, grab the kids; there's a motorcycle club coming, but this one seems different."

Most anyone who rides probably won't admit how much food is a part of the experience. Seth Diamond, chef and biker, has found a way to merge the two.

Chew on This

Here's the deal—we like riding, we like eating, but our idea of the former is ride hard and fast to our next destination, and if that's a place to eat, that means less talking and more eating. But Seth Diamond would rather we take our time with both and enlighten us on a thing or two between all that gnawing and potential indigestion. After all, the world does look different when it's not flying by at eighty miles per hour, and so does the food going in your piehole!

Seth is the host of *Food Biker*—a web TV series that has him riding his 2002 BMW R1200C (he affectionately refers to as "Ellabelle") to various food events and restaurants to learn about different techniques and recipes from chefs and food experts. For him, it's a passion and an obsession. For us, it sounds like a helluva good way to spend a weekend.

So how did this former med school student and entrepreneur get to be a roving evangelist for culinary technique? Seth said it started at a spring break in Key West about twenty years ago, where finding good food was more important to him than getting hammered or hooked up with a coed...or two.

"I was going to med school at the University of Cincinnati and just wasn't into the spring break party scene, so I rented a moped for the whole week and rode all over the area searching for the perfect key lime pie. That not only got me hooked on getting a real motorcycle, but also probably planted the idea for what would later become *Food Biker*."

As it turns out, when Seth went back to med school, he realized he wasn't much interested in being a doctor, but he was interested in food and motorcycles. The purchase of a bike later that year after the Key West trip began to put those two unlikely ingredients together.

His first bike was a 1976 BMW R75/6 he found in the local Autotrader in the mid-'90s. He didn't have more than $2,000 at the time, and the owner had it listed for that exact amount. So Seth decided to offer him $1,976—it was an offer, as they say, the owner couldn't refuse.

"When I saw the Beemer, it just seemed like the right bike for me. I had to get it."

Of course, like any self-respecting biker, Seth didn't let his new two-wheeled purchase live life as-is. He named it "Étienne" (French for Stephanie) and promptly began some significant modifications. He had the engine rebored to correct the compression. Put on a bikini fairing and added some bits from a larger BMW R/90 and got his hands on a period-accurate Corbin gunfighter seat, and essentially turned it into a café racer.

I wonder if Seth sees the irony in a guy who has a passion for food turning his first bike into a "café" racer?

When Seth left medical school, it didn't sit well with his family. Neither did the purchase of a motorcycle. His dad was a doctor, and both of his parents and extended family saw motorcycles as dangerous, and anyone who rode them was just asking for it. But Seth was now so far into it, there was no turning back, and he still had an interest in food beyond just consuming it.

In fact, good cooking had never been further away than his mother's and grandmother's kitchens, and he'd liked to cook since he was a kid. But as an adult, he realized he needed some professional training, so he made it official and attended the famous Le Cordon Bleu in Boston, Massachusetts. While he was in school, he also decided some real-world experience was in order. So he hit the road.

"I got on my bike with my knife roll and found a way to work with different chefs. It was basically like being an intern, but without the formality of it. That sealed it for me, and it's where the idea for *Food Biker* finally came from—travel by my motorcycle and interview different chefs."

Two opportunities were served up about the same time that nailed it for Seth—working on the food-themed television shows *Simply Ming* and *America's Test Kitchen*. The latter was where he said he received hands-on experience with culinary media that helped him fully flesh out the *Food Biker* concept.

"There appeared to be potential opportunities to continue working with both Chef Tsai [*Simply Ming*] and the *America's Test Kitchen* team after graduating Le Cordon Bleu. But I had this idea, and I really didn't want to let go of it. I knew it wouldn't be easy, but I had to give it a try and make it my own full-time venture."

On the surface, it's pretty simple. Guy on a motorcycle travels around and talks to different chefs and eats what they make. But Seth has put a lot more thought into it than that, and what he wants the show to do is much deeper.

From a biker perspective, he said he wants to show non-riders and newbies that you can ride safely if you minimize risk. You do that by being prepared, having the right equipment, and planning for possible disasters, all of which apply in the kitchen as well.

"There's also the idea that when you get out on the road, you're opening yourself up to possibilities. It's not just the sights and smells, but the people you meet. On a bike, there's nothing separating you from what's going on around you. You get a chance to interact with people in a different way. It makes traveling more personal, and I want that personal experience to come across in every episode."

He's also trying to get people to understand that good cooking isn't just about following directions.

"It's about learning good technique. I want the average viewer to understand that they are just as capable of cooking well if they take the time to understand how to do it well."

And what about his favorite chefs and a favorite meal?

"I love so many different places and cuisines I've sampled in doing *Food Biker*, so it's not fair of me to ever play favorites. However, it's always safe for me to say that solid Southern cuisine is always a desert island meal for me."

Seth said there are two top chefs that epitomize that style of cooking and helped inspire him to start *Food Biker*—Chef (and Sergeant) Robert White of Sgt. White's Restaurant in Beaufort, South Carolina, and Chef Robert Stehling of The Hominy Grill in Charleston, South Carolina.

"These two let me day-stage with them during my training, and they taught me a great deal in a short amount of time. I would probably have my last meal prepared by either one of these stellar chefs, and I'll be forever grateful to them for setting me on the right culinary path."

When Seth started putting *Food Biker* together in 2009, it was the height of the Great Recession. As he traveled around different areas, he said he saw firsthand the devastating impact it was having on small businesses. He also saw the power of eating together to break down differences and get people to talk to one another. So a bit of altruism gets sprinkled in with the riding and eating.

"One of the best ways to knock down barriers is to break bread together—sit across from each other at a table and have a meal. And if they try a new restaurant or diner they hadn't thought of before, then I will have also helped in a small way to keep that business alive."

Let's see. Slow down, break bread, and get to know one another. Seth Diamond you've definitely given us something to chew on.

The biker world is full of anachronisms, and Foster Kinn is no exception. A classical music composer with ties to Hollywood, he started riding motorcycles late in life, but there's no way you're going to get him to stop anytime soon.

100 Hundred Dollars and a Piece of Pie

Give Foster Kinn a hundred bucks and you might be surprised at what you'll end up with. Particularly if you're a waitress at a local LA diner or Denny's. Foster is an artist—music composer, novelist, and teller of motorcycle tales. And that periodic trip for a coffee and pie is where he sometimes finds his muse when it's not coming to him while sitting in a dark room or banging around the country on two wheels. After three to four hours, he'll pack up his laptop, pen and pencil, and head home...and that lucky waitress gets whatever is left after he's paid his bill from a single Benjamin or equivalent thereof.

For the past forty-some years, Foster has made his living making, arranging, and sourcing music for some of the most famous performers who ever laid down tracks—Barbara Streisand, Whitney Houston, and Chicago, to name a few. He's worked on movies like *Seven*, *The Hills Have Eyes*, and *Ghostbusters 2*; classic TV shows like *A-Team*, *Mad About You*, and *In Living Color*; and a multitude of commercials. His original compositions and arrangements have been performed by the Hollywood Bowl Orchestra, the Tokyo Symphony, and the Boys Choir of Harlem. He's also the musical director for the California Contemporary Ballet. So Foster, as they say, has musical chops.

"I got interested in music when I was around eleven through my older brother and sister, who introduced me to pop music. But I was drawn to classical. Then I saw Louis Armstrong on TV, and he was always smiling. I thought it must have been the trumpet, so that's what I ended up playing."

After graduating from high school, Foster attended the College of the Sequoias and, later, Cal State Northridge, where he said he really learned to analyze music. He also played in a dance band before finally making a go of it as an arranger and composer. But before you get the idea this guy is some tuxedoed dandy who turns up his nose at anything that doesn't smack of Mozart, think again.

"I like heavy metal, prog metal, because a lot of metal is like classical. Many of the metal musicians I've met have classical music training. When you're making money in a metal band, you're a mother-fucking musician!"

To drive home the diversity and intensity that makes up Foster's musical passions and interests, his answer to my question about his favorite classical composer is Ravel. Who the hell else, besides someone who really appreciates classical music, would say Ravel? He said he appreciates Mozart, but it's really his work ethic and integrity that he admires. Evidently, that guy wouldn't just write anything for anyone.

But one of Foster's most favorite genres to write for is ballet—that's right, tights, tutus, and toe crushing dance moves.

"One of the most beautiful things you can watch is a woman in a tutu dancing en pointe in a ballet. It practically brings me to tears when I see it done well."

But while he said he learned as a professional musician to never disparage another type of music, there is one form that he said he flat out despises.

"New age. I can't stand it. It makes me want to set my hair on fire."

Right there with you on that one!

Foster looks like the quintessential biker. Long white hair, goatee, Nordic tats, and a no-nonsense look. But his path to two wheels was hardly stereotypical. There was none of the typical ride until you get married, then get back into it when the kids are old enough to take care of themselves. He didn't start out on dirt bikes. And neither of his parents rode. As he points out, they were Danish immigrants who came to the US on their own, so there was no extended family when Foster was growing up in the bucolic town of Visalia, California. In other words, no uncles or cousins with motorcycles.

"I rode a bit when I was a kid, but never really thought of riding as an adult. It wasn't until about seven years ago that Vic, a friend of mine, kept bugging me to ride his bike. I finally caved, and when I got on it, it was enough to make me get one. So I took the safety course, and that's when I said to myself 'I get it.'"

So not long after that initial ride, Foster bought Vic's bike—a Yamaha V Star 650 with about 60,000 miles on it. But it wasn't long before he decided he wanted a bigger bike.

"I had this idea that a Harley would be a good bike to get. So I spent some time sorting out exactly which model. I eventually settled on "The Beast"—a deuce that just spoke to me. It was sitting in a driveway covered in dust, but it just seemed to say 'I'm the guy. Ride me.'"

So Foster bought The Beast but thought it would be funny to call it "The Babe," so he could say things like "I just rode in on The Babe," or "I've been riding The Babe all day...and night." You get the picture, but The Beast evidently wasn't having it.

He describes the whole naming thing in a book he published in September 2013 called *Freedom's Rush Tales From The Biker and The Beast*. I'm paraphrasing for brevity, but essentially, after Foster told The Beast his name was The Babe, a ride to the California coast was one small disaster after another—twisties he couldn't ride, lines he couldn't keep, a wide turn that planted him in the weeds... and a parking lot fall that left The Beast lying on top of him. Thankfully, the only thing bruised was his ego.

"It hit me that he must hate his name! I needed to apologize and come up with a new one. And I needed to do it fast, or I'd end up going down permanently. I thought back to when we first met and there was only one choice. I apologized, then announced that his name was, now and forever, The Beast. Since then, we've been problem free."

Freedom's Rush is a personal chronicle of the trips Foster has taken racking up miles and stories in all forty-eight states. It immerses you into how he has completely embraced being a biker, and how being on a bike allowed him to discover an America he hoped was still out there and meet people he believed still existed.

"When you get away from big cities, this is still an incredibly beautiful country, and the people are still some of the nicest people you'll ever want to meet. This is the country I was hoping it would be, and the people are some of the friendliest I could ever want to meet."

Since Foster came to riding relatively late in life (he recently turned sixty-three), I asked him how his family reacted to him riding long distances—mostly by himself.

"When I set out on my first multi-day trip several years ago, my son and two daughters both showed up to see me off. They're all adults with their own families, but they were clearly concerned. Now they've gotten used to it. Today, one of my daughter's rides, and the other is married to a man who rides. My son still doesn't like it, but that's okay."

There are many funny incidents he describes in the book. One in particular has to do with a waitress in Milwaukee who wouldn't let him order or have dessert until he ate his vegetables.

A big problem if, like Foster, you hate vegetables.

Another was a situation he found himself in once he crossed the California border into Oregon. He came across a group of women dressed in nothing but chastity belts and men in the equivalent of Speedos. They were evidently intent on changing the world.

It's worth buying the book just to get all the details. But I couldn't help but think that if this was how that horrible Nicholas Cage movie *Wicker Man* would have started, it might have been worth watching!

You don't have to know a lot about music or motorcycles to talk to Foster. If you're at least curious about either, you've got his full attention, interest, and willingness to share what he's learned from both.

Since motorcycles have always been equated with rock in its many variations, it's not a big leap to get why a musician and composer of even classical music would connect the two. Hell, he likes heavy metal! But I wanted to know more, so I asked him how he would describe the connection between the two.

"Music is about motion and molecules. You sit in a concert and feel the notes go by you. When you're on the bike, it has a mass moving through the air, pushing molecules. You don't just feel the motion of the bike; you feel it moving through the air, pushing molecules. They're both about motion."

I love that! But I find a bit more in his book about the link between the two that is worth calling out.

"...when you listen to music you step away from everyday life and the pervasive burden of seconds, minutes and hours, and into another world where seconds and minutes and hours have no relevance. Freedom!"

Boom! That's what I'm talking about! The same feeling you get when you're riding on the open road. Time becomes irrelevant. No wonder music and motorcycles are such strong elements in Foster's life.

So by the time we finished talking, he'd got me wondering what he'll come up with the next time he takes pen, paper, and a hundred bucks into a diner. Whatever it is, I'm sure it will have it's own rhythm with decidedly classical undertones... and some heavy metal thrown in for the helluvit.

At some point in a biker's life, there's probably going to be a charity ride. Chuck Furey did that idea one better by starting a ride of his own after the Boston Marathon bombing.

FUREY ROAD

Chuck Furey had a mission—to ride to all four corners of the United States to raise money for five different charities. He started in June 2015 and called it the "ONE Ride."

I know what you're thinking—sounds like an interesting thing to do, but why the four and what five?

The answer goes back at least as far as April 15, 2013—the day two brothers decided to set off a couple of bombs near the finish line of the Boston Marathon and created their own twisted version of jihad. It was a day when Chuck thought he'd nearly lost his daughter and found himself in the middle of the resulting dead, maimed, and confusion.

"I'd gone into the city to join the Andruzzi Foundation at the Forum Restaurant, near the finish line. I'd ordered a beer, was about to open it, and all of a sudden I heard an explosion and thought 'that can't be good.' Then just as I popped the top off the bottle, the next bomb went off, and all hell broke loose. The crazy thing is one of the brothers walked right past me earlier, and I had no idea what he was about to do."

During the few minutes following the explosions, Chuck anxiously searched for his daughter, who was working as a volunteer coordinator nearby, and his wife, who was with one of the main race sponsors—the Joe Andruzzi Foundation. They were all eventually united and unscathed, but not unaffected.

"I struggled for months to find a way to make sense of the events and take some kind of action. In the aftermath, I found it remarkable how our entire nation came together and donated money and services to help the victims and their families—people they didn't even know. I wanted to keep that kind of charity going, but I wasn't sure how."

This idea of doing something simmered for almost a year. But it wasn't until Chuck saw the dedication and training his daughter and her boyfriend went through to get in shape to run the 2014 marathon that the concept for a more defined effort started to gel.

"It was so impactful to see these two young kids train and participate in the run to raise money for the families dealing with the emotional and financial impact of cancer. They went from barely being able to run down the street to being able to run the entire marathon. I realized I couldn't do the run, but I could ride my bike a long way and still make an impact."

So Chuck decided to create a personal fund-raising ride to benefit local charities via that spirit of national philanthropy he first saw immediately after the bombing. Thus was born the ONE Ride—a 14,000 mile, peer-to-peer fund-raising odyssey to benefit charities that are diverse in their locations but singular in their purpose—helping families in crisis.

The charities benefitting from Chuck's fund-raising efforts included: the American Indian Cancer Foundation, Gilda's Club of Seattle, the Green Beret Foundation, B.A.S.E. Camp Children's Cancer Foundation, and the Joe Andruzzi Foundation. The money he raised was evenly split between all five.

"The cancer tie was both personal and professional for me. I spent a good part of my career working for Eli Lilly selling cancer treatment drugs to centers throughout New England. I had a cousin whose son died from cancer. My wife is on the board of the Joe Andruzzi Foundation, and my daughter is their volunteer and events coordinator."

That seemed to make sense, but why the American Indians, and why the Green Beret Foundation over other more well-known veterans groups?

"There are very few studies looking at a connection between cancer and American Indians. I'm hoping we can help correct that. I picked the Green Berets since I'd met one of their board members when I was at Sturgis and found out about the work they did helping vets within their group. So it seemed like a natural tie-in."

Chuck's goal was to raise one million dollars—he raised nearly $2,500 before hitting the road on June 8, 2015, from Ocean State Harley-Davidson to mostly ride solo for over 14,000 miles around the perimeter of the United States. What he hoped would help juice that effort was the seventy-fifth anniversary of the Sturgis rally.

"We were able to get the owners of the Buffalo Chip to throw us a party on August 7. We'd like everyone who's going to be in Sturgis to join the party and contribute to the cause. A $150 ticket got you a meal, a Def Leppard Concert ticket, and a real good time. If everyone there who knows a Green Beret or a cancer victim or survivor contributed even twenty dollars, we'd get pretty close to reaching our goal."

Chuck could have chosen any number of ways to cover all of the planned geography, but he chose a bike because he's nearly as passionate about riding as he is about extending this idea of neighbor helping unknown neighbor and worthy causes.

While he'll be riding his prized 2005 Harley Road King on the ONE Ride, Chuck's first experience on a motorcycle started much earlier, when he got a chance to ride his brother's 1973 Triumph Trident. Chuck had just graduated from college, his brother offered to let him ride his bike, and as brothers are wont to do, Chuck rode that bike then promptly went out and bought one for himself.

"That Triumph was a pain in the ass. It was hard to maintain. The clutch cable broke about every 2,000 miles, but I rode that thing everywhere during the three years I owned it."

A return to pharmacy school, though, initiated the need to sell the Trident. Then it would be a couple of decades before Chuck would own a bike again.

"Time got away from me, and so did my weight. But I really wanted to get back on a bike. So my wife made me a deal—'Lose the weight and you can buy a Harley.' So I joined a YMCA, and after four months, I'd lost forty pounds...just in time for riding season."

There was also another, somewhat more altruistic, reason to get back in the saddle. Chuck had worked on several fund-raisers for the CJ Buckley Fund. It was a Boston-area non-profit named after the son of a family friend who had died of brain cancer. The Joe Andruzzi Foundation and Outlaw Barbecue would periodically hold benefit events for the fund. Chuck would watch some of his friends do the benefit rides, while he stayed behind to help organize the barbecue.

"I didn't mind doing that, but I got tired of twiddling my thumbs, while these guys were off riding and having a good time."

So Chuck started watching Craigslist for motorcycles, and his wife started wondering if maybe she had misspoken.

"Right before I bought a bike, she admitted she didn't think I was going to go through with it. So I had to remind her—a deal's a deal."

The bike Chuck bought was a very low-mileage 2002 Road King with a tricked out paint scheme. He said he proceeded to put about 30,000 miles on it, riding mostly throughout the Northeast. He was about to do some more work to it when he went into a dealer and saw a newer Road

King that was closer to what he wanted, and is the bike he still owns.

"I call it my Purple Haze bike. It's had a lot of upgrades, and the dealers' gone through everything to be sure it's solid when I hit the road."

All of this is meant to point out that when Chuck puts his mind to something he sees it through and makes the most of it. He's racked up 30,000 miles on Purple Haze and that's mostly been riding through places like the Berkshires, the Catskills, and Laconia. Plus, he's been to Sturgis twice. So he's put about 60,000 miles on two different bikes in about eight years. That 14,000 around the US are going to be a piece of cake!

"When I get behind the bars of a bike, it's like my Zantex. I'm so aware of my surroundings. My Harley is my prescription."

A pretty apt analogy for a guy who spent most of his career in pharmaceutical sales.

I ask Chuck if there's anything about this upcoming ride that has him concerned or worried in anyway. After all, it's a lot of money to raise and a long ride to get there.

"Failure of the idea keeps me up at night. It's about the possibility of not accomplishing the fund-raising goals and not being able to help the charities I've committed to."

Chuck, my friend, you're on a mission. I doubt failure will be in any corner you may find yourself in on this trip. Godspeed and ride well.

[Note: Chuck completed his round-the-country trip in 2015 and raised thousands of dollars for the various charities he had made sure would benefit from his efforts.]

One of the most dynamic elements within the motorcycle community is the increasing number of women riders, and Arlene Battishil is no exception. Besides, how many people can claim to have put together an all-female band with a lead singer who backed up Bob Seger?

Impatience is a Virtue

"I'm in the gear business because I never was into big hair and pretty looks."

Attribute that one to Arlene Battishill, head of GoGo Gear (aka Scooter Girls), and if we stopped writing here, that quote would about sum up her story. But what fun is that?!

You spend a few minutes talking with Arlene, and you get the idea she was never one to follow the crowd. She started riding minibikes when most girls were dressing their Barbies, and she eventually graduated to riding Harleys in her late teens when most teens were riding with their boyfriends in their Camaros. And, by the way, she also wanted to play ice hockey when she grew up.

While her riding experience was mostly due to the kindness of friends who would lend her their scoots, she was never at a loss for two wheels when the feeling struck her. Then she went to college.

"I gave up riding and got into my career. I thought I had a lot to lose by getting on a bike. But I eventually realized I had more to lose by not riding."

The diversion away from riding spanned a couple of decades that included a degree from Wayne State and an eventual master's in urban studies and a PhD in political science from Temple University in Philadelphia. That actually sounds almost normal. But given Arlene's predilection to tread elsewhere, she was also in an all-girl heavy metal band during her late teens and early twenties.

"We called ourselves 'Tush' and thought we were going to be able to go to LA and make it big. But this is when bands like the Bangles and the Go-Gos were just starting to break out, and that pop sound was beginning to take off. We weren't playing that kind of music."

Arlene pointed out that one of their closest brushes with fame was that their lead singer was a back-up singer for Bob Seger. Shut the f*&k up!

In the true spirit of both Arlene's push against the norm and impatience with having to spend a lot of time learning something new, she said that she learned to play the bass because it only had four strings. (Good thing Tush decided on heavy metal rather than Russian folk. She might have learned the three-string Balalaika!)

Eventually, the pursuit of a more established career led to the retirement of Tush, and for a while, a life that resembled what some might call a turn toward normalcy.

"I was in my late forties managing a fairly remote project for a real estate developer in LA. Since I didn't always need to dress professionally, I decided it would be fun to get a scooter to ride to and from work."

So she bought a little 150cc job (pictured) and realized that whole idea of what she'd been missing by not riding.

"It was 2008, when the real estate market was going to hell. I got a decent severance package but wasn't sure what I wanted to do next. I looked around at gear for women, and it was a lot of crap. I couldn't find any that looked good, so I decided to figure out a way to make it."

She worked with a designer who found a way to work safety elements into women's gear—jackets and leggings women would actually want to wear and that would look good on or off the bike. But those good-looking jackets came with a price tag of three hundred dollars—somewhat out of reach for the average female scooter and motorcycle rider.

"Our original designs reflected the '60s and '70s, when women were feeling that they could be sexy, powerful, and fashionable. A lot of what we created originally had a lot of that influence."

It took a couple of years to get everything worked out, which means by 2011 they had great product, decent distribution, and orders were coming in—then the bike market went south. One of the last things to follow the Great Recession.

"I said, 'Screw it. We're going to get away from working with a distributor and sell direct to the rider.' What we learned as a result is that no matter what you make in the fashion industry, twenty percent of what you sell will represent eighty percent of your market."

That insight was driven home by Arlene's decision to start offering products for men and narrowing her overall product line. She'd already been selling a hoodie, but hadn't really pushed it to the male market, because she was originally marketing everything under the name *Scooter Girls*. And to her point, what guy is going to even check out what's available for him on a site with that name?

"When we pushed our Kevlar hoodie to men, they outsold the same product to women, ten to one. So then we decided to see what would happen with our base layer that we were marketing as leggings for women. We changed the product name for men to *base layer* and saw increased sales for that, too. So now, all we focus on are hoodies for men and women, and the base layer and leggings."

Before you think Arlene gave up that scooter to spend all of her time running her company, think again. She's racked up some serious miles on both that little scooter and her current ride—a Kawasaki ER6N.

She did a ride from Los Angeles through Tijuana to Cabo on small pre-production bikes. She's ridden a couple of non-confirmed iron butts on her Kawasaki (during a ride from Los Angeles to Philadelphia and Philadelphia to Nova Scotia), and she continues to commute on her bike on a regular basis.

"Not a lot of people do these long rides and definitely not on a sport bike. I was pushing the limit on that ride from LA to Philadelphia—doing over 100 mph at some points. But the three hundred dollar ticket I got along the way was worth it!"

Did we say Arlene likes to grind it out until she gets to her destination? No sightseeing the world's largest ball of twine for her.

Luckily for her company and its employees, she does stop to take in what she's seeing happening with her business and exercises a bit more patience in the process.

"Working on a PhD means you have to get really good at looking at data and knowing how to do research. I spent a lot of time early on with the development of the company, researching as much data as I could, and still do. That, and my past experience managing people and big projects, has helped me be successful despite the challenges."

She said Australia continues to be a big market for GoGo Gear due to the flipped seasons. Facebook is her biggest sales channel, while she reconsiders potential distribution deals. And she's seeing extreme athletes like Alpine skiers (basically roller-blading down a hilly street), base jumpers, and wing suit fliers starting to buy her gear. Go figure.

Even though she's periodically asked about new products, her only plan to expand beyond the current line for now might include adding products from other manufacturers.

"I won't create new products until I can be sure we can make back our development costs. Until then, I'm okay with focusing on our two major products and adding other manufacturers that I think are a fit."

We're pretty sure that Arlene's ceaseless energy and ability to dispel the notion that normal is the only way to do things will keep GoGo Gear going. Grind it out, Arlene. You'll get there before you know it!

You'd think that for as long as people have been riding two wheels, that there would be no more original ideas. Michael Kaiser has proven that idea wrong and can thank his kids.

Blame It on the Kids

The things we won't do for our kids. Take Michael Kaiser for example. Some riders might decide they don't want their kids to ride until they're adults. Others might do everything they can to start them out as young as possible to get them comfortable with it early on. Michael did the latter, but took it one step further. He started a company called KinderRider to make and sell street gear specifically for his kids and anyone else who wanted to keep their kids safe while riding.

"In 2006, I decided that a motorcycle was going to be my sole means of transportation. We still had a family car, but I rode everywhere I needed to go for work or errands. Sometimes that meant taking one of my two daughters somewhere on the bike. My wife agreed to that, but only if our girls had the right gear."

While Michael found no lack of boots, pants, gloves, etc. for kids riding dirt bikes, there was very little gear for kids riding as passengers on the street. Thus was born the initial idea for KinderRider gear, but he needed to make some prototype jackets and pants.

So during a trip to see family in Germany, he found gear for his daughters and brought it home. (Evidently, the Germans are more civilized when it comes to kitting out their kids for two-wheeled travel.) His girls tried it out and told him what they liked and didn't like about it. He used that input, combined with what he knew about gear from over thirty-five years of riding, and began looking for someone who could help him take that input and make jackets and pants.

It turns out that wasn't so easy. You kind of have to know somebody who knows a guy who...you get the idea. But he eventually found what he was looking for with a company he met at a tradeshow, and that company has been making gear for KinderRider ever since. In the "you learn something new everyday" category, Michael points out that there's a small area in Pakistan that makes nearly all of the motorcycle gear sold in the world today. But there were some other considerations he wanted to keep in mind.

"One of the most difficult design elements I had to work out was proper venting, so kids wearing the gear wouldn't get overheated. Think about it...an adult sitting in front of a kid is basically a big windbreak. So little to no wind flow for the kid behind you. I was able to not only design in better venting, but also incorporated a growth feature that gives each item more years of use as kids gets older."

Sounds like a lot better idea than getting your brother's old, sweaty motorcycle jacket! Just sayin'.

Michael said he also wanted to keep the price down to at or around a hundred dollars an item, since that seemed to be about the threshold people would be willing to spend. He's successfully accomplished that with his KinderRider line that includes jackets, pants, gloves, and boots. At some point, he also plans to diversify the line.

And while he admits he's not getting rich off of selling gear for kids, he believes keeping his kids and others more protected is worth it.

"One of my customers purchased a full set of KinderRider gear for his daughter, and a few weeks later, while they were out riding, they hit an oil patch in an intersection. They both went down, but he said the KinderRider gear did its job and actually held up better than his TourMaster gear. Needless to say, he's a return customer."

"I started riding dirt bikes when I was nine growing up or visiting relatives in Germany. I'd get on the back with cousins and uncles who taught me not only how to ride but how to be a passenger."

Given that experience, it was only natural that, when Michael was ready to get a bike of his own, he bought a dirt bike and owned several, including a Honda XR75 and a Yamaha Enduro.

"I really liked that little Honda, but that Yamaha was a basket-case from the time I owned it until I sold it. I hated that bike!"

His first street bike was one he took over from his dad—a 1979 Honda Hawk CB400. He would continue to move up the motorcycle food chain until he found himself the proud owner of a 1994 Harley-Davidson Low Rider Custom.

"That bike got me through college, literally. I was working on my engineering degree and needed the money to finish. So it was either quit or sell my bike. I sold the bike."

It would be twelve years before Michael would own another bike, but during that time he had friends that would let him borrow their bikes when the need to get some wind in the face struck him. Which brings us to 2006, when he decided to give up driving and start riding again...full time.

"I just decided that I didn't need or want a car as my personal vehicle anymore. So I sold my Jeep Cherokee and bought a Kawasaki ZZR 600 and proceeded to put 60,000 miles on it."

The Kawi gave way to a first-generation Ducati Multistrada, and Michael put nearly 60,000 miles on that. Today he rides a 2013 Suzuki V-Strom that he said is similar to the Duc, but performs better and has a better seat.

Meanwhile, both of his daughters still enjoy riding, and his oldest now has her license and is interested in getting a Triumph Bonneville.

"I hope my kids will always want to ride. But when I'm at a tradeshow, I still get people asking me how can I be involved in making it easier for parents to get their kids on a bike. They don't get that I'm really helping those parents who want their kids to ride to be safer doing it."

Considering how many miles Michael has racked up on bikes over the last nine years, he does have his favorite routes. That includes a ride he did last year from his home in North Carolina out to Arizona and back through Colorado. Then in 2012, he rode out to California with a return route that took him up to Washington and across the upper Midwest.

But if he could ride anywhere, he said it would be to go back to Europe and retrace a ride he did in 2012 that included Germany, the Czech Republic, Austria, Hungary, and Slovakia.

"I had these old pictures of where my dad and grandparents grew up near the Romanian border, so I wanted to see those places first-hand. I actually made it within a stone's throw of an old fortress that's in some of the pictures from when my dad was there as a kid."

We get back to the subject of his business, and I ask him if there's anything he wishes he would have known before he started it.

"If you have an idea, just go ahead and do it. You learn along the way, and either some government agency will tell you what not to do or you'll figure it out. You don't fail by trying."

Hopefully, Michael's kids are reading this. Sounds like good advice from a dad who's doing the right thing by them and others.

Sometimes our moms are influential in ways they can't even imagine. Just ask custom bike builder, Kevin Dunworth.

Loaded Gun Customs—Blame It on Kevin's Mother

Kevin Dunworth's mother made him do it. Call his shop Loaded Gun Customs, that is. Well, sort of. It's not like she was a modern day Bonnie and Kevin's dad was Clyde. And while Kevin grew up around guns, it's not like he's carrying all of the time today. It's just that when Kevin was a kid, most anything that was dangerous had the capacity in his mom's mind to conjure images of running around with a loaded gun. That included hot rods, fast bikes, and anything resembling either one. Sound familiar?

"When we were kids, every time we'd get close to doing something that would hurt us, my mom would say, 'that's like carrying a loaded gun.' So when I opened my own shop and I was thinking of what to call it, 'loaded gun' came to mind and it stuck."

Today, and some twenty-five custom builds later, Kevin and his band of merry builders in Delaware kick out righteous looking bikes that you can ride without worry—

great geometry, mechanics that work consistently well, and a level of fit and finish that screams "Raw! But slightly tamed!" As a result, he and Loaded Gun Customs have been featured in some of the most high profile media in the motorcycle and even business world, including Velocity's *Café Racer* (now titled *Naked Speed*), *Silodrome*, *Bike EXIF* and the *Wall Street Journal*. (Yes, the *WSJ* writes—occasionally—about motorcycles.)

Kevin admits his first builds may not have had the same level of finish as other customs, but those earlier bikes ran. They and the ones he builds now can be ridden as every day riders. That's because he comes at every build with a history of having been influenced by people who had that same kind of ethos, and a dad who plied him with back issues of motorcycle magazines from the time Kevin was barely into grade school.

"I was able to work with and learn from some people I really respected very early on in my career. Larry Mohan, for instance, who built some of the best flat track racers around for Triumph. And my dad, who mostly rode Harleys, but appreciated anyone who rode and was always having guys over who knew a lot about different kinds of bikes and were willing to teach me."

Kevin's first major build started out as a 1999 Buell Cyclone M2 Blue Streak, but he was tinkering with bikes long before that. His dad, who still critiques Kevin's builds, gave him a badly used Suzuki RM80 when Kevin was ten and told him if he could get it to work, it was his. And, thus, a custom builder was born.

"I worked on bikes and motorcycles as a kid, but by the '90s, riding motorcycles on the East Coast where I grew up wasn't really considered cool. I saw what was starting to happen with bike builds, though, and I wanted to try it."

What nailed it for Kevin was a ride he took to see a race in 1999, where he had a chance to meet Eric Buell. It was that meeting that steered him away from a fledgling career in the marine industry to make motorcycles his life.

It would take him five years to finally open the door on Loaded Gun Customs, and his first big sale was not a bike, but three hundred T-shirts. At the time, he was called Loaded Gun Custom Cars—Kevin was also into '60s' retro mods and drift cars—and his logo was the big draw. But then he saw the start of the café scene and that very few people were doing retro mods yet on bikes. So cars and T-shirts gave way to custom café racers, and Loaded Gun Customs had its purpose.

"I've always had an affinity for European bikes and culture. Café racers in the '50s and early '60s in Europe were the equivalent of the hot rod culture here. All the guys coming to our place on old Beemers when I was growing up probably helped feed that interest."

As Kevin got more involved in the café racer scene, he took his inspiration from builders like Brandon Holstein, Bryan Fuller, Ken Boyle, and Richard Pollock, many of whom are now his friends. He said Holstein's Brawny Built mono-shock Harley was what has inspired his own mono-shock builds today.

I asked him if he could recall a moment when he was first starting out when he went "Oh, shit, I can't believe I did that." He spends no time coming up with one that turned in his favor but could have gone south with just about anyone else.

"Earlier in my career, I decided to contact Race Tech to give them some input on suspensions. Turns out I had the owner, Paul Thede, on the line, and it wasn't until I was well into the conversation that I realized who I was talking to. He was very patient and is a friend of mine today, but it was pretty clear I didn't know what the hell I was talking about with a guy who knew more than I ever would. To this day, every time I sit down with him, I have to bring a dictionary because I'm usually in no-man's land when he really starts talking suspension. I can honestly say I've insulted my way to the top."

While Kevin may now be somewhat of an expert on suspension in his own right, he hasn't stopped there. He's learned about every element of building a bike so that he can tell a welder how to do something to make sure the paint job is right and vice versa. Consequently, he said that's earned him the apt title of "the great connector."

"I've never been afraid of asking guys who may not talk to one another 'how do you do that?' The custom bike world is pretty small, so when you get to a certain level, you have friends everywhere."

Kevin and Loaded Gun Customs has gotten to that level by building bikes that garner respect and attention from the right people. This includes kudos from none other than Eric Bostrom, one of motorcycling's most well-known racers. In an episode of the first season of *Café Racer*, Eric takes the Loaded Gun Custom's Triton café for a spin. He later called that bike the platform that sets the bar for vintage bikes.

Nice!

That attention and other subsequent appearances in various media have helped Kevin continue to attract a clientele that's not afraid to spend the money. And those clients, he said, run the gamut—from doctors to tattooed bikers.

"I can tell a guy who's looking at spending $40,000 on a CVO that I can get him a bike he'll be just as happy with for about half that. This is like buying an affordable Ferrari."

With so many older bikes to use as a platform, Kevin said his favorites are air-cooled twins—Triumphs, Beemers, even KZ1000s, although, he said he's interested to see what builders will do with the new 750 Harleys.

"I like older bikes because they force you to work at riding them. Modern bikes don't do that. They're doing most of the work for you."

And what about his ultimate build?

"I would love to build an American standard. Something like what Confederate or Arch are building. Something that would be fast, fun, and nimble, with the ability to change it out with race sets if you wanted."

Yeah, we'd like to see that, too!

The conversation naturally gets back to the whole café scene and whether this is a trend that has peaked or still has some life in it. Kevin admits we may be at the point where this has started to run its course, but he still has plenty of people willing to pay for his unique take on café racers.

"Loaded Gun Customs has been one of the shops pushing the industry. And there are a lot of other people doing some really cool work out there. So the interest in café racers isn't over yet."

While he doesn't express the kind of mania that some builders have or try to mimic, Kevin clearly isn't one to take it easy. When he's not working on building well-honed bikes or running Loaded Gun, he works as a brand specialist for Klockwerks. Plus, he has twin three-and-a-half year old daughters and a wife who he sometimes has to flip a coin with to see who gets to ride. All of which adds up to a not uncommon problem with guys like Kevin—his ride time is often limited to the few minutes spent testing a new build or a customer's bike.

But after nearly eleven years in business and having worked himself into that tight-knit group of builders previously mentioned, Kevin has had the time to learn more than his share of what it takes to be successful, and he has some advice for aspiring builders.

"Do it right from the beginning. When I first started the shop, I tried to be everything to everybody. When we tried to do a favor for someone we didn't know, we cut corners and didn't do our best work. I had older guys tell me this earlier, but I didn't pay attention."

And we think his mom would add something about loaded guns.

A motorcycle can sometimes create a defining moment. For actor Jayson Warner Smith, his cross-country trip on his Triumph helped him define the rest of his life.

When Jayson Warner Smith Learned to Fly

Riding a motorcycle has often been equated to flying. You bank into turns. You rush headlong into the wind, buffeted at times by the currents of air coming down from the north, drifting up from the Gulf, or screaming off one or more oceans. To really drive home the analogy, when you ride, you learn to let go of the idea of falling when everything tells you that you only have two wheels keeping you upright and the laws of forward motion might as well be dumb luck.

But to really fly, to get the kind of lift you need to soar, you have to go unencumbered...or as much as you can in a world that tells you accumulation, rather than divestment of things, is the sign of wealth and success. Jayson Warner Smith—actor, singer, and maybe even occasional dancer—learned that's what it meant to fly, and it took a cross-country odyssey on a 2001 Triumph Bonnie to teach him that.

"I was coming up on my fiftieth birthday last year, and I told my wife I didn't want a party. I wanted to take a trip across the country on my bike...alone. I'd already disconnected from Facebook earlier, and I wanted this to be a trip where I didn't have to feel like I needed to be constantly connected. So I did, and a two-week trip turned into five."

To get to how Jayson ended up riding from his home in Georgia to LA and back, you have to start with his great-uncle, Dan Simon, and the 1933 Chicago World's Fair. It seems Uncle Dan was also a lover of two wheels, and as a young man, he decided to ride his motorcycle from Georgia to Illinois to see the Fair—quite the extravagance for anyone in the middle of the Great Depression. Jayson would hear his great-uncle tell that story at family get-togethers, and he said to himself, "One day I'm going to take a trip like that."

Years later, about the time *On Any Sunday* was showing at the local theater, but having absolutely nothing to do with that or his Uncle Dan's ride, Jayson's dad decided to get him and his sister a bike—a little Honda CT70. Jayson said they rode the hell out of it until it eventually became his by default. But after a couple of years, he lost interest in riding, and it would be well over thirty-some years before Jayson would get a motorcycle again.

About the time Jayson was riding around on that little bike, his mom, being the sort of homemaker who wanted to broaden her son's horizons, decided to join with a group of other similarly-minded women. The result was the South Cobb Arts Alliance—which meant Jayson and the children of the other involved moms went to drama camp.

"I loved it. I didn't think initially that it would be something I'd do as a career, but once I got into it, the more I liked it."

As grade school class plays gave way to high school productions, Jayson found himself pretty enamored with the idea of being a thespian. He eventually made it through college and started picking up some acting gigs here and there. But it was a friend of his who convinced him to come out to LA and give Hollywood a try.

"I was in my late twenties, and my friend, John, was already in LA making it as an actor. I went out to join him and spent three years there. It was a struggle. And I really wasn't prepared for it. But I met some of my closest friends during that time, people I still keep in touch with today."

But close friends don't pay the bills, so Jayson made his way back to Georgia and started a window and blind company called Atlanta Blinds and Shades. He kept up his acting chops with more local theater, commercials, and an occasional bit part, but his acting career was more of a hobby than a vocation. Then in the mid-2000s, thanks to some smart work on the part of the Georgia state government, the floodgates of film and video production opened up, and more work followed for Jayson.

"This was at a time that my blind and shutter business was also taking off and things were going great. I had a big showroom; I was getting more acting gigs. I met my wife. Then the recession hit; and it hit me hard. It just destroyed me."

Jayson ended up having to close down his showroom, lay everyone off, and move his business back into his home. But he was still getting parts, some in higher profile projects like *Coma* and *42*, then he landed a role in *The Vampire Diaries* and then a recurring major part as Wendell Jelks in the TV series *Rectify*. It was about this time that he bought his Bonneville.

"About eight years ago, I'd started hanging out with some guys who rode Harleys. But my friend, John, had a 2001 Triumph. I really liked that whole look, so I eventually bought it from him, and that's what I rode on my trip and still have it today."

Until Jayson went all cross-country on everyone, the longest he'd traveled was a few days here and there. He had rented a Harley at one point for a long trip, but nothing like the over seven thousand miles he'd eventually travel as a newly minted fifty-year old. And to make such a trip, Jayson had to put aside some very important traits that, until then, had defined him since an early age.

"My nickname used to be 'Dad,' because I was known as the guy who planned everything, kept it all together. But I wanted this to be a trip where I'd be free of that. At one point, about four days out on the trip, I caught myself planning, and it was killing me. It took me about a week to stop doing that. I wanted this to be about just going wherever I wanted to at a pace that was my own."

One of Jayson's biggest hurdles was letting his wife, Lisa, know that his original idea of maybe being gone a week or two would actually stretch into five weeks. Since his only commitment was to be in LA for his birthday and in Taos for his friend's, there wasn't anything keeping him from being out longer.

"I wanted to disappear for that entire time. Not be connected in anyway. But of course, Lisa thought that still meant that I'd be calling or texting her every night. So that's really the only consistent connection I had the entire time I was on the road."

That was probably a good thing to do since, at one point when Jayson was starting to get cold feet a month or two before the trip, his wife told him to "get your ass on that bike and go. You may never have a chance to do this again."

So Jayson packed up the Bonnie, and as a former Eagle Scout, he did so prepared for anything. Other than a few nights taking advantage of AirBnB and an occasional motel, he camped most of the way and brought a pistol, just in case, and a bottle of Jack Daniels, just because.

"The only time I wondered what I was doing and thought of quitting was on day four. Once I got passed that, I never thought about it again. It had all been kind of a slog until I got into Nebraska and came across this incredible Kite Festival. There was something about that event that helped get me over that hump."

That learning to fly thing, perhaps?

Other than that temporary crisis of confidence, the only physical issues he had was twenty-degree weather in

Grand Junction, Colorado, and a broken foot peg in a South Dakota campground. He took care of both with true Eagle Scout ingenuity.

"It was so cold at night in Grand Junction that I was worried my bike wouldn't start the next day. So I wheeled it into my motel room. Unfortunately, someone parked right outside my door that night, and I couldn't leave until after eleven the next day. But it was too damn cold, anyway, so I didn't care."

And the foot peg…?

"I ended up in this beautiful campground near Mount Rushmore, and when I put the kickstand down with all of the gear still on the bike, it sunk into a soft spot and tipped over. After I got past freaking out, I realized the only thing broken was the foot peg. So I eventually figured out I could replace it with one of the passenger pegs."

Jayson's trip turned from days into weeks, and he was spending a lot of time with nobody to talk to but himself. There was the occasional stranger who wanted to know about his bike and where he was headed; the friends and his wife he met up with in LA and Taos. But it was mostly solo—unencumbered.

"I came back with the desire to start streamlining my life and the realization that Lisa and I didn't have to worry about what people thought we should be doing. So soon after I got home, I started getting rid of things I'd been holding onto for a long time."

That included a MasterCraft speedboat, a Fender Stratocaster guitar he'd had since he was eighteen…and their home. With no children to pass anything on to, he realized a lot of the rest of what he'd been hanging on to was stuff he thought he'd one day pass on to his kids. Instead, his niece and nephew are getting first crack at some of it. What's left will get donated or thrown away.

"I think anyone who's ever thought of doing a trip like this just needs to do it. And do it alone. It may seem selfish, but it taught me about letting go of caring what people think."

For Jayson, that epiphany has paid off. He said he's been in four movies and was shooting *Mena*, starring Tom Cruise. He's gotten more involved in local theater and started teaching at a local college.

I asked him if there was anything he wished he had brought with him on his trip. He thinks a moment then blurts out, "An Airhawk. The first several days I had to stop about every thirty-five miles because my ass was killing me. I eventually got used to it, but that would have helped."

Funny. I wonder if he sees the irony in the fact that the one thing missing on his trip where he learned to fly includes the name of a bird.

The motorcycle lifestyle has been depicted in books, movies, TV shows, and art—not all of which can trace itself to people who actually rode. Eric Hermann paints from experience, and that's evident in the detail he puts into every piece he creates.

Painting Is Not a Numbers Game

Stare at an Eric Hermann painting long enough and you'll realize that this guy's painting is the equivalent of reading a novel. There's a story going on with just enough detail to give you the gist, then you fill in the blanks with your own imagination. That ability to convey through acrylics and canvas stories relating the biker lifestyle is probably what's endeared him to a cadre of collectors, admirers, and corporations willing to shell out tens of thousands of dollars for his originals.

If you're unfamiliar with Eric Hermann's work, imagine what would happen if Norman Rockwell was born thirty years later and became a biker. While unrelated to a particular time when things and people might have been less, shall we say, "edgy," Eric's paintings still have a sense of nostalgia to them. They make you miss the feeling of freedom and screwing a few rules in the process. They make you want to get back on your bike and ride. Life's simple pleasures taken in whatever dose you decide to measure out.

"There are only two things I'm really good at—motorcycles and painting. And I hope to be doing both until the day I die."

While that might be an excellent closing line, it's really a better way to get things started. Eric is very clear about what he's interested in and what he won't waste his time on. It's hard to say whether he's been that way his entire life, but it's where he finds himself now.

He wasn't born into an artistic family. His dad and brothers were mostly left-brained machinists and mechanics, while he was the right-brained one, with paint in his veins and various shades of light in his soul. Surrounded by men who liked to tinker on bikes and cars, it seems that, if Eric was going to gravitate toward painting something, it would be what was familiar.

"I won my first art contest when I was in the fourth grade. But I drew mechanical things. Even all of my side jobs in art while I was in high school and going to college were mechanical related. So it was a natural progression for me to eventually paint what I do now."

When Eric left high school, he initially went to the Triton College of Fine Art and The Art Institute of Chicago. He said he put himself through college doing pin-striping. But it was in the Windy City that he met Bob O'Malley—an illustrator and instructor, and also former college roommate of Leroy Neiman.

"You probably won't find much about O'Malley, but I think his work was better than Neiman's, and he had a big influence on me. I also have an eclectic appreciation for other artists, but it's more about their specific style—why they paint a certain way—rather than any particular piece of their work."

Eric eventually left Chicago to follow a girl to Arizona, and while that relationship didn't work out, he did complete a BFA in Graphic Design at Arizona State University. He's been in the Grand Canyon state ever since, and currently has his home and studio in the small desert community of Cave Creek, near Phoenix.

But the path to becoming a world-famous artist was not a short or straight one. He's owned a few screen printing companies, a product design firm, and an advertising and marketing company. But none of that quenched his artistic thirst, and being in the desert no doubt became a bit of an allegory for a long dry spell.

"I finally decided I wanted to concentrate all of my time on being an artist. So we sold our businesses and relied on my wife's [Suzanne] income while I was pursuing a full-time career as a painter. It wasn't easy, and I had people telling me I wouldn't make enough money, including my parents. But I'm making more money now than most anyone else in my family. I'm not saying what they're doing is wrong or what I'm doing is right. But this was the right choice for me."

By all rights, it was a decision that paid off. Not only has the money followed the passion, but Eric's work has been shown at The Petersen Museum in Los Angeles, the American Motorcycle Museum in Ohio, and galleries throughout the world. Go to any major motorcycle rally—e.g., Sturgis and Daytona—and you'll find his art on display. You've probably also seen his work in ads, books, menus, on clothing, and as fine art prints. Hell, even Jack Daniels, Barrett-Jackson Auto Auction, and the Indianapolis Motor Speedway have commissioned him to paint specifically for them.

Not bad for a guy who got in trouble in grade school for drawing hot rods in class.

So what is it about his paintings that give them such an air of authenticity? There are other artists who paint motorcycles, but they don't capture the lifestyle the way Eric does. As he points out, painting a motorcycle in front of a museum is a pretty clear indication you don't get the lifestyle. But Eric also has an eye for detail, and he does a ton of research before he starts painting a subject that he may have thought about for a while before deciding that's what he wants to paint.

"If I'm going to paint a scene with an old panhead in it, I better have the number of fins on the engine just right, or I'm going to hear about it. Plus, I want people to work when they look at my paintings. I want them to find something new each time they do."

Authenticity also comes from experience. Eric grew up on dirt bikes and has been riding different kinds of bikes for most of his life. He was the youngest of four boys—all of whom he said were dirt heads. Consequently, his first bike was a Honda 100 Scrambler that he said he won in a contest.

"I wasn't old enough to enter, so I used one of my older brothers' names."

Eric owned and raced different makes and sizes of dirt bikes after that. Over forty broken bones later and a series of Hondas, Kawasakis, Harleys, and other V-twins, he has now winnowed his collection down to a KTM and a 1996 custom bagger designed by the infamous Jesse James.

"I love the KTM because I can ride that bike from my house to the Grand Canyon and never touch asphalt. The bagger was the only one Jesse ever designed and built. He needed the money at the time, so I offered to take it off his hands. Harley modeled the Street Glide after this bike."

Yes, Eric knows Jesse James and just about anyone of any notoriety in the motorcycle business. He belongs to a select group of riders called the "Hamsters"—originally cofounded by the grandfather of custom bike building, Arlen Ness. There are now over three hundred members from around the world—mostly industry leaders and company owners who must be sponsored in and have a custom bike to ride to even be considered. Each year they meet in Sturgis, and this year they're expecting over eight hundred people to show up for the annual Hamster get-together.

"When you go to the hotel where most of us stay, you'll see what builders are doing to push the envelope. These are bikes you won't see anywhere else. It's a great way to get a pulse on what's going on in the industry."

Sturgis is a big deal for Eric. He'll load up a good-size trailer with his work, bring equipment to print on-site, and arrive well enough ahead of time to get some riding in before he gets to work. His son, Dustin, now his director of operations, is helping him, and his daughter is flying up from Florida as well. Dustin's now familiar with the drill and has been going up with his dad off and on since he was fifteen. He's even competed in the annual hill climb. Eric's other son, Ian, also paints. Must be genetic.

As you can imagine, Eric is constantly approached by parents showing him their kids' work and asking for feedback. He's a patient guy with a consistent response.

"I tell them 'send your kid to college.' The whole experience of going kept me focused on my artwork. Education helped me immensely. It made me paint a lot and that's the only way you're going to get better."

Eric said there's not a day goes by that he doesn't get up ready to paint, and that he's been fortunate to know exactly what he likes to paint.

"My favorite painting is my next one. But I can still explore for another hundred years because I know I can always be better."

We hope he has another hundred years in him. The biker world has too many stories still to be painted...and told.

Chris Van Dyke's background would lead you to believe he'd be one of the least likely people to ride a motorcycle. But motorcycles, in various forms, have been a part of his life since, unbeknownst to his famous father, he first started renting bikes as a teen.

DEFY EXPECTATIONS

You would think that growing up with a famous singing, dancing, and acting father, Chris Van Dyke would have pursued the same. But that's why stereotypes often deserve to be blown up, crushed, and driven into the ground.

A self-proclaimed rebel, Chris at an early age gravitated toward riding motorcycles and carving his own path, with multiple forks in the road along the way. He said he didn't have the talent or inclination to act, even though he appeared on his father's show a few times. His talents and interests were aimed elsewhere.

"I started riding when I was fifteen-and-a-half because back in the '60s in California you could with just a learner's permit. So my buddy and I would take the money we earned from part-time and summer jobs and go rent motorcycles."

When Chris tells me that, I'm not sure which is more surprising—being able to rent a bike with nothing but a learner's permit or the fact that the son of Dick Van Dyke was working as a teenager—at jobs like selling shoes at Sears, construction, and cleaning up movie theaters at 1 AM. Again, so much for stereotypes. BOOM!

Evidently, Chris's parents were more intent on having their kids grow up with the same Midwestern values they had developed while being raised during the depression. That probably beat the alternative of watching them turn into the typical entitled progeny of the Hollywood famous.

"My dad's father was a door to door cookie salesman. My mom's mother was married seven times...several husbands who were killed as gangsters during prohibition in Chicago. I was blessed that my parents could afford to send me to a great college and law school, but they were very careful to teach me that I would only be happy if I did my own thing."

So Chris took doing his own thing to heart, especially when it came to riding, since it wouldn't be until he was well into college that his parents eventually discovered his side hobby—one that had gone well beyond renting bikes to owning them and chopping them.

"The first bike I bought was a Triumph 650 Bonneville that leaked oil, broke cables...it was just a pain in the ass to keep up. But my friend, Jim [Rickerborn], saw a picture of one that someone had chopped, so we decided to do the same to mine. Once we realized we could do that, we started buying old police bikes for a couple hundred bucks at auction, chopping them, and then selling them for spending money during college. Back then, a lot of the people who rode choppers were pretty scary, and we sold a few bikes to guys like that."

Chris graduated from Occidental College in Los Angeles, and went on to graduate from law school at Arizona State University. From there, he went to Oregon with a brand new BMW R90S and clerked for the Chief Justice of the State Supreme Court. After a couple of years at that, he became the Deputy District Attorney for Benton County, Oregon, then an Assistant Attorney General for the state of Oregon.

The first three years he lived in Oregon, he didn't own anything but a motorcycle. Wearing an Afro and an earring made him standout even further, and as he pointed out,

"Some people in the court system thought I was kind of cool. The older ones thought I was a jerk."

So at this point, Chris was in his late twenties, the '70s were well past their prime, and he started seeing some of the injustices that further awakened his rebel nature.

"The district attorney [of Marion County, Oregon], at the time, was a guy who rarely prosecuted a rape or child abuse case during his sixteen years in office. Everyone knew he was crooked. A fellow lawyer and I were talking about that on a car ride one day, and we both decided that one of us needed to run against him. We basically drew straws, and I won or lost—however you want to look at it."

Chris ran for office, and at twenty-nine, Chris became the youngest person in Oregon's history to be elected to a district attorney's office. But Chris lasted one term and decided to move on. He'd seen enough of what he calls the "exhaust of humanity." For him, the one saving grace was being able to get on a motorcycle and ride to clear it all away.

"Being a DA exposed me to all of the failures of modern society. Poverty, broken families, drugs. Eighty-five percent of people just doing something stupid; five percent who were just evil."

While he said he didn't have the make up to go past that one term, he did at least make an impact by establishing a professional code of conduct he co-wrote that is still in use today. It created more ethical standards for the attorneys Chris characterizes as those who can "fuck up people's lives or fail to prosecute those that should be in jail."

The daily grind of having to be at the scene of every single crime also put him front and center of some pretty high profile cases—most notably the I-5 serial killer—that grabbed the attention of Nike. While not the sports apparel juggernaut they are today, they were growing and making a name for themselves...and they needed an in-house attorney.

"Once I got there, it wasn't long before I was the one responding to a lot of media requests. So I went from being in-house counsel to running Nike's public relations department. A few years at that, and I eventually was also running marketing for a new outdoor apparel division they were starting."

Just to frame this up—Chris had gone from building choppers in college to holding public office to working at what was starting to become one of the biggest names in sports apparel in the country. He could have taken many different paths, but his was definitely a trail defined by doing his own thing!

While Chris was making a name for himself at Nike, he met up with Casey Sheahan, who went on to become the CEO of Patagonia. Casey eventually hired Chris to become head of marketing there. A position Chris held for three years.

But after nearly twenty years spent in the corporate world, Chris started looking to satisfy a desire for something more challenging. He'd racked up thousands of miles on several different motorcycles, including that RS90, an R100T, a Honda 900, and even a Heritage Softail. Rather than turn to a different bike or longer rides, Chris and his wife, Christine Shihadeh (her friends call her Chris), decided to do something completely different—they decided to go sailing.

"We sold everything—our house, our cars, and our furniture—and took off in October 2002 for Alaska, then Mexico. We crewed on another boat from Tahiti to Hawaii and then sailed down the coast of Chile and all the way to Antarctica."

Chris and Christine would spend three years at sea until they decided it was time to get back on land. They moved back to Portland, and Chris went on to form his own clothing company—NAU—got out of it during the height of the recession, went to work as head of communications for the World Wildlife Fund, then started his own public relations and branding agency (Songlines Communications) with close friends from his days at Patagonia.

"I recognized the power of wealth creation for social good and the need for non-profits to do a better job of telling their story. So that became the basis for starting Songlines and what we do with our clients today."

Chris had also started gravitating far more toward dual-sport riding than street. When a close friend wrecked a Ducati 1098 Chris had bought primarily for the track, that sealed it. BMW GSs became his main mode of two-wheeled transportation.

Besides riding a big dual-sport in as much dirt as he can get to, Chris camps, hikes, mountain bikes, and even goes four-wheeling. Yes, four-wheeling, which in this case means a tricked out Toyota Tundra that can take Chris and his wife back into the wilderness with a few more creature comforts than what he can fit on a bike.

But for a guy who has traveled throughout the world, racked up hundreds of thousands of motorcycle miles, and engaged in all manner of outdoor activities, his big wreck came in December 2012 while driving his Toyota Tacoma near his home in Bend, Oregon.

"I was going to work, and a deer came right through the windshield and hit my head and upper body head-on. Broke both my shoulders, most of the bones in my face, and caused me to be partially blind for a while. It took several surgeries to get everything fixed, but other than having to wear glasses now, I'm pretty healthy."

To give you some perspective—that deer not only messed Chris up, but it did nearly $17,000 of damage to the windshield and interior of his truck. Plus, the legs went through the roof. So imagine the kind of impact that occurred to create that much damage.

At that point, you'd expect that during and after Chris's recovery he would have re-thought some of his outdoor activities, particularly as they pertain to motorcycling. But not so fast. Remember, this is a guy who has made defying expectations and taking on new challenges a passion. As soon as he was able, Chris got back to riding, has ridden some tough multi-day backroad trips, and is now planning his next big trip—an eight-person, multi-week, guided motorcycle trip down the eastern slope of the Andes to Tierra del Fuego.

"Everyone on this trip will be familiar with each other and our riding abilities. So the challenge won't be so much in dealing with each other's personalities, but with what we'll encounter together along the way."

Some people are content to avoid challenges, no matter how simple or hard they may be. Others seek them as a way to continue to be more than just one of millions of other heartbeats on the planet. Chris's upbringing and his parents' desire to teach him the value of creating his own path have clearly led him to be one of the others and defy expectations along the way.

The motorcycle industry has its share of people who got into the business for any number of reasons. Bill Kniegge has his Uncle Otto to blame or take credit, depending on how you look at it.

More Than One Thing at a Time

Bill Kniegge has to have more than one thing going on at any given time—and manages to turn every one of them into a success. He proves that by reeling off the consecutive companies he's worked for, started, and sold in the car and motorcycle business over the course of a few decades—some of them simultaneously. His current company, Blue Strada Tours, is a case in point. They lead two-wheeled tours throughout the Southeast, and rather than be content with that, he recently branched out into Italy.

It might have something to do with the fact that, since he first started riding at the age of ten, he's never been without at least one motorcycle. His purchases have varied over the years, but the common element seems to be a proclivity to buy whatever catches his attention at the time.

Blame it on Uncle Otto.

"My parents immigrated to the US from Germany and settled in Davenport, Iowa. When I was ten, my Uncle Otto Kniegge brought his BMW over from Germany and took me for a ride. I was hooked."

About a year later, Bill bought his first bike—a Whizzer Sportsman. That began a long list of bikes that has included an assortment of new and classic European and Japanese motorcycles. Believe it or not, here's a *short* list:

1966 Suzuki X6 Hustler; 250cc (1966-1972)

1973 Norton 850 Commando (1985-1997)

2000 Cagiva Gran Canyon (2002-2007) (Bill's favorite adventuring bike)

1969 BMW R 60/2 (1992-2007)

1969 Yamaha CT1 Enduro

1970 Ossa Pioneer (1972-1974)

1975 Bultaco Sherpa T (1976-1978 First real trials bike for ten years of competition)

1972 Husqvarna 250 WR (1972-1976) (first real off-road bike...after seeing *On Any Sunday*)

1974 BMW R90 S (1976-1982)

1977 Husqvarna 390 OR

1972 Triumph 500 Daytona

2007 Suzuki V-Strom 650 / 1000

1995 BMW R100 GS/PD (real favorite)

But one of Bill's all-time favorites is a custom 1976 BMW R75/6 (dubbed "Old 'n' Fast") that Bill points out unconsciously ended up looking a lot like his Uncle Otto's. It even included custom-made panniers that mimicked the soft bags on his uncle's older Beemer. Unfortunately, finances forced Bill to sell Old 'n' Fast last year, after a multi-year run that racked up the miles and the attention. (Photo courtesy of *Motorcycle Classics*)

We get back to the subject of Bill's career in the automobile and motorcycle business, much of which reads like a litany of the top brands in both industries. His first job out of college was as a sales rep for Husqvarna, and eventually he became that company's head of marketing and sales. At one point they were bought by Electrolux (that's right, the vacuum cleaner company) and then were sold off to the motorcycle group of Castiglione.

"From there I went to work with Bell Helmet, when it was owned by the Winn Oil Company. It was the early '80s, and bicycle helmets were really not much to look at. We changed up the design, used new technology, and went from selling seven million to twenty-four million in three years."

When Bell got sold, Bill left to cofound a company (Accuride) with a guy he met during his daily train commute from San Diego to Fullerton, California. Accuride made drawer sliders, and working there was one of the few times Bill wasn't involved in the motorcycle business. While the company went through substantial growth, Bill eventually left and joined ATK Motorcycles as a marketing consultant. The company was making some interesting dirt bikes powered by Rotax engines, and Bill brought over some engineers he knew from his days at Husqvarna to add some additional design muscle.

Now here's where Bill's tree of motorcycle employment gets, shall we say, a bit complicated.

While Bill was at ATK, they bought a Swedish company called Highland. Two of the guys from there left to start another company and called it MCM Motorcycles, and Bill joined them. Their claim to fame was a lightweight, big bore V-twin adventure bike that debuted at the 1996 show in Cologne.

"We were based out of Costa Mesa [California] to take advantage of the availability of engineering and design expertise in the aircraft industry. But the bike itself never took off. So we sold off the engine design that turned into a project for Arctic Snowmobiles, and another for Volvo. Eventually, we sold the business to Mike Corbin and that formed the basis of his Merlin project."

At that point, while he'd rather not go into details, Bill said the experience soured him on the motorcycle business for awhile. So he checked out and rode Old 'n' Fast down to and around Baja. And as serendipity would have it, a lost piece of luggage led him to start another company—Motosports Panniers.

"I had that company for ten years before selling it to Saddlemen. We had designed a set of high-quality aluminum boxes and hard-fastening soft luggage and did pretty well with it. But when Saddlemen made the offer to buy, I thought it was time to try something else."

Somewhere between Baja and Saddlemen, Bill was working with some of his many long-time friends on different marketing programs on the side. One of which included six years with Ford Motorsports and Ford Racing. As a result, that meant spending a lot of time in Charlotte, North Carolina, going to races. Although he and his wife were long-standing residents of San Diego—they owned a small restaurant in Vista called the "Vista Ice Box"—they were ready for a change.

"What did it for me was riding in and around Charlotte and the surrounding area. People don't realize that the Tail of the Dragon isn't the only great ride near there. The whole area offers so many other options. It's just great riding."

Since Bill had informally been taking people on guided tours to track days at MotoGP at Laguna Seca in the past, starting a motorcycle tour business out of Charlotte wasn't that big of a stretch. Thus, was born Blue Strada Tours, a company that leads private and group tours in and around the mountains of North Carolina. Besides the Tail of the Dragon, that includes Snake Valley, the Blue Ridge Parkway, the Cherohala Skyway, and The Diamondback Route.

"I take as few as four and as many as fifteen. For a couple of years, I contracted with Edelweiss to do their Smoky Mountain Tours, but decided I'd rather lead small tours myself."

His rides are typically four to eight days, all twisty roads linked together by the Blue Ridge Parkway, which according to Bill, can turn into 380 miles of twisties and sweepers without a stop sign. And, amazingly, he said there's only been one incident during his time leading rides where anything went south.

"I got hired by Harley-Davidson one year to take dealer sales winners out. They were selling Buells at the time, so they sent me the Ulysses model, which is essentially a sport-touring bike. One guy got too aggressive going into a curve on one and went over the handlebars. Luckily, he wasn't hurt too bad. But that's the only time anything has happened during any of the rides I've led so far."

So with a near-perfect record of leading safe rides, and in typical Bill fashion of not being content to do the same thing for too long, he decided to start offering rides elsewhere. But while most tour operators might decide to try to keep it local—or at least in-country—he decided to go to Italy. And it was because of his experience with Bell.

"When I worked with Bell, I loved bicycling and once in awhile was able to ride in Italy. So at one point, I bought the Masi bicycle company with two friends. This was a huge brand in Europe in the '80s and was the bike the Russians rode when they won gold at the Seoul Olympics. So that gave me a strong tie to Italy. Plus, my wife and I realized we could go to Italy for about the same cost as going to Hawaii."

So Bill found a tour operator in Italy that he had met at a Cycle World Show, and they put together the first Blue Strada tour in that country in 2013. He organized two rides last year and planned for three in 2015. These are all typically five to seven days of about 125 miles a day. Earlier, this year, he also organized a women-only ride and plans to do more of those, too.

Bill said one of his best experiences with Blue Strada so far was having a moto journalist from Switzerland tell him, "Thanks for the invite...we really don't have roads this nice in Switzerland." North Carolina back roads better than Switzerland? Who knew?!

Since Bill has ridden so many different places, what's interesting is that he said one of his favorite solo rides would be back in California in the winter or spring from Borrego Springs to Palomar Mountain "for coffee" at Mother's Kitchen. It's a pretty short forty-five miles each way, but 4,500 feet of elevation change. "The best part is there's only one stop sign and hundreds of turns, plus, great coffee at Mothers!"

And what about an ideal group ride? He has a couple, but one in particular sounds near perfect because, if Bill is right, there are no cars! This one is in Italy starting at Olbia, Sardinia, and ending at Villasimius, Sardinia—a total of 190 miles, basically going from the northern tip to the southern tip of the island with what Bill describes as plenty of "mountain twisties and fabulous sweepers."

So where does he see Blue Strada going in the years to come?

"I'd like to get the company to where it's not quite so all-encompassing. Three tours in Italy and two or three in the Charlotte area. That would be ideal."

That seems like a lot of spare time left on any given day or week for a guy like Bill to have to fill. And he does. He has another company on the side called Wheel Jockey that makes a part for bikes that don't have a center stand. There are probably more ideas Bill hasn't even thought of yet.

So the next time you think you're too busy with one thing, consider Bill probably has several going at once. And is making sure every one of them does better than the last.

Mike Fitterling has found a way to combine his love of motorcycles and writing into a company that publishes the big stories from unknown bikers who might never have been heard from. And he's also a afficionado of old Japanese bikes.

Ride It, Write It, Own It

Some people enter the writing profession out of purpose. Writing because they have something to say, believing there are enough people who will find the way they combine words so fascinating as to want to actually pay to read it. (Some say this may be the ultimate form of narcissism. If so, then there must be some masochism thrown in as well!) Others come into it by dumb luck...or by taking a fork in the road they never saw coming.

How most people start riding motorcycles isn't much different. You don't plan on it. Someone gets you on a bike and BAM! you're hooked, then fated to wondering why those who don't get it, well,...don't get it. You ride believing everyone else should.

Which brings us to Mike Fitterling...

Mike owns Lost Classics Book Company, a publisher of long out-of-print books, many of which saw the first drop of ink in the late 19th century. Sounds like the kind of thing that may have put you to sleep in school, right? Don't tell that to the Rockefeller family. One of the great-grandchildren started the company and eventually sold it to Mike.

Chances are your grandparents, parents, and maybe even you if you're of a certain age have read some of the books in the Lost Classics line. We're not talking about the works of Shakespeare, Faulkner, or Plato. No, these are mostly texts and early learners with titles like *A History of the United States and Its People*, *Stories of Great Americans for Little Americans*, and *The Life of Kit Carson*. (And if you don't know who Kit Carson is, look him up. Clint Eastwood should make a movie about him!)

So what's this have to do with motorcycles? Well, Mike, being an eclectic kind of guy also publishes books about that topic under his Road Dog Publications imprint banner. These are mostly travel-related books written in the last few years and includes Mike's own book *Thoughts on the Road*, and *Bonneville Go or Bust* by Zoë Cano, and *A Tale of Two Dusters* by Kirk Swanick, among others.

"Road Dog is a result of my enthusiasm for riding that grew rapidly over a fairly short period and my publishing experience with Lost Classics. It became a way to create a business out of two things I'm most passionate about."

Mike didn't set out to be a publisher, nor did he begin riding at an early age. He slid into both a bit sideways.

"I got a degree in art from the University of South Florida and was doing reproduction covers for Lost Classics. They ended up hiring me to do that full-time, which then turned into becoming the managing editor. Eventually, the Rockefeller descendant who had started it decided in 2010 to sell it to me, and I've owned it ever since."

As for motorcycles, Mike said he'd always wanted a bike when he was a kid but could never afford one. His two-wheeled experiences then were limited to an occasional ride on a cousin's scoot. But that changed in 2002 when Mike, well into adulthood, spotted what ended up being a 1968 Honda CB350 (eventually dubbed Ol' Faithful) in a pile of debris at his father-in-law's modular home sales company.

"I offered to get it running for him and he ended up giving it to me. I taught myself to do all of the work on it and could say I finally had a bike!"

Over a two-year stretch, from 2002-2004, Mike worked on that bike to get it running as well as he could. Then Hurricane Charley hit Florida, ruining the roof on Mike's home and forcing a five-year wait before he could continue on the 350 from where he left off.

He still has that bike and recently rode it from his home in Florida to Tennessee and back…including putting it through the twisties that make up the Tail of the Dragon. And since he got to be so well-versed in fixing that Honda, he realized he also had a knack for wrenching.

"Much of the work I do on a regular basis is so cerebral and static—sitting in front of a computer and writing. Wrenching is almost the opposite, and you see the reward of your work in a more physical way."

To give you some idea of his wrenching ability, Mike happened upon another bike in bad shape through his father-in-law's nephew. It was a chewed-up 1986 Suzuki Savage with no saddle, cut-up exhaust, and non-matching side covers—a true rat bike. Mike put it back together, got it running, but never bothered to get it close to looking original.

"I thought that it was too far gone to be a beautiful bike again; there was too much rust and too many other cosmetic issues. So I basically turned it into what looked like a little chopper. I eventually sold it after my wife [Andrea] said I didn't need three bikes!"

That third bike was a 2011 Triumph T100 that Mike still has and recently rode 5,000 miles round-trip from Florida to eastern Canada and back, a trip he said was necessary at this point in his life.

"I had gotten so caught up in all of the negative I was hearing on TV and the difficulties I was having with my business, that I felt like I just needed to get out and find something positive. The trip restored my faith in people."

He said he specifically went to parts of the US and Canada he'd never been to before, including New England, the Saint Lawrence River, and Quebec. Along the way, he had people provide him with rooms, food...and hospitality in ways he hadn't anticipated.

"Everywhere I went, people went out of their way to help. I was reminded that when you can meet people face-to-face, differences dissolve away. Terrorists want us to be afraid and suspect everyone. If we continue to close ourselves off from each other, we're handing that to them on a silver platter. We can't do that."

Mike's wanderlust hasn't been confined to these later years in his life or travels on his motorcycle. As a young adult, he had his own sailboat, *Aries*, that he sailed for several years, including an extended voyage from Tampa, Florida to the Turks and Caicos, the Bahamas, and up the East Coast of the US. He also professionally captained the *Spirit of Ppalu* for Red Sail Sports in the Cayman Islands during the summers of 1990, '91, and '92.

When Mike talks about his past travels and even most recent rides, there's a wistfulness...perhaps a desire to be traveling even more. But as he points out, as a husband and a father of two growing children, you have to balance that need or desire with being a parent.

So while Mike's trip to Canada was one of the few times he allowed himself to hit the road for a long period on his own, he does rack up the miles for yet another publishing gig of his related to his interest and knowledge of old Japanese bikes. Besides Lost Classics and Road Dog, Mike is also the editor of *Vintage Japanese Motorcycle Magazine*.

"After I took over Lost Classics, I joined the Vintage Japanese Motorcycle Club and wrote a couple articles for their magazine—mostly pieces on 'how *not* to' do things when restoring a bike, based on the pain of my own experiences. Then not long after I started Road Dog Publications in 2010, the former editor left *Vintage Japanese*

Motorcycle Magazine rather abruptly. A board member of the club knew of my publishing and biking experience, so he asked me to take on the editor role. That has given me an opportunity to write about something I love and to ride to a lot of events any chance I can get."

Considering how much time Mike spends in the saddle and reading and editing other people's work, it's surprising he actually finds time to read anything just for fun. But he does, and his list of favorites is as eclectic as you would imagine it to be. There are the motorcycle adventure books like *Jupiter's Travels*, *Dreaming of Jupiter*, and *Lois on the Loose*. But his list also includes the works of Kurt Vonnegut (Mike said he's read everything he wrote), John Steinbeck, Ernest Hemingway, Somerset Maugham, Mark Twain, and Herman Hesse (*Siddhartha* was evidently a pivotal book for Mike).

Since 2002 when Mike first took a wrench to that little Honda 350 then later wrote about that experience, he's racked up over 100,000 miles traveling through a good chunk of the middle and eastern half of the US and parts of Canada. Keep in mind, those are miles spent on mostly just three different bikes. But he's yet to ride anywhere overseas. So not surprisingly, he said one of his ideal routes would be to ride from the northern to the southern tip of the UK.

If, as Mike said, the intent of Road Dog is to publish books that are as much about the ride as the effect of the ride on the rider, we're hoping he can take that trip. What he learns and writes about that trip will no doubt be worth reading.

A couple of chums build some interesting customs near Windsor Castle—then they take a break and ride across Europe...or as far as they can get before a complete breakdown of their bikes means they have to turn around.

Run Ryan, Run Riot

Not many custom bike builders can see a castle from their shop—let alone Windsor Castle, the oldest occupied castle in the world and one of the homes of the Royal Family. But that's exactly the view from outside the Run Riot shop—an up-and-coming British builder of stripped-to-the-core customs that break more than a few rules along the way.

Founded by Ryan Walker and friend, Rob Cross, Run Riot traces its name to some joking around they did with names in high school and the roots to Ryan's incessant interest as a kid in tearing things apart to see how they worked. Unfortunately, he didn't always put them back together.

"My dad was a carpenter, so I always saw him building things. I was more curious to see what was inside anything I could get my hands on. Unfortunately, most of what I took apart as a kid stayed that way, and my bedroom was typically full of spare pieces lying around."

Eventually, Ryan learned to put those pieces back together, which led to building BMX and mountain bikes. Contraptions, Ryan said, that drew more than a fair share of attention, but also gave him a base from which to start building motorcycles. In fact, he completed his first build before he could even ride. It made sense, since cars in the UK were too expensive then and still are today.

"We bought a Kawasaki Z305 when I was still fifteen. We got it into a friend's van and drove it over to my parents' garage. We immediately started cutting it up into bits and experimenting with different angles. Everything that could go wrong with it did, but that's how we learned."

Much of Ryan's focus at Run Riot is on the metal work—frames, sheet metal, and welding. While some of that is self-taught, he learned the basics as an engineering apprentice working at Heathrow Airport, outside of London. Rob helps with some of the metal and fabrication work, but primarily handles the mechanics. Philip "Squeak" Minkinnen does all of the operational and finance work, as well as the online element. The shop is also periodically inhabited by two or more friends, who do odd jobs and work on bikes as they can.

The majority of bikes you'll find in Run Riot's shop are older Japanese models, because they're relatively cheap and easy to work on. You might find an occasional Triumph or Harley, but nearly all of the bikes that come into and leave the shop were made in the '70s and '80s in the Land of the Rising Sun. The result is a happy group of merry motorcycle makers, who manage to create bikes that are about as stripped down as you can get. Speedo, turn signals, and side mirrors—who needs 'em?!

"If you can avoid getting caught, it's not a problem. The laws in the UK are a little iffy, so if you are pulled over, it's probably because you broke some other law, and the police are more interested in giving you a ticket for that than seeing if your bike is legal."

Oh, if it were only that easy in the US!

While Ryan's been building bikes for about ten years, he's still open to being influenced by a multitude of outside sources. In fact, his minimalist style came about from a trip he took several years ago to Japan.

"The idea there is to have no distractions. Strip away everything to only what's necessary. You'll see that in the bikes we build. But I also look at the work of serious engineers—guys who want to do everything properly."

Ryan names British builders Pete Pearson (Rocket Bob's Custom Cycles) and Vic Jefford (Destiny Cycles), and US-based Roland Sands (Roland Sands Design) as some of his inspirations.

The common factor here is a reflection of Ryan's own interest in making sure his builds convey a sense of quality and an extreme attention to detail. "I don't want it to look like we just took a bunch of old bikes, stripped them down, and put some new pieces on them. It's crucial that our bikes look as good as they perform."

Which brings us to how the custom scene in the UK compares to the one in the US.

"It's hard to put a finger on it—climate makes a difference. Lots of people like riding in the UK, but you're usually riding in rainy weather. Laws have also changed here—there is a longer theory [written] test, plus more complicated practical [riding] tests, and age restrictions. You can't ride just any-sized bike when you first get licensed. All of this is almost phasing bikes out because of how restrictive it's become. So the bikes that are getting built here tend to be smaller and cheaper."

Ryan said when his friends who don't ride see the bikes Run Riot builds then they start getting interested in having one. It's a way for him to help keep motorcycling alive and growing in his own country.

But before you get the impression there's way more seriousness than fun going on here, he starts telling me about a recurring trip he, some friends, and the rest of the crew at Run Riot have been taking every year since 2010.

They buy little 125s, get them running, and then see how far they can take them on the mainland. Ryan said the first year they didn't even make it to the south of France—too many breakdowns. The second year they made it to Spain. The next year they got to Belgium and back. This year was a breakthrough—Croatia.

"We picked these bikes because they're easy to work on, and since you can't go fast you stay off the main highways and stick to side roads. That means you also see more and tend to stop more frequently. We literally camped wherever we found ourselves when it started to get dark, and we ate whenever we got hungry. There's never a plan."

Though at twenty-six, Ryan has a lot more build years under his belt, he's still learning and has no intention of stopping any time soon. What helps is the loyal following that has supported Run Riot through some times that would have tried the more experienced.

The garage Run Riot operates out of now is the result of that network of friends and loyal supporters who chipped in over a couple years to help build it on an empty lot. That empty lot was their idea of a move up, after initially operating the shop out of the garage owned by Ryan's mother. She, by the way, is pretty supportive of his chosen obsession—his father...not so much.

"My dad had a friend who died while riding a motorcycle, so he's never been too keen on what I do."

As for the future, Ryan said he would like to see Run Riot develop a small product line. One that would help other people get into the custom scene themselves.

"For anyone who wants to do this, I'd tell them to not let people tell you it can't be done. Build what you like. Don't build for trends. Find parts of bikes that inspire you. Stick with what you want to do and build the bike for you."

As they say, a man's home is his castle, and perhaps Ryan's view of one of the most famous continues to inspire him to build his bikes and his business his way.

Cari Draft isn't just another female rider. She has her own fitness company, sells a line of healthy snack bars, and keeps it all going even in the dead of winter in Michigan. Not bad for someone who started out as a graphic artist.

Keeping Things Interesting

If you find yourself somewhere around or near western Michigan, chances are pretty high you'll see Cari Draft doing one of several things—working out, leading a fitness group, or riding her motorcycle—"Beast"—around the shores of the lake that shares the state's name—sometimes all in the same day and definitely outside at any given time of the year.

This is a woman who clearly isn't content to sit still and spend her days updating friends and family on Facebook. And freezing Michigan winters aren't about to keep her inside. Cari, as Larry the Cable Guy would say, gets 'er done.

While Beast—a 2006 Yamaha V Star 650—is the first and only bike she's owned outright, she has plenty of riding experience under her helmet.

"My little brother and I had dirt bikes when we were growing up. And I'd get on the back of my dad's Honda CB 900 and ride with him. I've ridden other bikes since, and every time I do just like the feeling of being on one. To be honest, when I'm riding now, it's one of the few times where I actually like doing something alone, rather than in a group."

While anyone who rides a motorcycle understands the overall appeal, there are probably as many different arguments for why some like riding in groups as there are for riding alone. But to give you some idea of how contrary it might be for Cari to prefer riding alone, consider the fact that she owns a personal fitness company—EcoTrek Fitness—that conducts both group and individual training sessions. So being with people is a natural part of her job and one she also seems to enjoy.

But changing things up is Cari's thing. Unlike most personal trainers who are intent on conducting classes inside a gym, especially when the weather starts to turn, Cari takes her classes outside, even in winter. The idea is to use elements of the environment—fences, rocks, trails—as part of the workout.

"I've always worked to be fit and leaned toward healthy living. So when I had my son, it wasn't hard for me to get back into that routine. When my friends started having children of their own and found it difficult to get back into shape, they asked me to help them and were willing to pay me to do so."

As her outdoor workouts grew in popularity, Cari decided to create a company that would bring her unique approach to more people. So she founded EcoTrek Fitness in 2006 with the intent of not letting weather—regardless of the season—be an excuse to not going outdoors to workout. As it said on her website, "I was determined to keep my 'peeps' moving into the winter months, and we found that if we dressed for the weather, we could workout outside all year long—even in Michigan!"

The EcoTrek sessions integrate a combination of strength training, cardio, and flexibility in a single seventy-five-minute workout, and every session is different. One might be at a local park and the next at a nearby trail. Everyone works at his or her own level, which eliminates any competitiveness or intimidation that might scare away some people.

Since formally launching the company, over 3,000 people have gone through EcoTrek training—most in groups and some in one-on-one training. Cari's success can probably be attributed to a number of factors: her unique approach to training, her overall philosophy that focuses on where her clients are at relative to their physical well-being, and she walks the talk.

There are a number of success stories on her website, but there's one she's particularly proud of.

"One of my clients was a guy who eventually lost 160 pounds, but it took him three years to do it. He'd had years of working an eight-to-five desk job and accumulating bad eating habits. Now he works out every day and has completely changed his approach to food. Being a part of those kinds of success stories is really gratifying."

Cari's training also includes a focus on nutrition, with one particular goal of eating fruits and vegetables every day. But she recognized early on that wasn't easy for a lot of people—they either weren't in the habit or didn't feel they had the time. So in 2011, she started a side business that spun off of that idea called EcoTrek Fitness Bars that makes some of the best tasting energy/snack bars around.

"I was able to partner with a company that was on the verge of going out of business. They were producing a protein-packed snack bar, but they were serving up over two hundred calories a bar, and I needed it to be below that. So we worked together to get it to 195 and also made the bars vegan, dairy-free, and gluten-free."

And that fruits and vegetables thing? Well, one bar contains the equivalent of six servings of both.

EcoTrek Fitness Bars can now be found throughout the upper Midwest, including Meijers' 220+ stores, the 50-store Wesco chain of gas and convenience markets, and assorted other locations throughout Michigan. They're also sold directly off the company website. That's not bad for someone who started out as a graphic designer with no intent of someday being at the front end of a successful fitness and snack bar company.

"When I was in high school, I used to do pin-striping and airbrushing for friends. That was when putting art on pickup tailgates was the popular thing to do. So I took that skill and became a graphic artist."

Cari parlayed her artistic skills into a twenty-year career as a graphic designer with the advertising department of a large grocery store chain. When she had her son, she decided it was more important to work from home to take care of him than go to an office every day. She made that choice work for her and her family, which eventually is how EcoTrek got started.

Then there's the BikeTime Calendar project.

BikeTime is an annual motorcycle event that was started in Muskegon, Michigan, in 2007. It's held the third weekend in July and draws an average of over 75,000 bikes and over 120,000 people. And like any self-respecting big biker event, there must be girls competing in bikinis...in this case that would be the Miss BikeTime Bikini Contest.

So in 2010, Cari got invited to participate in said bikini contest. While fit enough at forty-four to feel comfortable competing with the younger twenty-somethings, she thought the whole idea of a bikini competition needed a revamp. Why not, as she told the organizers, have them in sexy leathers or something else—anything but bikinis and definitely not trashy!

While her suggestion fell on deaf ears, she competed anyway and was a runner-up. Now she had the show organizers' attention.

"I got more involved and eventually became a judge. Every year I kept suggesting they drop the bikini contest in favor of a 'more is less' philosophy about what the contestants should wear. I finally suggested we have twelve winners, include guys, and turn the results into a calendar we could sell to benefit charity."

Cari's persistence eventually paid off with the 2015 competition featuring both men and women in biker attire—bikinis were not allowed. The resulting 2016 calendar features the winners of the competition—seven men and five women—each of them tastefully photographed by Cari with their respective bikes. (Given this is Michigan, Wisconsin's neighbor, most of the bikes in the calendar are H-Ds.) All of the profits from the sale of the calendars will go to the local Habitat for Humanity.

"The idea was to convey the biker lifestyle—avid female and male bikers—not just young women who looked good in a bikini on a bike. Once I got the approval to take that direction, I had less than sixteen days before BikeTime to pull it off."

According to Cari, the BikeTime organizers are now all over this idea for next year's event.

As for where she'd like to take EcoTrek, she said she's starting to focus more on corporate fitness and working to get more kids outside and away from their computers.

"I ultimately want to make getting outdoors more attractive to the public. Growing up, I didn't have to be told to go outside to play. But more people, regardless of age, seem to need that push."

Which brings us back to being a woman who likes to ride. While her advice for any woman who is thinking about getting a bike is worth noting—do your research, take a safety course—her description of riding pertains to anyone who wants to ride or who has contemplated doing so.

"When you're riding, you're breathing in the air, being ultra aware of everything around you—sights, smells, colors. You're really in the moment. There's no daydreaming on a bike...and I like that."

And that is no doubt how Cari keeps things interesting—no day dreaming, just get 'er done.

While some bikers can't wait to get a bigger bike, Andrew Pain has gone the other direction, and that hasn't stopped him from riding on some really big rides.

The Upside of Pain

What if there was a guy who rode a motorcycle all over the world, saved people when they were in trouble, then wrote about his adventures later? Sounds like a bit of a mashup of a modern day superhero right?

Well, meet Andrew Pain. Yes, that's his real name, which even sounds like it would fit a character in a graphic novel.

But this guy's for real, and he's taken great steps—some would call them painful—to become an expert at adventure traveling via a small motorcycle. We're not talking the 800cc and similar Beemers and Triumphs. We're talking 1980s' model Yamaha 250s. That, if you do the math, is about eighty percent smaller than the big behemoths from BMW and KTM, and even the slightly smaller Triumphs that have become popular since Ewan McGregor and Charley Boorman decided to go the *Long Way Round* and *Down*.

Andrew said he was always interested in riding—chalk it up to reading *Zen and the Art of Motorcycle Maintenance* in high school. (What is it about that freakin' book that gets into your system anyway?) But there were mitigating circumstances that kept him from making good on that desire until he was an adult.

"My mother didn't want me to ride a motorcycle at all, so I had to wait until I was out of college before I could buy one. So my first bike was a Yamaha SR250. Just like the one I own now."

Answering the call of the road, and a certain girlfriend in Georgia, Andrew jumps on that little 250 and proceeds to put about 6,000 miles on it with trips from his hometown of Milwaukee to Georgia, some cross-country excursions, and abundant tours of the Deep South. Amazing what two wheels and a girl will make you want to do.

The 250 eventually gave it up, so Andrew proceeded to go through a couple other bikes—a Suzuki GN440, a Yamaha XS1100, a BMW K100, and a Ural sidecar rig. Along the way, he became his own mechanic.

"When I first started riding, I knew nothing about motorcycles. I didn't know spokes needed to be tightened, chains needed to be lubed, valves needed to be adjusted. But I learned along the way, and a few people taught me what they knew."

That mechanical aptitude has come in handy on more than one occasion, since a motorcycle has typically been Andrew's only mode of transportation. Considering his predilection to riding long distance and the fact he lives in the Upper Midwest and rides in the winter, it became a necessity, which is kind of his justification for buying the Ural.

"I ride in the middle of winter, and heated garb is key. Literally, I have everything from socks to pants to jackets and gloves. But the roads get slick, snow builds up, and two wheels aren't that stable. So I thought a sidecar would be a good idea. I could also use the extra room. When I looked at what it would cost to get a sidecar for my XS1100, I realized I could buy a Ural, which is designed for a sidecar. So I bought a new Ural in 2007."

Then he put over 62,000 miles on it with a combination of three Iron Butts, a couple of cross-country rides, and general tooling around. He was planning on taking it up to Alaska, but realized it was too big for the kind of riding he wanted to do and would require too much work to get it into shape for long distance riding.

So he went back to a small bike, found a non-operable SR250 that had around 4,500 miles on it on Craigslist, and paid sixty-five dollars for it. That's not a typo.

"The guy wanted a hundred dollars for it, and it wasn't running. I took it home and discovered the vacuum tube had been disconnected, and there was a lot of lint in the carburetors from someone who'd probably tried to wipe them down with a cloth. Those were the only two things keeping that bike from running."

While Andrew had already planned on riding from Alaska to the tip of South America, his original intent was not to ride small. So he read anything he could on long distance adventure travel and what little there was on doing so with small bikes. He then set out in 2011 and traveled for a year throughout North and South America.

"This is really a good trip for first time long distance travelers. All you really need in terms of documentation is a passport and a visa. The roads are mostly paved, unless you decide to go off pavement—something I don't recommend. And other than Brazil, once you get outside the United States, everyone speaks Spanish."

During that trip he decided to write a book about what someone would need to know who wanted to travel long but with as little as possible. There had been plenty of motorcycle travel and adventure books published by people who'd used bigger bikes and taken as much as they could strap onto a bike. But Andrew found very little information for riders who were leaning toward a more minimalist approach.

"I started writing the book [*Going Small*] on my trip and finished it when I got back home. It sold fairly well, but it got mixed feedback. More experienced riders didn't think there was enough information, while newbies loved it, since this was all new to them. So I wrote an updated version and added some information and corrected others."

For most people, being able to take that kind of time off as an adult to just travel around is the stuff of pipe dreams. And it's not as if Andrew didn't have a job. In fact, he'd been working as a paramedic since college. But despite being able to take four to six week trips in the past, he wanted something more. It took an experience at work to get him to finally pick up and go.

"We responded to a call for a man who had owned a successful business but had never really taken any time off. He had recently sold his business, bought an RV with the intent that he and his wife would hit the road, and then within six months of retirement he got cancer. When I saw him, he was down to about ninety-five pounds and didn't live long after that. I thought, 'I don't want that to be me.'"

So Andrew sold everything he owned but the Ural, his book collection, and some family heirlooms. He put those in storage and then hit the road.

When he returned, he got another job as a paramedic, but now he was considered somewhat of an expert in minimalist adventure travel. Overland Expo and Horizons Unlimited started inviting him to teach classes. He wrote some more books—*Going Small 2.0*, *The Minimal Motorcyclist*, *10 Things You Should Know Before Buying an Adventure Motorcycle*, and a couple of volumes specifically about his trip titled *Pain, Curiosity and a Bear*. (The bear references a blue Teddy Bear he takes with him on all his trips.)

He also realized he wanted to try his hand at writing a couple of fiction books about what can best be called anti-superheroes. In other words, what if the superhero was really an asshole, and what if the villain wasn't such a bad guy after all. Those two books are the *Fall of Awesome* and *Under the Radar*.

And he met a woman (Sue) who has two daughters—all of whom share his interest in motorcycles and adventure travel.

"Sue had a Suzuki Boulevard when we met, but it got bogged down in a campground on one trip, and she realized a smaller bike might be better. So she now has her own SR 250. Her girls ride on the back of both of our bikes when we ride locally, but for our next long trip to Alaska, we'll drive in an older RV I bought and have the bikes racked to the back."

In a bit of irony relative to the guy with cancer who was the impetus for Andrew's really long-distance journey, Sue was diagnosed with breast cancer after he met her. While she is fine now—she's training to run a marathon—the lesson Andrew learned from the cancer patient who died before he could enjoy life is still fresh in both of their minds.

"The one thing I'd tell anyone who's contemplating doing a long ride is to just go. Quit what you're doing. Sell what you don't need and just go."

Sounds like a plan. Watch for our stuff on Craigslist and we'll see you all on the road!

They say another man's junk is another's treasure. Jeff Goorman has played that out in spades with some rebuilds of junked Harleys and Indians that most people wouldn't have tackled. Talk about persistence!

Keeping History Alive

To say that Jeff Goorman likes old bikes would be an understatement. His garage is a testament to a passion that he said has always been there. There are two old Harleys he's brought or is bringing back to life—not as museum pieces, but as daily runners. This includes a 1939 H-D sidecar rig that's nearly complete and a 1953 Panhead that's finished. Then there's a binder full of photos documenting a multi-year project he undertook to breathe new life into a 1932 Indian Chief that he eventually sold to a guy in Canada.

Some people undertake these projects for the challenge. Jeff's reasons run much deeper.

"I like taking a pile of stuff that seems like junk and turning it into something you can ride. But for me it's also about the history of these old bikes. Riding them is an experience in themselves. It's the conversations you get into with people; old guys who used to have bikes like these. When those old guys die, that history will go with them. I guess I'm trying to preserve that."

While Jeff may have always been drawn to old bikes, he didn't start out on one. In fact, like many kids in the '60s and early '70s, his first two wheels and an engine was a mini-bike his parents bought him when he was in the third grade. He later moved up to a Suzuki 90cc trail bike, followed by a Suzuki 185.

"My step-dad was into trials bikes, so at the age of twelve or thirteen I started riding those, too. You could say I competed, but I was never good enough to be that competitive. But I kept riding dirt bikes until I finally got my first street bike when I was twenty-one."

That first bike was a 1983 Honda Shadow 750 that Jeff bought off of his step-dad who got the newer and slightly larger Shadow 800. Jeff said he rode that 750 for about four years before he bought a Kawasaki GPZ750 in what became his sportbike phase. That "phase" eventually led to the purchase of a 1997 Yamaha YZF1000.

"This was when I was an adrenalin junky. I'd ride like an idiot up through the mountains outside of Denver with guys who were racers and way more skilled than I was. I eventually realized that trying to keep up with them was a recipe for disaster for me."

So Jeff went a completely different direction. He bought a 2000 Honda Valkyrie. A bike he still owns and rides today.

It was about this time that Jeff also decided to do something about his attraction to old bikes. He bought a 1974 Norton 850 Commando that was being sold for parts at auction. After a three- to four-month intense rebuild, he turned it into a 950 Interstate.

He eventually entered it into some shows in Colorado and took a couple of firsts, a second, and a third place over just a two-year period in '06 and '07. Not bad for a first rebuild and a Norton at that.

"I had some help from a buddy's dad who was a big Norton guy. His name was Carl Graves, and he taught me a lot about working on those bikes. We used to show together and got to be very close. But when he eventually passed from prostate cancer, I sold the Norton."

Sometime later, Jeff bought the 1932 Indian Chief. When you see pictures of the bike before the rebuild, you'd swear it was pretty solid and wouldn't have required as much as what Jeff eventually put into it. Ah, the wonders of paint, putty, and heavy-duty lubrication!

What Jeff uncovered were holes in the gas tank, heavy pitting and holes in the fenders, and some extensive engine work that required far more effort than he originally thought was going to be necessary. But he hung in there with that bike, and after a three-year, complete ground-up restoration he sold it to that guy in Canada for a little over $50,000.

"That was before the new Indians came out. That's driven up the price of the older bikes even more. So if I had that bike today, I could probably get even more for it."

Jeff's passion for old bikes doesn't just begin and end in his garage. He's also president of the Rocky Mountain chapter of the Antique Motorcycle Club of America. Earlier this year, he and his wife, Teresa, trailered his sidecar rig to Wisconsin to join some other antique Harley owners for several days of riding through the back roads of the state.

"A two hundred mile day was a long day. Most of these old bikes aren't meant to go more than about fifty-five miles an hour. The roads back when they were made weren't built to go fast on, anyway. We rode with local people and visited different garages. There were people who had old H-Ds from the early 1900s and were really riding them. It was pretty great to see all of these old bikes on the road."

To get some idea as to just how much effort Jeff puts into restoring his bikes, you have to look at some of the before and after pictures of his Norton build and that old H-D sidecar rig. Jeff pays attention to detail and has built up a network of other restorers who barter their skills with each other.

The skills Jeff has developed weren't just acquired with that Norton project. It's something he'd built upon since he was a teenager when he started working at a Denver-area classic Rolls Royce/Bentley shop. Eventually, he would parlay that experience into becoming a certified GM mechanic, a job he held for ten years before becoming a deputy with the Jefferson County Sheriff's Department.

"I didn't set out to be a mechanic or in law enforcement. I actually always wanted to be a fireman. But I couldn't pass the oral boards for the fire department. So I decided to try the law enforcement boards and passed. Being in the sheriff's department was the best experience I could have had. I learned to handle high-stress situations and was involved with some pretty high-profile situations, including the Columbine shooting.

After four years, Jeff eventually left the sheriff's department and fulfilled his dream of becoming a fireman. He's now an engineer with Littleton Fire and Rescue. It's a job he said he probably couldn't have gotten into without his law enforcement experience.

We got back to talking about his garage, and I asked him what he started out with in terms of tools. Being a mechanic for so long, this could be some good insight for others wondering what to do with their own garage. His response wasn't too surprising.

"As a former mechanic, I'd already built up a pretty good collection of tools. I really like the older ones because they were made to last. But the one thing I didn't have was a motorcycle table lift. When I started on the Norton, that's the first thing I bought."

A final look around Jeff's garage and you notice that, besides the old Harleys and that 2000 Valkyrie, there's a 2004 BMW GS. Jeff said that is his daily rider, but he admitted he's probably put more miles on his 1939 Harley.

"I build these bikes for me, bikes that I like. When I think of old motorcycles, I see a rigid-frame machine. A solo seat. That's what I envision as an old motorcycle."

Right there with you, Jeff. And glad to see that there are people like you who won't let that vision die.

Lorne Cheetham has made a name for himself by putting together some incredible custom bike shows in England. But the road to get there, like most, had a few twists to it.

Boredom Sucks!

Sometimes boredom can be a funny thing. It's kind of the great proving ground for stupidity. Really dumb people who are bored typically do even dumber things. While smart people either find themselves at a loss—or they finally use the down time to do something really interesting. There's typically no middle ground.

Lorne Cheetham is a smart guy, passionate biker, and long-time event director who found himself blasting around on the frustrating roads of boredom one day. Rather than stay there and possibly succumb to doing something stupid, he got the hell out and brought with him the idea of putting together a series of custom bike shows that would be unlike any other shows seen on his side of the Pond. The result is a series of what are now three shows he puts on throughout the year—Kickback Chelsea, Kickback Stoneleigh Park, and The Festival of Bikes.

"When I started this five years ago, it was literally out of boredom. A group of my mates and I were riding one weekend, and one of them suggested that I use my event experience and passion for motorcycles and put together a custom show. It's now turned into a full-time job, and each year every event keeps getting bigger."

Lorne credits his brother with getting him into motorcycle riding. At the age of ten, he jumped on the elder Cheetham's BSA Bantam, and it was full throttle from there. He later developed a love of motorcycle racing, but admits he was more interested in what Kenny Roberts and Barry Sheene were doing off the track than on.

In 1977, at the still impressionable age of seventeen, he got his motorcycle license and his first road bike, an FS1E. Before that he owned a Puch Maxi scooter, which he cut everything off that wasn't needed and turned it into a "forester." But it was riding a Honda 185 that nearly ended his motorcycle riding days.

"I don't really remember what happened to this day, other than I'd had the bike about eight months and I was riding it at night in the middle of winter. I later learned that someone had pulled out and hit me. I broke my left arm and shoulder, and lost most of my teeth."

Not long after, Lorne was back to riding. Perhaps it was boredom that made him do it.

Then came the '80s and a realization that girls in London preferred guys with cars to guys with bikes. Plus, all of his mates were into cars. So Lorne ditched motorcycles for a time and got a car. But everyone who rides knows eventually two wheels will call you back. For Lorne they called in a big way.

He went on to own a 1977 Kawasaki Z1000, a Harley Sportster bobber, a Triumph flat tracker, a Harley shovelhead chopper, a vintage Norton/Ariel brat, and a 1978 Triumph Bonneville. His current ride is a Moto Guzzi V7 street tracker, because he likes the dependability of having a newer bike.

"I got into the whole chopper and custom bike scene through Hunter S. Thompson. I read everything he wrote, sometimes more than once. So I had my mind set on a

Harley Sportster, but I didn't want it to be stock. So I found a picture of one I really liked, took it to Si Harris, the legendary builder, and said 'can you build this?' And he did."

That's right; Lorne was riding a custom Sportster built by Si Harris of Attitude Customs.

But riding a series of bikes, custom-built or not, doesn't qualify as experience to create a custom bike show. That's where Lorne's background as an event manager came in. He spent over two and a half decades putting together events and exhibits for different companies. That gave him a pretty good idea of what it was going to take in terms of logistics, venue, and manpower to put on a decent custom bike show. What Lorne wanted to do, though, was have a show that had something for everyone.

"I really wanted to embrace everyone who's into any kind of bikes. If you come to one of our shows, you'll see custom-builts you won't see anywhere else. Some of these are from first-time builders, others are built by guys who've been at it awhile."

Lorne said his shows have been growing steadily and now attract between eighty to a hundred builders and forty or more exhibitors featuring aftermarket parts and lifestyle-related apparel. The Kickback Stoneleigh Park show, in April 2016, was entirely dedicated to picking the top builder in the UK.

"We used to be affiliated with the AMD World Championships, but they got a little fractured. They now have the world championship set for the INTERMOT show in Germany next year. Our show now has six different classes, including one that recognizes young British builders under thirty."

There's a bit of a custom approach to the shows Lorne puts on, too. He tried having past winners be judges, but that didn't pan out—too much favoritism. Judging for the national custom show is now by a handpicked group that includes three award-winning custom builders—

Pete Pearson of Rocket Bobs, Larry Houghton of Lamb Engineering, and Paul Milbourn of Paul Milbourn Customs—plus two members of the press.

The builders enter for free, but Lorne does charge exhibitors. It's also free to attend the Kickback Chelsea shows, but attendees are asked for a donation when they leave.

"It might be a bit of a stereotype, but I've hired some attractive women to be at the exit with a donation box in hand. They ask attendees to pay what they think the show was worth."

Obviously, putting on a custom motorcycle event is different than, say, a trade show for the plastics industry.

In some ways, the level of diversity mimics what's going on in the custom scene worldwide, with no dominant single style. As Lorne pointed out, British builders are being influenced by other builders from throughout Europe and elsewhere—particularly Japan, Germany, Spain, and even Ireland.

"When we first started in 2010, we saw a lot of stretched-out choppers. But now it's everything from café racers to urban brats to bobbers. The big thing now is that guys are looking around at what engine they may have sitting around. They'll take an AJS or an old BSA engine and put it in a custom frame. It's a really stripped-down approach."

Lorne explained that his shows are really a blank canvas for builders to show whatever they want—especially young builders. One of the things he said he learned is how to exhibit the bikes so they look like art.

"I want the bikes to be cool. I want them to be underground and edgy. I know there's a fine line between doing that, yet making it open to everyone. But I think we can make that happen."

Making that happen doesn't come easy. It's a full-time job. With the Kickback Chelsea show only a few weeks away, he's already working flat out on the national championship custom show at Stoneleigh Park. Help comes in the form of friends who are builders, an illustrator who does the artwork, and he recently hired Zoë Cano as his sales director.

Time and again, when we talk to people whose passion is motorcycles that often means giving up or at least cutting back on the one thing they really love—riding! Lorne is no exception, what with the full-time demands of his job and the fact that he's a father of three. A ride on Sunday when the weather cooperates seems to do it for him for now.

Either way, there seem to be no room or place for boredom where Lorne finds himself today. The custom bike scene in the UK, at least, should be grateful.

From hairstylist to the stars to designer of quality women's riding apparel, Ginger Damon has seen a lot, and she's out to empower women riders who want to be more than a passenger.

Go Your Own Way

If you've ever been to Bakersfield, California, there's a strong chance you'd just want to keep going. It sits at the southern end of the Central Valley of the state and is dotted with oil pumps and is a landscape that looks like the aftermath of a bad mixed-drink hangover. Some notable former inhabitants include the Supreme Court Justice Earl Warren, who headed up the commission that looked into the shooting of John F. Kennedy; now deceased country music star Buck Owens; current heavy metal favorite Korn; Pro Football Hall of Famer Frank Gifford; and one of the founders of the Mexican Mafia, Rodolfo Cadena.

All of this is a lead-up to understanding why Ginger Damon would find any way possible out of the city where she was born and raised, and eventually end up launching a motorcycle apparel company for women called Gigi Montrose Moto Couture.

"If you were seventeen in Bakersfield, you were probably pregnant and working at Albertson's. No one seemed to have any hopes and dreams. So I was determined to do something else."

That something else turned out to be hairstylist for Sebastian International, where she had a client base that eventually included some of the most famous people in Hollywood in the late '80s and early '90s—Sheena Easton, Paula Abdul, Jane Fonda, and members of the Jackson family—any of those names ring a bell?

Turning the tresses of the rich and famous eventually lost its appeal, but rather than start a new career, she took her talents down the street and became a hairstylist for the film industry. In fact, she can actually claim Academy Award recognition as a result of having been part of the hair and makeup team that won for its work on *Star Trek* with Chris Pine and Zoë Saldana.

"I didn't set out to be a hairstylist. Early in my life, I wanted to be an attorney. But I heard a lot of nos, a lot of 'you can't do that.' So I got pissy and said 'Okay, then I'm going to be a stylist to the stars.' So I set my sights on that, but was also into competitive saber fencing. I made friends at Sebastian International through fencing, and soon after I started working there, I was styling hair for these very famous people."

Growing up in the country outside of Bakersfield also laid down the roots of Ginger's eventual passion for motorcycles. A friend had a little yellow moped that Ginger said she rode whenever she could. Her friend grew tired of the little scoot, but not Ginger. She continued taking it out of her friend's garage and tearing around the neighborhood, until the parents finally put a stop to it.

"I eventually got a car when I got older, but I was still around bikes for a while through a girlfriend who was building her own Harleys from junkyard parts. We were all just curious back then and grew up with people who knew how to tinker."

It was some time and miles spent riding and flying in just about everything but a motorcycle before Ginger would actually get on two-wheels again. She said it was on the movie set of *Next* (featuring Nicholas Cage) when she saw stunt girls "doing these amazing stunts."

"They were all like little cheerleaders, and the main one was Jennifer Caputo, a really well-respected stunt lady at the time. I thought it was so fascinating. I wanted to do that."

So Ginger told the stunt girls she wanted to learn, and by the afternoon they had her riding around a nearby parking lot on dirt bikes. Ginger later went to a dirt bike school to learn more and she said she just took to it. But her travel and work schedule didn't let her put the time and energy into it the way she wanted. Not being one to compromise, she held off pursuing it any further.

A few years later, she felt she'd gone about as far as she could with her hairstyling career. She'd traveled the world, worked with movie stars and royalty, and was looking for something new, but had no idea what that would be.

"What attracted me to the career I'd been in was the beauty and power. There was an understated elegance earlier on, and I wanted to be one of the people who made that statement. The stylists were in control. They were the rock stars. But that was changing, and I wanted something different."

The next phase of Ginger's life would start with a year off spent at an archeological dig. When she returned, she got involved in community policy in Los Angeles. This rekindled her earlier desire to go into law, but again, was told she was crazy for considering it. She even had a professor who told her she needed to apply her experience into something more transferable.

"I happened to know a guy at the time who was starting a custom motorcycle shop. I used my organizational ability and knowledge about the LA permitting process to help him get set up. In exchange, he offered to build me a motorcycle."

While that guy never did make good on his offer, Ginger's involvement with the motorcycle community started to gain some traction. She started going to local motorcycle events, and while she was not yet a bike owner, she dressed the part but with her own sense of style.

"I'd go to these motorcycle events and dress up in what I had. People started commenting. Girls would say 'I need to dress like that.' The guys would say, 'I wish my wife or girlfriend would dress that way.' When I started actually looking for a real motorcycle jacket for me, I couldn't find one. So I made one myself."

That first jacket, plus the comments she heard earlier, inspired Ginger to start a company that would make stylish motorcycle apparel strictly for women. Thinking her friend at the motorcycle shop might be of some help, she told him, and he basically told her it was a dumb idea. So Ginger left and never looked back.

She then met with a banker friend of hers and told him her idea. He wanted to know if there was even a market for women's motorcycle apparel.

"Right then, this woman rides by on a motorcycle and did so several times during our meeting. After that, I kept seeing motorcycles and fashion coming into play, and I knew I was on to something."

But there was something missing as Ginger began building her fledgling motorcycle apparel business—the proper name and her own bike. She credits Marilyn Manson with the former and Craigslist with the latter.

"I had worked with Marilyn and was intrigued by the combination of names he and his band had come up with. I'd always been a fan of the movie *Gigi* and the song *Bad Motor Scooter* by Montrose, so the name of the company became Gigi Montrose Moto Couture. I call it Prada meets the Rolling Stones."

As for the bike...it seems Ginger quickly recognized that some serious cred was missing if she did not ride—her past and limited experience with that little yellow moped, junkyard Harley parts, and dirt bikes in parking lots notwithstanding. So she promptly turned to that leviathan of all that's used—Craigslist.

"I really wanted a Triumph. It was probably because everyone I liked rode them—Steve McQueen, Fonzi, Ann Margret. I'd even met Ann, and I knew she was passionate about motorcycles. So when I saw this two-year old T100, I just knew I had to buy it."

Turns out, that T100 was a deal. At two years old, it only had 5,000 miles on it, and Ginger got it for $7,000. She's been riding it as much as she can ever since.

When you listen to Ginger talk about what inspires the designs she's creating and will be selling through Gigi Montrose, it's not surprising she chose a Triumph. She consistently mentions the idea of evoking a sense of timeless elegance and feminine power. She credits her experience attending Dia de Dona in Italy—a one day celebration of women by men that has nothing to do with mother's day—and her aunt, whom Ginger said was one of most elegant women she knew.

"I saw that when women rode, it was a borrowed identity. I decided I didn't want to be the girl in that jacket; I want to date that guy in that jacket. But how do you compliment that? How do you make a statement in an industry that already has an identity?' Being that I'm a new motorcycle rider, I had to ask who do I aspire to be? Who are women I can identify with? I dug back into my roots and designs from the forties for inspiration and created apparel that has a strong sense of feminism and individuality."

Ginger would love nothing more than to eventually see her start-up become as large as well-established companies like Schotts or Belstaff. Her apparel reflects that, and with a focus on quality that also translates into a price that may be out of the ballpark for some women riders—$1,500 to $2,000 for a leather jacket and $450 for a denim/textile jacket. But keep in mind, Ginger's intent on making a statement...and helping other women do the same.

"All of my life has added up to this moment. Every time I open an article or see a news magazine, I'm reminded I'm on the right path. I spoke to a couple of young girls not long ago who saw me with my bike. I told them, 'You can ride a motorcycle. You can be pretty. You can be anything you want to be.'"

What Ginger probably also told them is that often times that means going your own way; something she's had no problem doing since at least getting on that little yellow moped in the country outside of Bakersfield. Maybe one day Ginger Damon will be added to that list of famous former residents.

Lee Block has been riding nearly his whole life, including racing professionally, but it's how he's led his life off the track that has made the biggest impact.

Life Doesn't Always Fit Like a Glove

On Father's Day, 1988, Lee Block was entering the second lap in a race at Loudon riding a Honda VF Interceptor when he experienced the worst crash of his professional career. He broke both wrists, a leg, and had several other injuries.

He went home a few days later, and once he was out of the casts, he went through months of physical therapy. At one point, his girlfriend, Michelle, who would go on to become his wife, had to do everything for him...and we mean everything. That's some serious love and dedication!

Some people might give up racing after that, maybe even more. Others keep going and get more determined. Count Lee among the latter.

The crash happened three years into Lee's racing career. He'd go on to race three more years and ride in over 150 races before putting his racing gear away, all except the gloves—he still has the pair he wore when he crashed.

"When my first daughter was born in '91, I decided to quit racing. I didn't want her to grow up not knowing who her father was. But I never stopped riding motorcycles."

Lee's dad might be the one you could point to as having started it all. When Lee was ten, Mr. Block bought Lee a Rupp mini-bike. Little did Lee's dad know what kind of future that little Rupp would create for his son. But as a rider himself, he probably didn't think about it.

A dirt track where Lee and his buddies had raced each other on their banana-seated bikes became the perfect place to bomb around on the Rupp. A year later, the mini-bike was replaced by a small Enduro, and Lee never looked back. What's crazy is Lee and the guy who had that bike as a kid are still friends to this day.

But none of that bombing around in the dirt would lead to an immediate career in racing. Lee went to college, majored in air transportation management, and then found himself working at a Honda motorcycle dealer in Connecticut. This was the time when the Honda Interceptor was out and was a favorite track racer.

"That was such a cool bike, and parts were relatively cheap. So I decided to set up a business selling these spare parts. I was initially working out of my mom's garage, and the business was called Connecticut Cycleworks. I eventually got a vendors license and began selling and installing parts in the paddocks at Loudon Raceway [now New Hampshire Motor Speedway]."

What made it work is that Lee focused on supplying the guys racing in the stock class. Parts were both easy to come by and install, so selling and installing at the various tracks where this class raced was relatively simple.

Sometime in 1985, Lee made his way out of the paddock and onto the track. Thus would begin his racing career, which took him to most of the major venues on the East Coast, including Talladega, Daytona, Road Atlanta, and Bridgehampton in Rhode Island.

At one point, he was ranked in the top ten at Loudon's AMRR racing organization, which included piloting the Honda VF 500 Interceptor, and later a Honda 600

Hurricane and a 500 Superbike. The Hurricane is what he was riding when he crashed in '88.

A lot has changed in racing since the '80s. Classes have come and gone. The technology in the bikes is far more advanced; so is the gear. And racers are pushing themselves and the bikes in ways they really couldn't thirty years ago. Does Lee miss it?

"I was always kind of scared when I raced. It was definitely exhilarating, and I really loved the faster tracks. Other than Loudon, Daytona and Bridgehampton were probably my favorite. But I often thought about what would happen if I crashed. When I had my accident, it was a big wake-up call that took me three more years to answer."

When Lee left racing, he went back to running Connecticut Cycleworks for about three more years, followed by a stint at a sportswear company, then Fox Racing. Both jobs must have shown him he had an affinity for everything from marketing to sales to the ever-exciting world of inventory management and supply-chain operations. It wasn't nearly the adrenalin rush of dragging a knee on asphalt, but the guy had a growing family to support!

After a few additional positions at companies related and unrelated to motorcycling, Lee found himself in 2010 as head of operations for Element Case, Inc. This is the company that introduced the Vapor Case for the iPhone that was current at the time and still makes some pretty interesting cases for the current models.

Somewhere in the middle of all of this, he also had a dirt bike rental company called Monterey Motorcycle Rental Company, and he started building quite a stable of bikes that now includes the following:

'97 Honda Z50
'04 TTR 125 (Sarah's)
'08 WR250F
'00 XR650L
'75 CB400F

'83 VF750F
'86 SRX600
'97 TZ250 GP bike
'02 GS1150
'13 CBR300 RR (former Ari Henning championship/ lap record bike)

Life, according to Lee, was pretty good. Then it took a slow, but ugly, sweeping turn.

"In 2012, Michelle was diagnosed with ovarian cancer. I was commuting from Gilroy to Redwood City [California], which was about three to four hours or more a day. I wanted and needed to spend more time with her."

It didn't help that Lee's mom had passed away a year earlier, and by this point Lee and Michelle had been married for twenty-six years and known each other for thirty-five. This was the woman who took care of him after he took that crash at Loudon, and they had two daughters entering early adulthood. That Bay Area traffic was the last thing Lee needed to deal with.

So Lee came upon an opportunity to meet with the folks at Roadrider, who was the US importer for RacerGloves out of Austria. They introduced him to the parent company, and he took it from there.

Lee opened up the RacerGloves USA office a few minutes from his home, and put all of that prior marketing, merchandising, sales, and related experience to work expanding the company's presence in the US. He built the back end of the website, focused on just carrying the company's premium line of products, and came at the product line from the standpoint of the rider. But when he turned on the site...nothing happened.

"It was a couple of months before any significant traffic started coming to the site and orders started coming in. I'd just sit there waiting for something to happen. We eventually did okay that first year, and this year is off to the best start yet. It's off the hook. But those first few months were tough."

Meanwhile, Lee's wife continued to fight cancer, but she eventually succumbed in 2015. Anyone who's lost a loved one or friend to this messed-up disease can relate to how Lee must have felt. He no doubt has had his moments, but rather than dwell on his loss, he seems to be circumspect about the outcome.

"We had a great life together, and I'm glad I made the decision to be able to spend the time with her."

Since Michelle's death, Lee fills up his days with plans on how to expand his business and what new lines to add, hitting a track day once a month when he can, and thinking of the future. He and his daughter, Sarah, ride together on occasion. His other daughter, Lauren, is more into bicycles.

Given his background and the varied events that have made up his life, it seems appropriate to ask Lee what, if anything, racing has taught him. His answer has none of the requisite ideas of freedom, wind in the hair, go your own way, but they fit a man who believes he now has more at stake.

"It taught me discipline, the ability to fix things, and responsibility. I know the consequences of going too fast, so I don't have to do the crazy stuff anymore. I'm far more about self-preservation and good thinking."

As far as what Lee's riding future looks like, his favorite bike is that '02 GS1150 sitting with the others in his garage, and his dream is to ride something like it across China. That's a long way from that racetrack in Loudon, New Hampshire, but patience seems to be something else Lee has probably learned. Eventually, he'll make that trip, and it will somehow fit just fine with the life he's led so far.

Imagine riding flat out as fast as you can on two wheels on a salt flat, where top speeds are hitting close to 200 mph. That's how Erin Hunter Sills spends her off-time when she's not working at Facebook. Here's how she got there.

What "Cider Run" Means to Erin Hunter Sills

Erin Hunter Sills is somewhere on a deserted highway in Nevada hitting speeds as far north of a hundred and sixty as she can push her bike to go. This is how a world speed record holder in multiple categories prepares for her next run at Bonneville.

She readily admits that going fast sits somewhere in the chain that makes up her DNA...but it probably took her dad to give it a bit of a boost.

"We weren't wealthy, but my dad always made sure he had the fastest car he could afford. When I was around six, he started taking me out on the back roads of Ohio and drive as fast he could. When he'd tell my mom he was 'taking me to get cider,' I knew that meant we were going for one of those fast rides."

Who knows how long it took for Erin's mother to catch on to the inside cider reference, but the raw feeling of speed clearly made an impression on young Erin Hunter. It just took a while for it to fully manifest itself on two wheels.

Erin wouldn't buy her first motorcycle until around 2000—a Honda VFR800, not particularly fast, but still considered one of the best bikes Honda has ever made. Besides, Erin was looking for a starter bike that would be fun, comfortable, and a good ergonomic fit. Going faster than hell would come later.

A year later, the Honda was replaced by a Yamaha SV-1, something more in line with going fast. This was a bike that could do zero-to-sixty in just under three seconds and had a top speed of 167 mph.

Somewhere in this time frame, Erin met Andy Sills—a man whom she would go on to marry and who had established himself as one of the leaders in the idea of getting on two-wheels and riding like a bat out of hell across a plane of salt.

The two of them fed off of their hunger for speed and a full throttle desire to live life on their own terms. So when BMW came out with the speed eating HP Sport in 2008, Erin promptly bought the first one that came to the US and gave it to Andy as a present.

"I still have that bike, and it has over 30,000 miles on it. What that bike did more than anything was to make me appreciate BMW and the way their bikes perform."

A BMW is what Andy and Erin rode as the first two people to attempt a land speed record riding two-up at Bonneville. They hit a combined speed of 181 mph on a BMW S1000R in 2011, which gave them the *Guinness Book of World Records'* credit for the fastest two people on a motorcycle.

Andy was the pilot on the first pass with Erin on pillion, and they hit a top speed of 182.385 mph. Erin piloted on the return pass and managed 180.503 mph. Thus, the average of the two gave them the 181 mph for the record.

"Keeping a bike in a straight line as just the pilot is tough enough, but imagine having someone on the back. It's an entirely new set of possibilities for margin of error that have to be taken into account."

To give you some idea of what this entails, here's a brief description Erin gave in another publication soon after she and Andy got the record:

"Elbows are tight to the body, toes are pointed, knees are slammed to the horizontal axis, and even the minor folds in the second-seat rider's leathers pull like a freight train opposite the direction of travel. For the second-seat rider, it becomes an epic battle to remain tucked and motionless, relaxed yet vigilant. At 180 mph, one wrong move by the second-seat rider can become a back flip off the tail into the jaws of a fire-breathing dragon. If the second-seat rider moves their helmet ever so slightly, the pilot's helmet responds like an uncontrolled bobble head. If the second-seat rider opens a knee while adjusting position, that appendage will not go back to center unless we scrub speed and slow it back down again."

In other words, one false move and you're either going to die or go horribly off course.

Anyone who thinks that the majority of the preparation to go this fast is focused on the bike and that the rider just has to open the throttle and sit still for a few seconds needs a serious rethink. Let's start with getting into the mind-set of hitting 180 to 200 mph.

Back in the day of the original café racer scene, hitting a ton (100 mph) was the big goal. But when asked, Erin can't remember the first time she hit one hundred. She said it was probably on that Honda VFR, but her speeds come in ten-mile increments that don't really settle in until she's over 120. At 120, most riders will probably want to back off, but Erin's just getting started.

There's also the idea that this kind of sport still requires physical conditioning. She said she's always been fit so maintaining a weight-lifting and cardio routine is easy for her. She also practices yoga, which reminds her she needs to breath, during a run.

"I've done runs where I'm panting at the end of it, and I

realized that I was holding my breath the entire way. Yoga helps me get over that, and meditation helps me visualize the run and what I need to be thinking about. I owe it to my team to be as prepared as they are to do the best we can possibly do. You don't get a lot of chances out there."

Contrary to what you might think, Erin said the last thing you want to do is look at the speedometer. Your head needs to be somewhere else—both physically and mentally. Depending on where the speedo is located on the bike, a change in helmet position to look could throw off your speed by a wide margin. Depending on your frame of mind, the idea of knowing how fast you're going is similar to a tightrope walker looking down. (For anyone who's seen the movie *The Walk*, you'll understand the reference.)

That level of preparation didn't lead to just one speed record for Andy or Erin, it has led to well over nineteen world and national records between the two of them; and it wasn't always on big one-liter bikes. In 2003, they worked with Jack Costella (a world famous land speed record holder) to create a purpose built 100cc streamliner that Andy went on to pilot to 141 mph. Erin broke that record a year later with an 80cc engine, which gave her the distinction of being the fastest woman with a world record on a streamlined motorcycle. As for Erin's fastest time ever—try 200 mph.

Unfortunately, a non-racing motorcycle accident cut short the couple's mutual passion for going fast and their life together. It took Andy's life and the person who Erin said was not only the love of her life, but also the main person she credits with being her biggest influence.

"I wouldn't have gotten into this sport without him. I wouldn't be successful without him. He's still in my helmet—even on daily rides."

While Erin and Andy were breaking land speed records they also decided to help attract more women to the sport. Soon after they won their first BUB-sponsored event at Bonneville, they realized how few women were participating.

There were only four at the time. So they started the SheMoto Award that gives an annual thousand-dollar scholarship to a woman in the sport and another thousand-dollar award to the person who most encouraged that person's passion. It's been going for ten years now.

"It's about recognizing a woman who most embodies what it means to be a land speed racer. She can be an actual racer, someone just starting out, or a woman involved in promoting the event. It's about persevering as a woman in a very male-dominated sport."

When Erin isn't being one of the fastest women on two wheels, she enjoys a successful career as director of consumer insights at Facebook. She points out that Facebook has been a big supporter of her passion for speed, and that support is one of the reasons she decided to work there.

"When I went to talk to the folks at Facebook, it seemed like a good fit. The company encourages everyone to celebrate their passions, rather than hide them. And when you think about how easy they've made that for the average person to do, it makes sense that they would do that with their own staff."

Every sport has its euphemisms and analogies relative to work and life. Team sports stress the concept of collaboration, knowing when to back off and give the "ball" to someone else. Individual sports focus on the concept of self-motivation. On the surface, you might wonder how does that apply to chasing land speed records. Considering what's involved, Erin's response makes sense.

"You have to understand your own strengths—what you can or can't do. I'm a phenomenal pilot and rider, but I'm not an engineer or tuner. I need the people who can do that. The same goes for work. I understand what I can do well, and I hire really smart people who can do what I can't and be passionate about it."

Then there's the future. The passing of someone as close as Andy was to Erin might make some think twice about their chosen passion. Not Erin. If anything, it only seems to have made her even more focused.

"I have two goals—bring home the production 1000cc record for BMW by breaking 201 mph and become a member of the SETA 200 mph club. They have strict rules for doing so, but I think I can get there."

With Andy in her helmet and more than a few backroad "cider runs," Erin will no doubt achieve both.

In 1916, two sisters set out to ride their motorcycles across the United States. They became the first to do it on two separate bikes. 100 years later, their relatives retraced their route.

Women Can Ride

Adventure is a funny thing. Particularly when it comes to motorcycles. There are as many definitions of it as there are riders. For some, it's a day ride down a new route or a dirt trail. Others find it in casting aside as many worldly goods as possible and riding across unfamiliar terrain and foreign countries. But however it's defined, adventures create immortal bonds and stories that deserve and demand to be shared and retold...and sometimes they can be so significant they make history.

One hundred years ago, Adeline (Addie) and Augusta (Gussie) Van Buren went on an adventure that did exactly that. The Van Buren sisters became the first two women to ride individual motorcycles across the United States and the first women to ride to the top of Colorado's Pikes Peak.

The Van Buren sisters undertook their adventure at a time when women didn't have the right to vote, it was illegal in some towns for women to even wear pants, and good luck finding a paved road. Europe was embroiled in WWI and US involvement looked to be inevitable.

None of those seemed like good reasons for the two young women to stay at home. It made more sense to the sisters to prove that if the US got involved in the war, women could do their part as motorcycle couriers. So on July 4, 1916, they set out from Sheepshead Bay, New York, on newly purchased and highly vaunted 1000cc Indian Powerplus motorcycles and headed into what was mostly a wide-open country. They'd finish their 5,500-mile trip a little more than two months later in Tijuana, Mexico.

At the time, the US had a population of just under a hundred and two million, less than a third of its current size. Stamps cost two cents. Gas was sixteen cents a gallon. Albert Einstein would complete his general theory of relativity. Charlie Chaplin would sign a contract awarding him an astonishing $10,000 a week (about $230,000 in today's dollars). Pancho Villa, roving bands of renegade Indians, and occasional cattle thieves made travel in the American Southwest potentially dangerous. In other words, the country was still a mixed bag of civility and untamed west, and so was the route the Van Buren sisters would be traveling.

None of that deterred them. They weren't in it for the glory; they were out to prove a point. And while they successfully completed their trip with no significant mechanical issues—one of the tires on the two bikes supposedly made it the entire way without ever needing air—the sisters' point was lost on the US government. Women were meant to stay at home.

Here we are one hundred years later; women have equal rights, the last key element of Einstein's theory was just recently proven, and any mega star in sports or entertainment is making as much or more than Charlie Chaplin did then. And thankfully, what the Van Buren sisters accomplished is not going to go uncelebrated.

This coming July, Alisa Clickenger will lead a group of mostly women riders along much of the same route. Sure, they'll have the advantage of paved roads, modern motorcycles, and hotels and motels along the way, but it's the spirit of the ride, not the conditions, that's important.

It's no surprise that Alisa took this on. An avid rider and experienced tour guide, she's had her own set of adventures with extended cross-country and cross-continent rides of her own. But none that would have the scope or significance of a 100th anniversary celebrating the accomplishments of two sisters who had society and the elements telling them they shouldn't when the two of them believed they could.

"As an avid rider, I'd gotten this idea to do something like this, especially for those women who think they can't. About two years ago, I came across the Van Buren sisters' ride again and decided I needed to stop talking about it and do it. I wanted to lead one hundred women across the United States to commemorate the anniversary and encourage women to try something they might not have thought they could."

Yes, that number is correct—on hundred women riding across the country on motorcycles in what Alisa has dubbed the "Sisters' Ride." We'll get to the logistics of that in a bit.

Meanwhile...one of the most incredible elements to this ride is the fact that Alisa was able to get some of the sisters' descendants to join her—Addie's grandson, Dan Ruderman; his wife, son, and daughter (great-grandchildren of Adeline); and Gussie's great-nephew, Bob Van Buren and his wife. Interestingly enough, Dan and Bob had never met until this last summer, even though they were raised on the same stories of the sisters' feats and live in the same general area in Massachusetts.

Until, a couple years ago, Dan had ridden a motorcycle once and Bob was, for the most part, an occasional rider. But both convey a similar adventurous spirit that could have only come from the genes of their respective great-aunt and grandmother.

"My grandmother [Addie] wouldn't let my mother touch her motorcycle, let alone ride it, so I grew up with the stories, but not with the personal experience of riding," said Dan. "The closest I got was riding one a friend of mine had in college. It was an old AMC Harley-Davidson, and I ended up riding it into a cornfield. I got off and never got on another one."

Today, Dan works as a sales consultant for LexisNexis and lives about a two-hour ride from Boston. In 2014, with the 100th anniversary of his grandmother's ride two years away, he and his son, Skyler, decided to take the motorcycle safety course and get their licenses.

"I didn't know what that would mean or how far either of us might ride by the time the anniversary came around, but it seemed like the thing to do."

Dan and his son successfully passed all the requisite tests. Dan bought himself a used 2003 BMW 650GS, and his son a used Honda Rebel 250. That bike soon gave way to a Honda CB500, that his son has since put 10,000 miles on riding around the country. Must be in the genes.

While Dan may not have long-distance motorcycle experience, and he admits to being a bit of a klutz and not very handy mechanically, he said he and his wife both enjoy riding.

"We call it wind therapy. Sometimes, I'll get on my bike and ride for hours, just turning left when it seems like it's time."

He fills in some gaps about his grandmother that only a relative could. Like the fact that her grandfather's parents weren't too keen on their son marrying someone of Dutch decent.

"My grandfather, Jim, was sent off to a Catholic seminary to avoid marrying Addie. But she was so determined that they be together that she hired a private investigator to find him. Once she did, she went there and convinced him to leave and marry her. She was someone who evidently was always determined to do the right thing."

Bob is the more experienced rider of the two. He started in 2002 with the purchase of a Harley Low Rider, then eventually rode that with his wife, Rhonda, in 2006 for the ninetieth anniversary of his great-aunt's ride. The sixteen-day effort included a trip to Sturgis to see the Addie and Gussie induction at the Sturgis Motorcycle Museum and Hall of Fame.

"We wanted to try to capture what the sisters did and thought we would have a lot of riders on that ninetieth anniversary ride, but most of them dropped out before we started or left along the way. We didn't have much of an itinerary, so that may not have helped."

Today, Bob is a retired engineer who teaches physics at the local community college. Twelve years ago, he formed a company to preserve and promote the integrity and history of what the sisters accomplished and what they stood for. During that time, he said different people have approached him to turn the sisters' story into a movie. One came close, but he said they wanted to make so many changes to the story they eventually turned them down.

If he could identify anyone on his side of the family who was most like his great aunt, he said it would be his daughter, Sarah.

"She created her own degree, started her own dance party company in Europe, and is the art director for the Hudson Basilica. For her, it's all about experiences. She'll be creating some of those when she joins the anniversary ride on her own bike in July."

There will be at least six Van Buren descendants on the Sisters' Ride: Dan Ruderman and his wife, Ditte, son Skyler and daughter, Sofie; and Bob and Rhonda Van Buren, and their daughter, Sarah. If Alisa's vision for the ride becomes a reality, one hundred women, maybe more, will be joining them on July 3 to track as much of the original sisters' ride as possible.

What Alisa is planning is nothing short of extraordinary. If you've ever bothered putting together a day-ride of more than say twenty people, imagine multiplying the length of time by twenty and the number of people by five, then figure out where they're going to eat and sleep in different states along an over three-thousand mile route that won't necessarily always follow a direct line. It's not for the faint of heart or badly organized.

But there must be some Addie and Gussie in Alisa. She's approached this project with the same sense of purpose and a hard-core case of don't-tell-me-I-can't. But that's not to say she hasn't tried to figure out how to make it easier on herself and those who will join her. Here's where her previous experience running and leading tours has come into play.

Fully-guided riders will be in groups of no more than six or seven, with someone leading each group. As long as each small group follows the local and state traffic laws, there's no need to let the police or highway patrol know a big group of bikers will be riding through city streets and taking over a quarter-mile or longer stretches of state highways.

Self-guided riders can ride at their own pace. Once everyone leaves the designated meet spot in the morning, they can ride as fast as they can legally get away with or as slow as they desire. The only caveat is to be at the base hotel at the end of the day for whatever is planned. So the entire group of riders will never be riding completely together. Brilliant!

With five months to go, Alisa's biggest concern is not what's left to do, it's how many opportunities keep coming up from other groups that are hearing about the ride.

"The more contacts we make, the more opportunities we have. At some point, I'm going to start having to say no. But I'm not quite there yet."

The ride the Van Buren sisters completed one hundred years ago has left an indelible mark that has positively impacted their families today. Each side has their own set of pictures, stories, and influence. When asked what their grandmother and aunt taught them, both Dan and Bob give different answers, but their responses seem to encapsulate the spirit and intent of their relatives.

Dan hones in on the concept of expectations. "Growing up, we were never told we had to do a certain thing or be a certain way. My grandmother taught me and our family that we could be whatever we want."

For Bob, it's about determination. "They taught me service to country and not giving up. The sisters could have given up, but they kept going."

Alisa is obviously not part of the family, but she is clearly doing this to honor what the two sisters accomplished, and by doing so she hopes to achieve even more.

"I'm hoping we can attract women who will come out and hear our stories about transformation on two wheels. If they've ever had a tickle about trying a motorcycle, I want this to give them the impetus to try."

This sounds a lot like a quote attributed to Gussie after she and her sister completed their ride: "Woman can if she will." For the women who have ridden and created their own adventures since, and those who will do so in the future, that saying couldn't be more appropriate.

[NOTE: Alisa Clickenger completed the Sisters' Ride in July 2016, and by all accounts it was a huge success.]

Don't tell Antonia Bolingbroke-Kent that girls aren't supposed to ride in remote places on small motorcycles by themselves. She's liable to convince you that there are even more remote places yet to see on a small set of two wheels.

Riding with Ants

Before you think this is about a journey with insects and how some poor rider got stuck trying to get rid of them, let me quickly dispel that. This is the story of a woman who goes by "Ants" and who has made a habit of putting herself out there in a way most people, let alone most riders, wouldn't.

Let's get one thing straight; Ants (her full name is Antonia Bolingbroke-Kent) does not have a death wish. In fact, her desire lies more in the reality that there are untamed roads and places out there that are quickly becoming obliterated by progress and whose history is rapidly fading. She wants to get there and experience them and the people who live near them before it all goes the way of the Dodo and common sense.

"I was brought up in a very rural part of England. I rode horses, climbed trees. I was very feral. So I had this built-in love of the outdoors and nature. When I was in my teens, I went to a really pressurized school and didn't care for it. As soon as I graduated from college, I decided that I didn't want to have a job that wasn't interesting."

The taste for adventure, at least the travel part, was probably as much to be blamed on nurture as nature. Ants's father is an antiquarian book dealer who travels all over the world in search of old tomes. Her mother is also a global traveler and recently bought a home in Romania. Then there's the grandmother who traveled to and lived in Peking in the 1930s and a grandfather who was evidently "mad about motorcycles."

Ants does have a sister who evidently didn't get the same genes. She's an interior decorator with two kids who Ants said wonders what's wrong with her.

Traveling by motorcycle was not her first foray into the somewhat unknown or less-traveled parts of the world. The motorcycling element wouldn't happen until 2006 when she and her good friend, Jo Huxster, rode a tuk tuk nearly 12,600 miles from Bangkok to Birmingham, England.

"I had managed to start making a career of being a travel journalist and adventure writer in my twenties. That included traveling to some quirky places and working for an adventure travel company called "The Adventurists." So you'd think that I would have jumped at the idea of this trip. But the first thing I thought about was the security I was going to give up by going."

Two things convinced Ants to discard that thought. First, her friend Jo had been through six or seven years of treatment for depression and mental health issues. This trip would be a celebration of being better. Then another friend committed suicide. That convinced Ants she needed to live life and continue to put herself out there. So off Ants and Jo went in their tuk tuk.

Keep in mind, a tuk tuk is basically an engine-powered rickshaw. The one Ants and Jo rode in their *Guinness* record setting trip was no different. And theirs was painted pink—making it highly visible across the remote landscape they traveled on their way across the Asian and European continents.

Their adventure lasted three-and-a-half months, and besides achieving the world record, they also managed to raise 50,000 pounds for Mind, a mental health charity, and published a book about the experience—*Tuk Tuk to the Road*—but not before experiencing multiple earthquakes in China, numerous mechanical breakdowns, border passage issues, Russian men stopping them for a quick breast grope, and drunken men trying to get into their hotel room. Other than that, Ants said their trip was "mostly trouble free."

Really?

By this point, Ants had been bitten by the riding bug. But her newfound passion didn't take her into the realm of big adventure bikes or even mid-sized versions. No, given that tuk tuk wasn't powered by much of an engine at all, she gravitated toward Honda Cubs.

"They have character. They are idiot proof. And they're practically indestructible! You can literally pick them up, drop them, get back on, and ride off."

So Honda Cubs, with their little 90cc engine, became and still are Ants's steed of choice. That's what she and her boyfriend, Marley, took on a three-week excursion around the Black Sea several years after her tuk tuk adventure.

"We had both fallen in love with Cubs and were wondering where we could go for three weeks on them without much preparation. So we painted our bikes in different cat prints, got spandex pants to match, and off we went."

It's clear that while many riders would tag this as a proper adventure, Ants considers this a ride like any other. Part of that comes from the way she personally defines what traveling to different places means to her.

"So many people go on these trips and think that if you go to the cities, that's the adventure. But you have to get away from the cities to really find out what the people are like and learn the real history of the place."

She also pointed out that having worked in the adventure travel industry she's noted a distinct difference between how most men approach adventure versus the way she does.

"Male adventurists are all about getting someplace first or fastest. It's about the athleticism. I go because I want to learn about the interesting stories that you can find out when you take your time."

But there's a bit of an contradiction there when it comes to another of Ants's motorcycle trips. That one involved a Ural, not a Cub, and a short period of time to see if it was possible to ride to the Siberian Arctic in the winter.

"We bought a crappy old Ural off of an old convict, fixed it up as best we could, and dressed in multiple layers to ward off the cold. Since the bike was constantly breaking down, we had to push it a lot, which helped keep us warm. After a week of breakdowns and getting stalled out in villages, we finally had to scratch the trip."

While that ride was unsuccessful, it did lay the groundwork for the Ice Run—an adventure ride organized by The Adventurists that takes you by old Ural across frozen Lake Baikal. The fine print warns that people have been dismembered and even died there in the past—not the typical ride to Sturgis!

And neither is the Ho Chi Minh Trail ride Ants has written about in her latest book, *A Short Ride in the Jungle*, detailing her 2012 trip down the road that for many is a symbol of both Western failure and Vietnamese defiance.

The idea for the trip began earlier while she was producing an episode about the Trail for the BBC series *World's Most Dangerous Roads*. Her inherent curiosity and love of history was piqued, and she decided that she would return to do the trip without support vehicles, medics, a riding partner, or translators. She was going to ride it alone.

As she had with her other trips, she found a used Honda Cub and someone to get it ready to ride, including a nice pink paint job. Other than riding one section of the trail with some male friends, she did mostly adhere to riding it alone.

"When I was previously on the Trail, I realized how quickly it was changing. It's history and the people who were tied to it were disappearing. There were so many stories I wanted to discover."

Ants downplayed some of the issues she faced on that ride—more groping men, periodic breakdowns and flats she had to take care of herself, and grabbing some shut-eye in places in which most would have never set foot. None of that deterred her from accomplishing what she set out to do—ride the Trail, learn what she could of its history while there were people left to tell it, and discover something about herself along the way.

"I learned I'm capable of doing more than I thought and that I can do things on my own. I always think of myself as a bit of wimp, but very few things are as scary as you make them in your mind."

On February 1, 2016, Ants left for her next adventure, exploring the remote northeast Indian state of Arunachal Pradesh. From 1950-1998, the area was closed to foreigners, and it remains a fairly unexplored and seldom visited place.

In her blog, *The Itinerant*, she describes it like this:

"Today this disputed region, is the most linguistically and ethnically diverse area of South Asia, home to 28 different tribes and 111 sub-tribes, many of whom—thanks to Nehru closing the state to outsiders in 1950 and the inaccessibility of its jagged, forested terrain—have retained their unique cultures and animist beliefs. Shamans still fly through the night, tigers have magical powers, hidden valleys hide portals to other worlds, spirits and demons abound and the gods are appeased by the blood of sacrificed beasts."

Sounds like a perfect adventure for Ants, although this time she said she'll be on a slightly bigger bike—a Hero Impulse with its massive [sic] 125cc engine.

What final advice does Ants have for anyone—male or female—who may have held off taking their own adventure?

"Stop making excuses and just go. It's easier than you think. Don't let your fears beat you. And, if you can't afford it, just put it on the credit card."

So the next time you think that three-day trip up the Pacific Coast or a week in Sturgis is an adventure, think of Ants traveling alone on a little bike in some remote part of the world. Now *that's* an adventure!

If the adventure mood should strike you, you can join Ants when she returns from India and takes up running her own adventure company, Edge Expeditions.

Sometimes you have to get knee deep in the thing you thought you wanted before you find the thing you should have started all along. That's Edward Wilkinson's story and he's sticking to it.

Get Out of Your Own Way

Edward Wilkinson was supposed to be working on Wall Street. A degree from Columbia and what was probably some familial urging pointed that direction. But after a few months in an internship there, he realized that fit about as well as a five-pound sack around a fifty-pound pile of you-name-it. So he went a different direction, one that's taken him on the back roads of the lower forty-eight, Alaska, and Canada and into a career developing products for like-minded adventure riders.

And it all started on a Puch Maxi-Luxe with a 2 hp engine his parents helped him buy when he was a teenager growing up in Connecticut.

"My dad raced motorcycles in California and had crashed enough to tell me it was too dangerous. So the deal was he'd buy me the Puch if I agreed to always wear a helmet. Once I got the Puch, I immediately made some changes. I put on a luggage rack and a two-gallon gas tank. I took the pedals off of it and put on a longer banana seat—anything to make it seem more like a motorcycle."

The Puch lasted through several years of long rides until Edward's interests started to lean elsewhere—white water rafting, mountain biking, road biking, and endurance rides—just about any way to get Edward outside and keep him there instead of being on a motorcycle.

When Edward ended his short stint on Wall Street, he got a job in an outdoor recreation store, where he was eventually noticed by Merrell, the shoe and boot company. He worked his way up through several positions there, still staying clear of motorcycles, until he saw something on a business trip that would change that.

"I was in Bangkok, and I noticed all of these people on mopeds hauling everything from entire families to pigs to plate glass windows. There was a BMW dealer in the hotel where I was staying, so I decided to go in. Well, I fell in love with a GS650 Dakar. So when I got back to my room, I went online, found one at a dealership in Chicago, and had it shipped to my parent's home back in Connecticut."

The problem was that Edward hadn't told his parents because he still had a couple of weeks of business travel to take care of, and he didn't have a license. His dad was the one that called Edward and told him the bike had arrived.

"When I got back home, I got my learner's permit, found some old motorcycle gear from when I had the Puch, and started bombing all over the family farm. It just felt completely natural to me."

Edward said he rode that single-cylinder thumper everywhere, including many four-hundred-mile round trip visits to his parents from where he lived in Vermont. But what was missing was a real adventure, something that would really put him and the bike to the test. So he promptly went to Nova Scotia.

"It was out there, and it was an island. But the trip went badly. It rained during most of it, and at one time I had to ride through the night in the rain. Just brutal. Then the clutch cable went out, and I had to have one delivered. But other than the clutch cable, the bike handled great."

Despite the weather and technical issues, Edward was bitten by the moto-adventure travel bug. He had that 650 for three years before it developed an electrical problem. Turned out it was a mouse nest in the exhaust, which taught him to never leave an open-ended exhaust in the winter again!

He traded up for a BMW 1150 GS then a BMW 1200 that he'd found on ADVRider. Unfortunately, that bike was in the shop almost more than it was on the road. Three broken final drives and camping out at his local dealer eventually got him a newer, more reliable GSA model kitted out with bags and other extras.

"I named that bike 'The Beastie,' and it made me feel like I could do anything I wanted. I just became addicted to riding. I couldn't stop."

Edward was still at Merrell and saving up his vacation each year so he could go on multi-week trips, rather than a week here or there. He had accumulated four weeks' worth of time off, put his request in...and they nixed it, saying they couldn't have him out for that length of time. So the next day, he quit.

"They didn't expect that, but it worked to my benefit. I was overseeing about a third of their product line at the time. So they said if I stayed and finished the new product line, they'd pay me through the end of the year, plus my Cobra [health] coverage for the year. I did that, then took off."

That's an understatement. Without knowing where his next paycheck would come from, Edward proceeded to spend the next four months riding through all of the US national parks, through sections of Canada, and eventually ended up back at his parents place in Connecticut, by way of Tucson.

It was about this time that he met Alisa Clickenger, a fellow adventure rider, who'd already started developing a reputation for interesting and long adventure rides. She eventually became his partner, and the two of them started planning a joint Trans-America Trail (TAT) trip, which Edward completed riding a DRZ 400.

At some point, Edward's story gets so far off-road that it's hard to keep up with where he and one of his different bikes were at any given time. But at one point, he found himself unemployed and at Port Orford, Oregon, where he heard about the Continental Divide Trail, which he promptly turned around and rode to see if he could complete that. That whole addicted to riding thing.

While on that trail and during a stop in Breckenridge, Colorado, Edward had a chance to try a KTM. He liked it, but not enough to buy it on the spot—that would happen on the second to last day of the Trail when he found himself in Silver City, New Mexico.

"Alisa had joined me later on that ride, and we were looking for a tube for her Suzuki, so I found myself trying another KTM. I really liked that bike, so I traded my DRZ in and wrote them a check right there."

Now most dealers couldn't do that without some serious checking around. Which the dealer did and found out that Edward was well-known by the folks at Twisted Throttle. So Edward had himself a new bike and was completely satisfied. Unfortunately, Alisa wasn't.

"She was ticked because she thought I'd rather buy a new bike than follow her on her trip down to Argentina. It really wasn't about the new bike, though. I'm just not that interested in riding in foreign countries. Besides, my trips are more like military death marches and hers are far more 'free.'"

So Alisa headed off to ride down to Argentina, and Edward got rid of his BMW in favor of the KTM.

Some more riding and a quick passage of time, and Edward found himself in Alaska, but with gear he wasn't too happy with. He'd had some Klim pants that he liked, but they really weren't made for adventure motorcycle riding. So he started to think that if they could make specific clothing for that market, they could be onto something.

Edward put together a presentation that convinced the company of the benefit of making waterproof, abrasion-resistant apparel for the adventure and off-road rider. Klim was so impressed, they hired Edward to head up the development of that line of clothing. The deal was he could get it started in May and complete a ride in Alaska he already had planned in June that year.

He and Alisa rode up to Dawson Creek, Alaska, with some spec Klim gear to do some product testing. They took what they learned from that experience back to Klim, and Edward was hired to oversee the development and introduction of Klim's entry into the adventure riding market.

"Things were great at Klim until they were bought by Polaris. It's not that Polaris is a bad company. They just added more bosses, which meant more meetings and less control over the product. So I started looking elsewhere."

Elsewhere ended up being Scorpion, where Edward works today.

"After the interview, I was in Steamboat Springs [Colorado] and had actually forgotten about Scorpion when they called and offered me a job. It meant moving from Idaho to Los Angeles, which meant we needed an address to move our furniture to. We looked at a map, picked a spot in LA, and while Alisa was riding in Africa, I had everything packed up and moved. It took a few months to get used to, but we're in the middle of the North American motorcycle magazine market, and most of the Japanese brands have their headquarters in this area."

Edward and Alisa have since moved to another part of Los Angeles, and today he still saves up as much vacation time as he can to go on the long backcountry odysseys he finds so appealing. He now has several bikes he can choose from and create whatever adventure he wants. That includes an '05 Honda XR650R, an '05 KTM 950 Adventure, an '07 KTM 950 Super Enduro that he's kitted out with a combined set of tanks to give him a 450-mile range and a Warn winch to get out of multiple "you name it" situations. His daily commuter bike is an '07 Honda CBR600RR that allows him to lane split with ease, and he also has a 2015 BMW S1000RR that he describes as his "scare yourself silly on the weekends" bike.

Given how ingrained backcountry and cross-country riding is with Edward, I thought he'd have a good idea of the main items anyone should bring with them and/or never pass up. Here's his short list:

Water—at least a couple of liters (two gallons a day)

Gas/fuel—never pass a gas station

Be able to fix a tire—even if it's tubeless; carry a tire repair kit and compressor or CO_2 cartridge.

Sounds like good advice, but I also wondered what adventure riding had taught him in general. While his answer could be just as pertinent to anyone who likes to ride their bike long distances, on- or off-road, it's a reply anyone who rides can use when asked the same question by those who don't.

"If you ride cross-country on a motorcycle, you realize how big this country is. You find out how the people change from one part of the country to the next. On a bike, you interact with people. You smell the smells. If you just fly and stay in a hotel, you don't get that."

For someone who's crammed as much riding into the last decade and a half as Edward, that's insight worth noting.

Adventure riding has become one of the most popular types of riding on two wheels there is. For Tony Huegel that means finding adventure in what was once the Wild West of the United States.

Answering the Call of the Wild

The backcountry has always had a draw for a particular type of person. Mostly it's either people who grew up used to being in it or as close to it as possible, those who want to escape for at least a short time from the mayhem of urban life, and those who just want to escape, never to be heard from again. Tony Huegel is mostly the first, a lot of the second, and none of the last.

He grew up in the San Francisco Bay Area in the '60s and '70s when land that is now covered in tract homes was nothing but open grazing land. When tiny towns like Danville and Walnut Creek were small bergs that were more about agriculture than shopping. Today, he lives in Idaho Falls, Idaho, and has turned his passion for adventure and travel into becoming an expert on what he calls "wild land travel" by motorcycle or SUV throughout the West.

"I learned to ride dirt bikes and eventually confiscated my brother's 1962 Honda 305 Superhawk when he was sent to Vietnam in '67. I didn't have a driver's license, but I rode that bike all over the backroads in the area then. It created this insatiable desire for adventure."

Tony said he didn't have the Superhawk for very long. Once he could afford to, he bought a Honda 350 Scrambler and later a Kawasaki, and proceeded to ride up and down the coast, into the Olympics in the Northwest, and anywhere else his motorcycle could take him.

"That was the beginning of this need to get out there and explore. I eventually got out of riding, but hitchhiked and rode freight cars across the country, rode an old car to Guatemala, backpacked in the backcountry, and hitchhiked across Morocco and Algeria."

Eventually, Tony put his thumb and feet to rest and got a job as a reporter in Lander, Wyoming. He got married, and he and his wife moved to Ukiah, California, where he continued work as a reporter. But while Ukiah is a small town with lots of forests and backcountry nearby, it was lacking one thing—snow. Turns out that Tony's wife was a big skier and wanted to get to someplace that had it. So the Huegels moved to Idaho Falls.

"This was supposed to be a two-year stop. We've now been here for thirty. A job brought us here, but access to public lands and having access to so much backcountry has kept us here."

That backcountry access eventually drove the purchase of an Isuzu Trooper, which allowed Tony to take his growing family into the backcountry any chance he could get. Eventually, he started keeping track of these trips, which led to starting a company called "Backcountry Byways," and he produced a series of guidebooks tracing various routes throughout the West only accessible via four-wheel drive.

"This was in the '90s, when the SUV craze really started to kick in. Because I had all of this quasi-wilderness experience, and Idaho had a lot of backcountry dirt roads that some people may not have been aware of, I decided to start Backcountry Byways to help get them there."

One thing led to another, and the more Tony got into the backcountry, the more guides he was able to publish. This now includes guidebooks for California, Colorado, Utah, Washington, and the Sierra Nevada. Each guidebook gives detailed information on routes, historical background, and options for non-driving activities like hiking, mountain biking, and camping.

These guide books opened the door for Tony to write about off-roading for other outlets like *National Geographic Adventure*, *Road and Track*, *Popular Mechanics*, *Four Wheeler*, *4WD & SUV*, *San Diego Union Tribune*, and the *San Jose Mercury News*.

But something was missing. Tony had been at this for about twelve years but hadn't been on a bike for years. All of his backcountry adventures for the last three-plus decades had all been in a cage. But in 2005 that changed when he got a call from a group out of New Jersey that wondered if he could put together an adventure ride for them in Idaho.

"I didn't have any real ADV experience. But I did have my past dirt bike riding and backpacking experience. By this time, I had been getting tired of bombing around the back roads in my SUV, so that call re-fueled an interest in riding again. I created an Idaho route for them, they shipped their motorcycles to Missoula [Montana], and they rode 2,500 miles through Idaho. They've come back to me several times for other routes since."

And so was born the adventure riding version of what had primarily been guides for the SUV enthusiast. While those guides are just as applicable to adventure riding, what they didn't include was information about where to go to get even further back into what Tony refers to as "wild lands"—places that potentially only someone on a bike, on horseback, or on foot could go.

So what Tony did was buy a 2008 Kawasaki KLR and start exploring on two wheels. This has since led to licensing plug-and-play versions of his guidebooks and helping groups and individuals plan wild land adventures, either based on his own experience or customizing specific trips based on what a particular rider or group wants to do.

"People read books like *Jupiter's Travels* and think that's what all adventure traveling is about. It's not. The kind of adventure travel described in books like that is really more about immersing or exposing yourself to different cultures and people, rather than really getting into true wild lands—places most people will never see. That's what I'm offering."

Tony said he doesn't lead tours. Since he's creating routes through public lands, he said there's too much expense related to organizing and insuring group rides. What he does is provide adventure riders will all of the information they need to ride a route on their own. If it's a route he's not done before, he'll create a custom one that he'll ride himself first to make sure all of the information he's putting into the route is as up-to-date as possible.

"If you're going to the expense of shipping your bike somewhere to ride in an unfamiliar area, you don't want something to go wrong. If you're one of my clients, nothing will go wrong."

That kind of customized service doesn't come cheap, but Tony said it's really like having trip insurance. Prices can vary from $750 to $1,500 and up, depending on the length of the route and how far Tony has to travel to get to it. But what his clients receive is a detailed picture of the route and the elimination of any surprises and obstructions that can force the end of a trip.

Tony continues to make all of these trips on his KLR. You'd think by now he might want to upgrade to a bigger adventure bike. While the KLR is known for its durability, it's absent a lot of the bells and whistles of a newer Beemer, KTM, or Triumph.

"My KLR is like the motorcycle version of a 1975 Jeep CJ-5. It just goes. It's relatively easy to work on and not so heavy that I can't get it off the ground if it falls. You can't say that about many of the new adventure bikes out there."

Being able to pick up your bike is one of the things Tony insists is critical to adventure riding. That short but essential list also includes: a water filter, a lightweight tent and sleeping pad in case you have to spend the night, and the ability and kit to fix a flat. That list doesn't include a SPOT locator.

"People ask me about them, but I don't carry them. I think they give you a false sense of security...that you can get yourself into something or ride a particular way and the locator will make sure someone can get you out of it. I'd rather know that I'm riding in a way that isn't going to jeopardize my ability to get me out of any situation I might find myself in."

Considering Tony's years of experience both driving and riding in the backcountry, you'd expect him to have one story after another of close calls. He said most of those happen when he rides around town. But the most precarious, the most dangerous aspects of riding in the hills, he believes, is hunting season.

"Hunters drive fast and aren't expecting to see anyone. I was coming around a corner in the backcountry one time on my bike and one of these guys was coming right at me. All I could do was to find an out and hope I had enough room to avoid hitting him. I did, but the guy didn't even stop to be sure I was okay. I tell all of my clients to be really careful during hunting season."

He said the biggest adjustment street riders have to make when riding in dirt is traction control. As he pointed out, "Traction's better on pavement, so if you try to ride in dirt like you do on the street and don't take that into account, you're going to have problems."

Tony said he was reminded of that when he got back into off-road riding. He took a corner too fast, and while he didn't crash, he came close enough to learn his lesson—redefine traction control and watch your speed!

For the adventure rider who may want to just take off into the wild and see what fate might have in store, Tony's guides and guidance might be considered a bit of a crutch, perhaps taking away some of the adventure. But considering how difficult and expensive it can be to get into the wild lands today, that guide might just be the best money spent to make sure you complete that adventure. As Tony mentioned, consider it a bit of an insurance policy.

Meanwhile, Tony continues to be in search of the perfect wild lands route. He offered to take us along on a new Sierra loop he's created. Since our desire for backcountry escape is mostly driven by a desire for at least a short break from the din of urban living, we'll be hard-pressed not to take him up on it...come summer.

Albie Espinola looks more like a punk rocker and talks more like a London DJ, but underneath is the soul of an artist intent on finding every opportunity to paint his passion.

Boxer, Biker, Painter

What makes writing about riders located around the world difficult is being stymied by distance and reliant on technology to get some sense for the person beyond their response to the questions posed. Such is particularly the case with Albie Espinola—an artist, biker, and Londoner who could be hanging with an eclectic mix of young clubbers one night and bikers of varying ages the next. One look at his Facebook page and you'll see what I mean. Who wouldn't want to hang with Albie for a week?

If you get a chance, here's what you'll notice—besides that wild bleached-out Mohawk. Albie's a guy that may seem like he doesn't take himself too seriously. Maybe it's that constant Cheshire grin. But a look at his art and you see that nothing could be further from the truth. That cat with nothing but a grin to leave behind shouldn't be mistaken as a sign of "I don't give a damn." Think of it more like "I'm having a freakin' good time. Why the hell aren't you?"

This is a guy who didn't start riding because someone got him on a bike at a young age. It was more of a result of disgust with public transportation in London.

"I never owned a car and realized I didn't much care for taking the bus to get around. So I got my motorcycle license about twelve years ago and have been riding ever since."

Albie's first bike was actually a Typhoon—a little 125cc scooter made by Piaggio. He moved up from there to a Vespa GTS, which at 300cc had more than twice the engine capacity and served up more power. But as it is, living in a city the size of London, that scoot took a beating when someone crashed into it while it was parked. That left Albie wondering what to get for his next ride. He went decidedly bigger by buying a Harley Sportster.

"When I got my Harley, all I thought about was bikes. Then I started riding with different groups. I don't belong to any, but I started hanging out with the American Motorcycle Owners Club [AMOC]. That gave me a really deep insight into the motorcycle culture that's influenced my art today."

There was never any doubt in Albie's mind that he would be an artist. It was something he said he wanted to do since he was a little kid growing up in Notting Hill. But going from there to establishing himself as an artist who paints the motorcycle lifestyle meant being influenced by three entirely different environments—studying art at Central Saint Martins college, working in the London club scene, and boxing. That's right, boxing.

"Boxing is like being an artist in a way. You can't fake it. You can try it if you haven't trained for it, but that will show itself once you step in the ring. You have to rely on yourself. That's what an artist does."

Albie never became a professional boxer, but he has boxed in multiple events as an amateur, and currently teaches young boxers at two different gyms in London.

Quite a difference from helping market one of London's hottest clubs, the Tonteria. This is a Mexican-themed tapas bar that serves tequila shots on a toy train and where Prince Harry is known to have partied on a fairly frequent basis. It's this experience that led Albie to decide to pursue being an artist full-time.

"I was really into the club scene, but it wasn't that fulfilling. I was doing art on the side, getting some positive reaction to my work. So I thought, 'this is what I need to be doing with my life.'"

That led Albie to start painting what he saw in the London motorcycle world. He did a portrait of some of the guys in the AMOC. He's painted individual bikers. He showed up at a local Harley dealer and did live paintings of the bikes there.

"My paintings have changed since I first started. I want them to be more narrative, to tell a story. So I recently did one of a father, his daughter, and the dad's bike. That was much more than just two people and a motorcycle."

Albie counts a number of famous artists as his influence, including David Mann, Monet, and the entire impressionist era. When you look at his paintings you can see that influence. This isn't realism, this is Albie's view of the world that he's now adopted and that's beginning to embrace him.

To get a real sense of how he approaches his art, you need to watch Albie in action. You don't have to go to London to do that. He's made it easy by capturing himself on video painting a number of pieces in time-lapse images that speed up the whole process.

You feel like you're watching someone attacking his work, only this canvas is stretched across an upright easel, rather than the floor of a boxing ring. He jabs with his brush—an upstroke here, a punch of color there. But the end result is unexpected. There isn't a hard-edged, bloody knockout at the end of a few rounds. There's a slightly softer view of what can seem like a tough world to an outsider. And that's okay, because painting it otherwise would be a little too much on the nose.

Albie said he would eventually like to see his work in famous galleries like the Tate in London or the Museum of Modern Art in New York. For now, he's showing his work wherever he can—custom motorcycle shows like Kickback Chelsea and up-and-coming London cafés like the motorcycle-themed Bolt. He's also selling his work online.

In a world where predictability is often shattered by what seems to be the insane, Albie's showing the world that predictability can often be shattered with a view of the world punctuated by a grin. At least that's the impression he's left on us from several thousand miles across the Pond.

Frank Esposito is well-known in the motorcycle industry. His life reads like a Hollywood movie… and the inspiration for how he's decided to lead the last decade or more of it actually was. Read for yourself how he came back from the dead more than once and is still riding today.

What Doesn't Kill You...

In 1963, on what was probably a warm summer day somewhere in Pennsylvania, fourteen-year-old Frank Esposito swung a leg over a Sears Allstate moped and learned to ride. That small bike and a big grassy field awakened a passion for motorcycles that would, over the next fifty-some years, take Frank into the upper echelons of dirt bike racing, land him on the up and down side of the motorcycle business, and nearly kill him.

And not once did he consider spending his life doing anything else.

"I remember when my sister and my future brother-in-law took me to my first flat track race. My parents were very strict Catholics, and they sent me along on those dates as a form of birth control. I was standing up against the rail, and the first time those bikes came screaming toward the first corner, I was just in awe. I had to find a way to race."

Over the next fifteen or more years following that initial baptism by dirt, Frank managed to race in nearly every type of off-road event you can imagine—motocross, scrambles, enduro, and flat track. Once introduced to enduro racing, that became his primary sport.

"My parents were big on education, so they sent me to a prep school and made sure I went to college. But all through those years I raced every chance I could get. If I could have done nothing else but race, I would have. So I ended up with a degree in mechanical engineering and was also building bikes on the side and got pretty good at it."

Not long after college, Frank gathered up his racing and building experience and started his own dealership in the Philadelphia area. He called it "Cross Country Cycle" and he initially sold Ossas and built bikes for other people. A few years into it, he added BMWs.

At one point, Frank said he had one of the most successful Ossa dealerships in the country and was even working with the company in their research and development arm.

But this was the late '70s, and no one saw the Japanese coming. They started dumping bikes like YZs and RMs on the market that were selling at retail for half of what it cost to buy a European bike. Frank and other dealers like him took it in the shorts.

"I had over six hundred bikes I couldn't sell and owed my OEMs hundreds of thousands of dollars. I lost everything, and my wife [Sharon] and I ended up having to move out of our home and into an apartment."

Frank said he could have declared bankruptcy and kept his house, but his dad, who had a successful butcher and slaughterhouse business, steered him clear of that with a very simple and direct declaration.

"He said, 'you declare bankruptcy; you're not my son. Espositos pay their bills. You'll find a way to make it out of this.' So I said, 'Screw this, I'll make it work.'"

Some may think Frank's dad was too harsh, but that kind of toughness and line-in-the-sand approach was more than likely what helped Frank reach the elite status in enduro racing and later some of the highest levels in the motorcycle business. It would also more than likely bring him back from the dead.

It was 1981, and Frank had been at JC Industries, a regional motorcycle parts distributor, long enough to have become their national sales manager. He was still racing on weekends, and that Memorial Weekend found him at the Moonshine Enduro event in Pennsylvania.

He crashed. Not a spill or a flip, but a hellacious shattering of his body that left his rib cage separated from his spine, bones sticking out where they shouldn't, and blood leaving his body faster than the doctors could keep it in.

Frank also took a short trip to the other side.

"It took me twenty-five years to tell anyone about it, I thought people would think I was crazy. But I had a near-death experience. I was removed from my body and saw Sharon, who was pregnant with our third child at the time, sitting beside me. But I had this incredible sense of peace, that this is who and where I'm going to be. But there was my wife, and I was thinking in the third person: 'He needs to live. Just get back in that body and take a breath.' And I did."

Then the real pain of recovery began. Frank would spend three weeks in intensive care and three months in the hospital. Over the next two years, he had over forty surgeries to mend his broken body. And there's where you'd think the miracles would have stopped, but Frank's life is not an ordinary one... and neither are the people who have been in it.

Once Frank could start seeing visitors at the hospital, John Cassis (the JC Industries owner) came to see him. At this point, Frank was wondering how the hell he was going to support his family, since he had no idea when he was going to be able to get back to work. JC solved that dilemma for him.

"He provided me with a steady income throughout my recovery. It was incredible, but as soon as I could get around, I had Sharon drive me to my sales calls. I wasn't going to let anything stop me from doing what I needed to do."

While Frank was still on the mend, JC sold his business to Bob Nickel, who'd also bought Ed Tucker Distributing (which later became Tucker Rockey). Bob wanted to be sure Frank was part of the deal he eventually made with JC to buy his company.

Frank would go on to spend twenty years with Tucker Rockey, and he eventually became its president and COO, but not before another near-death experience that would have kept most people down and potentially out for good.

See, Frank not only got back to work after that crash in '81, he also got back into racing, and not just casually. He's a competitive guy, and casual riding just wasn't his style.

By 1991, he was back to competing in races at an A-level, and in one particular event, he went down, hit his head on the ground, but didn't think much about it. That kind of thing, he said, was fairly common. But he started getting severe headaches, went to a doctor, and what should they find but a brain tumor the size of a lemon.

It turns out it was benign, but it did require five separate cranial surgeries to rectify, and at one point the doctors didn't think he'd live. When he did, they thought he'd be permanently brain damaged.

But as Frank said, "I already had enough brain damage to make it into management."

Again, Frank was faced with the stress of wondering how he was going to support his family of five and all three of his kids in their teens through his recovery.

"Bob Nickel came into my hospital room, just like JC did, and told me not to worry about it. He wanted to make sure my family and I were taken care of."

That generosity also belied a directness that Frank saw on more than one occasion with Bob, but in ways that were highly beneficial to his career.

"Before Bob made me head of sales for Tucker Rockey, he invited me down to the company headquarters and offered me the job. He knew Sharon and I didn't want to leave Pennsylvania, but he made it clear that if I turned it down, it would be the dumbest mistake I ever made. He did give me twenty-four hours to think about it."

Later, Bob would promote Frank again by having him look in the mirror in the passenger visor of his car and tell him he was looking at the next president and COO of the company. To top it off, Bob paid for Frank to get his MBA from Wharton School of Business at the University of Pennsylvania in Philadelphia to help him be a better business leader for the company.

Frank did make another racing comeback after his brain tumor, and he started participating in the Colorado 500—basically a masochistic, multi-day enduro ride through some of the toughest riding in the Colorado Rockies you can imagine. It's an invite-only event, although there is a spot on the entry form for rookies to apply for those who feel up to it. About three hundred or more riders participate, but only a handful finish. Frank's participated in it twelve times.

And if one grueling, multi-day slog in the backcountry fighting rain, snow, heat, and cold isn't enough, Frank has also participated in the *Cycle World* Trek. Last year was his ninth one. One look at a picture of a worn-out Frank and you can see that this event can take its toll.

Today, Frank lives in constant pain from the crash that happened thirty-five years ago, but he said he's learned to manage it and is in terrific shape. He's made a couple of job changes since leaving Tucker Rockey and is now the head of marketing and sales for Scorpion.

His accolades and other positions read like the who's who of the motorcycle industry:

American Motorcycle Association Charter Life Member.

Dick Bettencourt Spirit Award for lifetime contribution to off-road motorcycling.

Motorcycle Industry Council Board of Directors since 2002.

Motorcycle Industry Magazine Aftermarket Leadership Award.

Joseph E. Parkhurst Award for motorcycling.

Frank is characteristically modest about his accomplishments but highly appreciative of the recognition he's obtained from his peers and the industry. But when asked about what seems like miracles in his life—the people like JC and Bob who helped him and his family when he needed it most, the recoveries he's made when most didn't think he would—he's quick to point out a life lesson that directs his success to this day.

"I'm no hero, and I don't want to be portrayed as one... my wife and the people who supported and mentored me deserve all of the credit. I've learned that being of service to others is what really matters. There's no greater purpose."

This may be a lesson that some would think Frank learned the hard way, but it's a lesson that's stuck. And it's one the rest of us can take note of and hope to come as close as Frank has to living it.

You can find women and girls of all ages doing many things today that only boys would have been doing a couple of years ago. But nearly forty years ago, Pat Jacques was one of the few girls that were racing motocross and beating the guys at what some thought should have stayed a boys-only event.

A Life at Full Throttle

There was a popular country western song in the late '70s titled *Mommas Don't Let Your Babies Grow up to Be Cowboys*. Sung by Waylon Jennings and Willie Nelson, it bemoaned the dire outcome of boys who took up the cowboy life as opposed to growing up to be "doctors and lawyers and such."

Today, there are mommas and daddies out there who probably might and still have applied that song to riding motorcycles—dirt, street, or otherwise—rather than riding horses. Thank the god of two wheels Pat Jacques parents didn't, because the motorcycle world would have been a bit less interesting if they had.

This is a woman who, as a teenager, raced motocross professionally against guys and some very accomplished women, then later switched to ADV riding, and now uses her past and current experience to get mostly women to at least give riding a try. It started when she was eight.

"My dad gave me and my brother a mini-bike for Christmas, and we rode that all over the place. Then when I was eleven, I made the honor society, and my dad was so proud of me, he asked what I wanted. Of course, I said a motorcycle."

That motorcycle would be a candy apple red Honda SL100, that Pat said her brother ended up riding as much as she did.

"I made a big deal about telling him he could own half of it if he showed her how to maintain it. He agreed then got on it and rode off! I'd get home from school and just ride, ride, ride."

It wasn't long after that Pat took up racing in powder puff competitions in South Carolina. She started winning, and someone in the family realized she needed a different bike. So the SL made way for a Honda Elsinore 125. Pat said not only did she really take to racing, but so did her brother, who became a top-ranked East Coast rider.

When Pat was fourteen, she had the opportunity to train with world-famous racer Rolf Tibblin, who was giving a clinic in Georgia. As Pat tells it, Rolf told her she was better than most of the boys.

A couple of years later, Pat's dad surprised the family and took them out to California so Pat could race in the Women's Nationals. It was a defining moment.

"We didn't have a lot of money, so my dad had bought a used RV, and that's what we traveled in. I was now racing 250s, which put me in direct competition with Sue Fish [Hall of Fame inductee], who was one of the fastest women riders in motocross at the time. I was leading her in one race, my goggles were pulled down away from my eyes, and a spectator threw water in my face. I ended up going off the course, but now people realized who I was and I had a target on my back."

Pat said the next few races showed her that most of the women racing on the West Coast weren't riding at the same skill level as the guys she'd been racing against back east. Even though they were professional riders, they weren't riding like it.

"When I was riding with intermediate or pro male riders, I could read their line. But the women riders rode all over the place. I don't have any hard feelings about how some of my races ended up as a result, but it showed me I had the ability to win."

Pat went on to race throughout the Southeast, including the Carolinas, Florida, and Georgia. The biggest race she was ever in was the 1977 AMA Winter Nationals in Gainesville, where she finished a respectable ninth-place overall.

Keep in mind, this was when things weren't nearly as progressive for women as they are now. Did she get any grief for being a "girl" racing with men? Not as much as you might think.

"When I was younger, it wasn't a big deal. Maybe it was because my brother was out there. But I never really thought about it. When I got older, I started getting hassled. Some of the guys would work hard to bump me off the course, but I'm pretty competitive. I hung in there with them."

Here's an example. She was racing in a qualifying heat with her brother. She saw her brother cartwheel down a hill and came up on him lying on the ground. For all she knew he could have been dead. Her instinct was to stop—it *was* her brother. But she kept going. All of a sudden she heard someone "hot on my ass. Blocking every single line. I was doing everything I could to stay ahead. Turned out it was my brother."

He ended up in the last chance qualifier, and Pat took ninth overall.

Pat's performance, however, wasn't the only thing that made her stand out. Seems her dad was a professional wrestling fan at the time and figured his daughter needed a name and a specific look. So he took the Suzuki RM250 she was racing, sanded the paint off the gas tank, repainted it a brilliant gold color, and called her the "Golden Girl with the Golden Curls on the Golden Bike!"

Unfortunately, despite her ability, by the age of eighteen Pat was forced to retire from motocross racing. The race schedule just got to be too much, as did the early wear and tear on her body.

Nine years later, she got back into motorcycles; only this time she was racing Speedway. Racing the no brakes, methanol alcohol powered bikes was fun, but she soon returned to racing motocross. That lasted until she was thirty-two, when she demolished her knee and knew it was time to stop or she'd probably not get on a bike again.

"This second round of motocross racing was when I experienced some hassles from guys. But I soon got to be friends with some of the better riders, including Dave Newell, who was five-time Colorado state champion. Traveling and racing with those caliber of guys got most of the others to back off."

Eight knee surgeries and an eventual knee replacement forced Pat off of motorcycles and out of racing. She said she had to fight her naturally competitive instinct to race, but knew instinctively she had to stay away from it if she was going to stay healthy.

While you might be able to take the woman off the bike, you can't take the bike out the woman—especially someone like Pat. Eight years after quitting riding entirely, she bought a Honda XR350 as a fortieth birthday present, but rather than immediately locating the nearest track, she stayed with "puttering around on forest service roads."

"Adventure riding has become a great way for me to unplug. Here you are seeing some great scenery, you're outdoors meeting interesting people, and having some great conversations."

Bitten by the ADV bug and a desire to get back to riding more frequently, Pat bought a Kawasaki KLR 650, a bike she acknowledges most people like, but one she said she hated within three months of owning it. So she got rid of it and bought a BMW F800 GS.

"That was the best bike I ever owned in my life. I didn't want the bigger 1200, because I wanted something that felt more like a dirt bike. I took the 800 to a *Cycle World* Adventure event and was doing some crazy, fun stuff on it, but I realized that the smaller bike was kind of typical for a woman and I wanted more power, so I got rid of the Beemer and bought a KTM 1190R."

While Pat was off and on motorcycles as an adult, she taught people to ride horses and mountain bikes, and to cross-country and downhill ski. She also became an empowerment coach and an IT consultant, with her own business called "Double Diamond Technologies." But her real passion has become using ADV riding to help women gain confidence.

"When women can recognize their own physical strength, that they are self-reliant, and accomplish this [riding motorcycles], then that's empowering."

Not content to leave it at that, Pat is now making a forty-year old dream come to life with her first ever ADVWoman Rally to be held this July 2016 in Granby, Colorado. All of the instructors are women, and they'll be teaching courses on topics like dirt bike and adventure bike essentials, trail side repairs, and fitness. It's also a way for her to meld her coaching and motorcycle experience into a single event.

"There's never been an adventure rally in which all instructors are women. I wanted this to be about women helping each other and women helping themselves. This rally is a vehicle for self-discovery, empowerment, and for women to feel self-directed, self-reliant, and capable."

But not everyone has parents who let their babies grow up to be cowboys...or dirt bike riders. Especially their girls. So what does Pat tell women who've either been told they shouldn't or couldn't ride, or who have told themselves the same?

"Follow your heart. Follow your dreams. Life's too short. It's not that hard if you have the right teacher. It's safe, and the payback is so incredible."

Waylon and Willie couldn't have sung it any better than that.

The concept of Midwest values is typically illustrated by hard work, lack of complaints, and genuinely being willing to help when someone needs it. That pretty much sums up Robert Pandya and the way he's lived the several decades he's spent making a living in the world of two wheels.

Necessity Made Robert Pandya

Necessity, as they say, is the mother of invention...or the reason why some people start riding motorcycles in the first place. Take Robert Pandya, for instance. Here's a guy who most anyone who's spent any time in the motorcycle industry will know or know of. But he didn't get there by racing bikes, building customs, or owning a major dealership. He got there through hard work, knowing when to jump on an opportunity...and by necessity, at the age of eighteen he bought a motorcycle.

"I didn't really get on a bike until I bought a 1983 Suzuki GN250 in 1986 and convinced my urologist dad to co-sign for me. I couldn't afford to get a car, so that bike was my only option. Until then, the only time I'd spent on anything with two wheels was on a mini-bike that I crashed into the side of a building."

Now you might think that Robert's urologist dad could have afforded to get his kid a car. But that's not how Robert was raised. He has a Midwest upbringing and the values that go with it. Work hard. Be respectful. Pay your dues. And Robert did all of that...and then some.

With no experience, but a lot of will and determination, he rode the little Suzuki out of the shop and eventually took it with him when he moved from where he was raised in Illinois to Dallas, Texas. It became his sole means of transportation, but for him that wasn't a bad thing. Late nights after getting off work as a movie projectionist, he'd ride around Dallas playing his portable cassette deck. Simpler times.

"That bike didn't let me do anything stupid on it, but I eventually got rid of it and bought a Yamaha Radian 600—a fantastic second bike. I still didn't have a car, so that bike was my only transportation for a long time. The Radian was what started my real enthusiasm for bikes. It was just fun enough to put a big grin on your face."

Eventually, he moved from Dallas to Austin, and reality and a girlfriend meant the bike gave way to a car. So he sold the Radian, bought a Toyota Corolla, and later managed to squeeze himself onto a Yamaha YSR50 he bought while working at a local Yamaha dealer. That bike got stolen, and Robert found himself without two wheels for the first time since riding that Suzuki out the door.

About this time, Robert was working his way through college as a photographer. One day, he said he found himself meeting with a couple to go over what they wanted to shoot for their upcoming wedding. He noticed a bike underneath a cover in their garage.

"I ended up shooting their wedding for a Honda FT500 Ascot. I think I got the better deal, because that couple is probably no longer married."

As Robert grew his photography business, he also accumulated more bikes. That included a Honda CB1 inline sport and a Honda Hawk GT, the latter of which he and his brother, Manny, raced throughout Texas. (He still owns the Hawk and said he'd like to turn it into a vintage track day bike at some point.)

It was that Honda Hawk and his photography skills that helped launch him into his current role of being one of the more popular faces of the motorcycle industry.

"I started posting a lot to the Honda Hawk forum [HawkWorks] and eventually became the publisher for the newsletter. That got me connected to different people in the industry. About the same time, a friend of mine was trying to get his Aprilia dealership going, so I took all of the photographs for him and happened to meet Bill Stone, who was head of marketing at Aprilia at the time. Bill eventually hired me to move from Dallas to Atlanta and work with him at Aprilia."

Here's where Robert both jumped at an opportunity and worked hard to make the most of it. But his transition was, shall we say, a bit nerve wracking.

"I remember sitting in my office the first day or two thinking, 'What happens when they find out I'm a complete idiot.' So I go into Billy's office and let him know I don't know what I'm supposed to do. Billy just looks at me and tells me he figured I'd come around to admitting that at some point. So he hands me a list of reporters and said 'start contacting these people.'"

So Robert did, and that led to him getting to know some of the better known names on the media side of the motorcycle business like Mark Hoyer and Don Canet. He also started going to track days on behalf of Aprilia and learned more about who was who on that side of the business. His first track day request for a bike was for the 2003 Aprilia Mille.

That gig eventually meant additional work with Moto Guzzi until both marques were bought by the Piaggio Group about five years after Robert had originally started working with Aprilia. He also picked up part-time work as spokesperson for the International Motorcycle Show (IMS), and that's what eventually led him to the same role for the entire motorcycle industry.

"I'd work for Piaggio during the week then the show on weekends. Tracy Harris with the IMS, Jeff D'Entremont of Advanstar, and DeeDee Taft of Spin Communications started getting me opportunities to speak for the show and eventually the entire industry. So all of a sudden, I was getting quoted in the *Wall Street Journal* and elsewhere."

Robert eventually left Piaggio over a difference of opinion as to the direction the company was taking, but not before he worked with Bonnie Strawser of Sportbike Track Time to institute the first female track day event through Aprilia called "Femmoto."

"Aprilia was a very product-focused company, so the idea of a customer-based event, and a female one, was not an easy thing to get approved. But once they started it, they saw the value of it. Even today, if I was to go to just about any company and say, 'We're going to get a broad range of women with little experience to ride track days,' people would think I was crazy."

Departing Piaggio allowed Robert to become even more thoroughly entrenched in the motorcycle world. He started his own public relations agency and was partnering with Spin Communications for the IMS shows in the United States, plus doing side projects for Buell and eventually working for Victory.

"What's interesting about Victory is that when I first started with them ten years ago, they were just as product-focused as Aprilia, but they also had a customer consciousness. My Midwest upbringing helped me appreciate that and the stability that a company the size of Polaris brought to what they were trying to do with the brand and the company."

Since joining Victory, Robert has been involved in Victory's highest profile introductions like the Vision—a bike that most either still love or hate—the naming and introduction of the company's bobber-style Highball, and the Cross Country platform.

Then Polaris announced they had bought Indian, and it was only natural that Robert would help the company launch their version of the iconic American brand.

"It's hard to imagine anything else as significant in this business as relaunching the Indian Chief and Indian Scout. Those names are part of the fabric of the US. I knew this would be one of the biggest things in my career. We were bringing back the spirit of Munroe, the Scout on the Wall of Death. Most people don't understand what it takes to get a new platform on the market. This was huge, and it helped that most everyone in the industry thought that Polaris was the right company to make it happen."

With so much on Robert's proverbial plate, you'd wonder when he finds time to ride, but he does and some of his rides are of the epic kind. Take the Go Big Ride he did on the Trans-America Trail back in 2009 with a group of well-heeled types who thought they were far better prepared than he.

"All of these guys were riding pedigreed Dakar-type bikes, and all I had at the time was a Suzuki DR. So I bought a KTM MXC450. They were all convinced I was going to blow up, but other than frequent oil changes and valve adjustments, I never had a problem. Most of them did. But since I was hired to be the photographer and videographer for the trip, I did have to eat their dust multiple times."

Then there's Elnora...

In 2014, Robert got the bright idea to save one of the earlier Indian Chief prototypes and modify it to retrace the cross-country route of Erwin "Cannon Ball" Baker as a nod to the 100th anniversary of what would later inspire the Cannonball Run. Hall of Famer Don Emde and former dirt tracker and now writer Joe Colombero organized the ride, and Robert joined them while riding the prototype "dual-sport" Indian affectionately named "Elnora."

Nearly a year later, Robert got the engineers to tweak Elnora even further, and they took it to El Mirage, where it topped out at just over 130 mph. Then, this past summer, Robert got Indian to agree to give up twenty-five bikes, some with sidecars, to allow military vets to ride or be a passenger on the way to Sturgis for the Veterans Charity Ride.

Is this Robert having fun or also poking a bit of a finger at that other iconic American brand?

"I don't look at Harley as competition so much as a friendly rivalry. I want every manufacturer to find their voice, including Harley...although Polaris does crush it when it comes to product diversity."

With exposure to so many different bikes, it's only natural to wonder if Robert has a favorite. His answer shouldn't be too surprising.

"Tell me what you want to do, and I'll tell you what I think is the best bike to do it. Although, if I had to be down to one bike, it would have to be a dual-sport. I think everyone should have one. It gives you the best of both worlds, and with relatively little effort, you can change up that kind of bike for just about any use."

The conversation gets around to the current state of the industry and the plethora of bikes and choices out there now. The trend Robert sees is one toward bikes that are less about size and output and more about fun and entertainment.

"To get more younger riders we have to push the entertainment side of riding...the idea that this is an analog experience. I can see the day when you might have a Google car in the driveway that the owner doesn't give a shit about engaging with, and then they have a motorcycle, because that's what's going to make them still connect with what's around them."

If it's not evident, what Robert has managed to do is to meld his values and passion for motorcycles into his job and position in the industry to the point where they all appear pretty seamless. But there's also something that runs even deeper, thanks to his mother.

"She passed on to me this sense of history or making sure that I appreciate it, and a desire to create something lasting and significant. The Femmoto event—getting women on the track—and the veterans ride with Indian are those kinds of moments for me."

Will history, by necessity, credit Robert with creating these events or any of the others he's been part of or yet to participate in? We don't think he cares. His Midwest values will probably just want to be sure they leave a positive mark for as long as necessity will allow.

[NOTE: Since this story first ran, Robert has left Polaris and is pursuing new two-wheeled ventures.]

Liz Hardy has probably spent more of her adult life as a passenger on a motorcycle than many people have as a rider. That's just fine with her.

A View from the Back

Most people who are obsessed with motorcycles eventually handle that by buying one and riding it. But Liz Hardy took it a different direction. She's made a point of spending time strictly riding on the back, or pillion, as it's typically referred to everywhere else but in the US, and she's trying to get others (mostly women) to realize that it's a pretty good position to be in.

In fact, Liz has a blog called "Pillioness" where she extols the virtues of pillion riding and passes on some other useful motorcycle-related insights, as well—all part of her effort to help women love motorcycling.

The New Zealand to US time zone differences made it difficult to connect in any way other than email. So we shot Liz some questions, and here's her mostly unadulterated response. Our takeaway: the view and ride from the back has its virtues.

How long have you been riding pillion?

"I'm into my twenty-fourth year of it. It's a serious addiction at this stage!"

What was your first experience like when you did?

"It was like being in Dr. Who's tardis—just rushing

through space and time faster than the speed of light! Everything was more intense—I could see more clearly, smell everything we passed, feel the temperature of the air. It was unlike anything else I'd experienced."

Who were you with? And what kind of bike were you on?

"A very furry man named Pat took me for a ride on his black Harley Sportster. I married him a couple of years later! He's had lots of different bikes since we've been together, but we've been a Triumph family for a long time now, and we have a new 'baby'—an Indian Scout." [NOTE: the Indian Scout seemed like an odd choice given the Triumph reference, but Liz said both she and Pat just fell in love with the old school design of the Scout, so much so she wrote about it in her blog.]

What prompted the idea for pillioness.com?

"Pillioness is actually pretty new, but it came out of years and years of talking to men who ride and women who won't. I always ask male bikers why they ride alone. Ninety-five percent of them say their wife won't ride with them—but they wish she would!

"I also talk to the women who won't ride. Their reasons for staying away from bikes leave me speechless. The most common are:

"'I don't know how to ride.'

"'It's too scary.'

"'It's boring.' or, my personal favorite...

"'I don't want to mess up my hair.'

"Their answers always make me crazy—they're missing out on the coolest thing in the world! You don't even need your own license—and who cares if your hair's not perfect?

"So I made it my mission to help women see the motorcycling light.

"This way, everyone wins—the lonely male riders get to ride with their best friend and life partner. And the women get to experience how riding on a motorcycle is truly life changing."

Have you ever ridden a bike on your own?

"I never, ever have. Which surprises many people, because I'm not really the shrinking violet type."

Do you have any desire to a ride a bike on your own today?

"Nope! I love riding pillion. I'm not mechanical—at all, and I don't have that all-important Spidey sense that good riders have—they can anticipate what's about to happen on the road. I call it Biker ESP.

"But I'm not a passive passenger who just dreamily watches the view. I'm more of a copilot. I spot hazards on the road that Pat might not see, like a stray sheep that's broken through a fence or a plain-clothes police car cruising a little too close to us.

"When we're on a road trip, we talk together about the route, the roads, and how many kilometers we'll cover every day. And I always sort out the accommodation in advance. Pat's in control of the bike, but the experience is a real team effort."

Does anyone else in your family ride?

"My stepchildren do. They came over from Australia to see us for Pat's birthday a couple of years ago with their partners, and we did a cross-country family bike road trip.

"It's a lot of fun to flip your biker children the bird as you roar past them on another bike! But everyone has to be careful not to laugh too much while riding..."

What's the longest ride you've ever been on?

"A few years ago, we rode from the southernmost point of New Zealand to the northernmost place—with a few side trips built in. We did about 5,000 km in a couple of weeks.

"It was brilliant! The North and South Islands of New Zealand are very different—it's much colder in the south and gets pretty hot up north. So packing for two different climates was a challenge.

"But we got to tear along a perfect white stretch of sand in the North Island called Ninety Mile Beach. Pat's Triumph Scrambler's never been the same, but the ride was awesome!"

What's the fastest speed you've ever experienced while riding pillion?

"210 km/hour [130 mph] on a 1996 Triumph Trophy! Whoo hoo!"

Have you ever ridden outside of New Zealand?

"We lived in Australia until we moved to New Zealand twelve years ago, so we did a lot of riding over there, too.

"Summer riding in Australia is brutal. In the city, you sit in heavy traffic watching the road actually melting into a sticky black mess. And country riding is like moving through a furnace. The hot, dry wind burns your face, and the roads are long and straight and endless, with flat brown bushland as far as the eye can see. You have to be off the roads by dusk as the kangaroos and other wild critters come out. Hit one of them on a bike, and you'll be bleeding to death in the middle of nowhere."

What kind of work do you do?

"I teach various online courses, ranging from Communication to Adult Education, to students all over the country. Plus, I work on my three websites in addition to Pillioness.com. I have a site for online teachers and another one about cats."

How did you get into that line of work?

"I wanted to use my various degrees professionally. (I have a PhD in English and a few other degrees and diplomas.) I'm passionate about education and the doors it can open. I have a lot of ideas and love to write, so my three websites give me outlets for those skills, too.

"I've tried office life, and it makes me positively homicidal. So I work from my home office—which gives me the flexibility to take off for a Wednesday afternoon ride when the sun is out!"

What is the main message you tell people who don't want to learn to ride a motorcycle on their own, but might want to learn how to at least ride pillion?

"Riding on a motorcycle is not like anything else in the

world. There's no other experience like it. And it's as easy as climbing onto the pillion seat.

"The perceived obstacles are either in your imagination, or are totally fixable.

"If you're worried about:

"Safety—Wear all the protective gear, and ride with a person you trust.

"Comfort—Get a better pillion seat and a backrest!

"Rough culture—You don't have to drink a bottle of Jack Daniels for breakfast. I've never met a nicer bunch of people than the riders we know.

"Being bored—How is it possible to be bored while zooming through the world with your favorite person?

"Men-only culture—Once you get on board, riding becomes a couple thing. And it's the best thing you could ever do for your relationship."

So the next time your significant other comes up with a litany of excuses why riding pillion isn't for them, Liz has just as many responses as to why they should at least give it a try. But do yourself a favor and start out easy. Trust us. freeways, particularly in California, are probably not a good first step.

With the increase in the number of women riders has come a proliferation of women's motorcycle clubs, groups, and organized events. Stilettos on Steel is a group, not a club, and they want to be sure everyone understands that distinction and what makes them different.

Stiletto on Steel—Women Empowering Women to Ride

During the late Middle Ages, the stiletto was a favorite weapon of mercenaries, knights, and ne'er do wells. It was designed primarily for thrusting, due to its needle point and narrow blade. Stick it in, pull it out, back away, and your done.

Four or five hundred years later, some masochistic shoe designer decided to incorporate that small, narrow, and long concept into a high heel design that became a symbol for sexy and powerful women. Keep in mind, that to be considered a real stiletto heel, it has to have a solid steel or alloy stem—how else to support any kind of weight on such a narrow platform?

Today the word *stiletto* is probably far more apt to call up heels rather than knives. Which is no doubt why the original founder of the women's social riding group (they emphasize it's not a club) Stilettos on Steel decided to work the name into the title.

After all, there are some apt analogies here. This is a group founded on the idea that any woman—regardless of age or aptitude—could ride and probably deserved to at least know what it felt like. All it might take is the unwavering, steel-like support of other women who had already proven to themselves that they could do it. Think empowerment on two wheels.

Anne Zube—President

Look no further than the group's mission statement—provide an all-female motorcycle riding group empowering women to ride safely, strongly, and street smart—to see the analogy.

All of which are what attracted Anne Zube, the current president of Stilettos on Steel, to the organization in the first place. Although not the founder, she's put her heart and soul into the group in the roughly five years since she took over what was a small, slightly organized amalgamation of women in Milwaukee who may have been more interested in the idea of motorcycles rather than riding them.

"I'd finally gotten my license and found this group on Facebook. I'd met the lady who started it as a social riding group just for women. There were only about ten members who actually rode a motorcycle, and there was just no structure or process to keep them or to attract new members."

Anne started making suggestions as to how to change that. But she said the founder had no money and no real time to do much with her ideas, so she offered to give the whole thing over to Anne, who promptly began applying her business experience to making it grow.

"Our timing was right. It was the 100th anniversary of Harley, the number of women riders was starting to grow, and we were offering them something they couldn't find elsewhere—a social riding group with none of the strings attached that more formal clubs required."

Within a year, the group grew to forty-five paid members

and actual sponsors. Anne found some women outside of Milwaukee who were interested in joining, and some of them became regional coordinators. Today, there are several hundred members belonging to chapters in Wisconsin, Michigan, Minnesota, Indiana, Florida, Connecticut, Colorado, and Massachusetts.

The first four make sense, they share a few borders between them. But it's a long way from Milwaukee to Denver, and even longer to Florida. What gives?

Well, it turns out that Anne was doing a pretty good job getting the word out about Stilettos on Steel. So women riders in other states started reaching out to her to make their case for starting a chapter.

Here's where some groups might let anyone interested move forward—few questions asked. But Anne is all about making Stilettos legit, so becoming a chapter leader doesn't come without some requirements.

"I walk them through what we're all about and what we expect of them. They have to be able to use a computer and know how to post on Facebook, and read and reply to every question. We also have an officer training page to make sure they have something to reference when they need to."

Clearly, interest is one thing, but being serious is something else entirely.

Anne seems to have come naturally to her position in what she said is the largest women's social riding group in the Midwest. She grew up on a farm, rode horses and bikes, and loved having that feeling of wind in her hair. She said she was always a motorcycle enthusiast, but it wasn't until she turned forty that she became a motorcycle rider.

"After spending my life watching everyone else ride, when I turned forty I decided to learn how to ride myself. I think my husband was a little nervous at the time, since he doesn't ride, but I did so well in the motorcycle class that my instructor used me as the one to lead the others in the drills!"

Anne didn't have a bike at the time, but her husband later surprised her with a day-long use of a rented Harley 883. He was taking the kids on a short trip, while she spent the time on the bike by herself.

"I was terrified when I first got on it, but once I got familiar with it, I really loved it. When I had to return it, I actually cried. I thought, 'what am I going to do now?!'"

"Now" ended up being the following spring, when Anne rented another Harley, this time the much larger Heritage Softail. She had it for two days and fell in love with it. She then found one for sale that she really liked, but it was $5,000 over the budget she was working with.

"I told my husband that he was my soul mate, but this was my soul bike. I ended up buying it in 2010 and can't imagine riding anything else. I'm a mother, a wife, and I have a job. Now I have a network of fifty or more women I can contact to ride, and even more when we put on events."

Lori Mosher—Michigan Officer

Of course, Anne doesn't run Stilettos by herself, and even though it's based in Milwaukee, members aren't required to own a Harley or any particular bike for that matter.

Take Lori Mosher for example. Like Anne, she started riding late in life—three years ago, to be exact. She said she was always interested in motorcycles, had periodically ridden on the back of them, but never really thought she was capable of riding one on her own.

"When I turned forty-seven, I got on the back of a friend's bike, and when I got off, I decided that was it. I eventually took the riding course with my daughter. She passed; I failed. But I went out again, passed it, and later bought a used Honda Rebel—something to ease myself into."

As Lori got more comfortable with riding, it didn't take long for her to realize she needed more power. So bye-bye Rebel; hello Yamaha 650!

Today, Lori is head of the Michigan area for Stilettos on Steel. There are now eight chapters within the state and over one hundred members. Most of that growth occurred since Lori took on her role two years ago.

What's interesting is that, like Anne, Lori's husband doesn't ride, either. But he supports his wife's newfound passion, clearly not the stereotypical arrangement where it's the other way around.

Lori said she isn't sure why it took her so long to finally ride on her own, but she said she now can't think of what it would be like to not ride and not be involved with Stilettos on Steel.

"I'm not really sure what kept me from riding—maybe a lack of confidence. I needed to believe that I could do this myself. Once I did, that feeling of empowerment was overwhelming. I remember a 350-mile day trip I did by myself. That isn't long, compared to what some people may ride, but for me it was a big deal. What I felt afterward stayed with me a long time."

And in case you're wondering what Lori does when she's not riding or encouraging more women to believe they can, she and her husband run a construction business.

Burklin Nielsen—National Operations Director

When a motorcycle pulls up next to someone in a car at a traffic light, several thoughts might run through the person in the cage. For Burklin Nielsen as a young girl, it was hope—hope that someday she could be that person on the bike.

"I always wanted to ride, so I finally took the course through the Motorcycle Safety Foundation in 2010. About the same time, I started to notice ladies posting pictures on Facebook of a motorcycle photo shoot. They were all rad chicks with rad bikes!"

Those ladies ended up being the Stilettos on Steel in Wisconsin. At the time, there were no membership dues and members weren't required to own a motorcycle. So Burklin joined and started to become more and more involved.

At the same time, she went from riding a Honda Shadow ACE 750 to a Yamaha Midnight Star 1600. There was a Harley Springer in there at some point, too.

"The mission of Stilettos is what inspires me. I believe all women should know the feeling of empowerment and freedom that comes with riding. Anne and I have put every free moment into growing Stilettos. We love every member, every story, every accomplishment, every milestone. Our lives wouldn't be complete without Stilettos."

As for Burklin's background, she's a divorced mother raising a daughter and works full-time as a consultant project manager and analyst for a large food manufacturer. She's also a Cross Fitter and competitive bikini athlete.

Of Stereotypes and the Future

Clearly the members of Stilettos on Steel do not fit a particular stereotype. If there was one to be filled by those in need of such a thing, it's that these are women who were more than likely strong in their own right but became even more empowered once they threw a leg over the saddle of a bike, twisted the throttle, and rode down the road experiencing the sense of freedom that knows no gender, ethnicity, or affiliation.

Anne's vision is to eventually make Stilettos on Steel a household name and continue to be associated with something positive. She's organized the group in a way that makes it seem bigger than it actually is, but that means everything's in place to continue to handle the growth that going national entails.

With women like Lori and Burklin to help lead the way, that could happen. But probably more important to them, and all of the members is the sense that they are empowering women to do something they might have thought they couldn't, and they're learning to do it right. Like the stiletto, that's an idea that's both sharp and timeless.

There are people who think that because they ride a bike that makes them a biker. But a 100-mile trip and a lunch stop on an occasional weekend doesn't make you a biker. David Mead is a biker, and here's why.

Posers Not Allowed

Reading through the stream of consciousness emails racer and builder David Mead wrote to help tell his story, one can't help but think about a line from an old Monty Python skit that went something like, "I was born at an early age."

Here's an example: "It all started as a child, my father, from industrial Birmingham, home of many a British bike manufacturer, rode old Brit bikes as a means of transport to get to his place of work, and to take his racing pigeons in a big basket on a home-made large rack and let them out to fly home. He would then go as fast as he could to beat them back. We never had a car till early '70s."

There is so much subtext and imagery in there—old Brit bikes, racing pigeons carried in baskets, no car. Try to imagine a guy fifty years ago riding around the midlands of England with a basket of pigeons on a BSA Bantam!

Before the Bantam, there was an Ariel VB600 double sidecar rig that became the equivalent of the family car. Picture that, too, for a minute. Seven people (David's dad, mom, and five kids) and the family dog tooling around England on a weekend in the '60s in a big double sidecar rig.

This was far from David's only exposure to motorcycles. Seems his mother was the third oldest of twelve and already had those five kids by 1959. Her brothers, on the other hand, were younger and had more time on their hands. So like a lot of rebellious teens did in England back then, they became Rockers.

"On one-hundred mile visits to Nan and Grandad down in London, it was great for me to see my uncles and their café racers. One by one, they married and the wedding parties were all rock 'n' roll and '60s' music."

David's uncles, as they say in the States, were the real deal, and he counts them as some of his many different influences growing up. Each one has a unique story.

I turns out that his Uncle Kenny rode, but gave it up when he hit a churchyard wall and came to lying in a cemetery. His Uncle Jim evidently looked like Tom Jones (the singer, not the main character of the novel of the same name) and married David's Aunt Pauline (on his mother's side). Jim and Pauline would visit David and his family in Birmingham riding a 650 Triton outfit, complete with a single seater sports sidecar. One by one, Uncle Jim would take David and his sisters for a spin around the neighborhood.

Most kids growing up in the US at the same time might have gotten their riding start via a mini-bike or dirt bike. A sidecar rig driven by a Rocker named Jim sounds a little more interesting!

David's dad was ex-Army and worked a series of jobs, including truck driver, post office worker, and an engineer in a Lucas factory. His mother, meanwhile, worked just as hard, if not more so, as a school cook and, later, as a factory worker, bicycling four miles one way to work, then carrying shopping on her way back, "...while the men watched TV."

David said the first bike he rode himself was a Honda step-thru the local kids had found at a nearby golf course. The first bike he owned was a 1973 Yamaha 200 he paid 250 pounds for in 1977. A year later, he bought a 650 BSA, which became one of the first bikes he tore down and rebuilt, but not without running into a bit of a problem.

"Some skinheads found out where my garage was, broke in, and smashed up the place. I had the BSA stripped down. All the parts were placed out and cleaned for reassembly. But they scattered them all over the floor. So I went around catching up with them, and they turned out to be kids—fifteen- and sixteen-year-olds. I could not touch them, but I did put some fear in them, so that every time a bike went by their neighborhood, they would run in all directions in fear it was me coming for them."

Learning to wrench came from several different influences. His dad would earn extra cash by working on neighbors' cars or bikes, the latter of which would sometimes find their way into the family kitchen or under a makeshift tarp outside.

Then there's the older guy on David's newspaper route who would take the time show him his bikes—a new 750/4 and a Z900. All of that guy's friends rode similar bikes, so David got to know many of the popular Japanese-made bikes of the day.

Later, David would take on an engineering apprenticeship, but was bicycling, instead of riding, ten miles a day to and from work. This is when his influences included what he describes as "long-haired greaser-types with old '60s' café racers and standard old Brits with silly big ape hangers." One of these "greaser-types" would eventually sell David an older 650 BSA.

And, thus, the seeds were sown for David's long-term interest in bikes....and perpetual tinkering.

"At nineteen, while in a modern bike show room with a friend, I spotted a bright red café racer tucked in a corner, gathering dust. A closer look revealed it was a '59 Triton. I got a loan for 500 pounds and bought it. I stripped it, rebuilt it, and still have that bike today."

From there, David said he went through all of the bad-ass biker stuff. He joined a bike club and got into big fights during the resurgence of the Mods and skinheads in the late '70s and early '80s. He pointed out that he and his best mate, Dennis Evans, were the only two that rode old British iron with clipons and rearsets. (The two have now been friends for nearly fifty years.)

"I had a great couple of years then, but with the fun came the hassles. I had a reputation for not backing down. I'm a loner now and have to deal with it."

Then there's racing, which wasn't part of a particular plan for David. Like so many things, it just happened. He rode a '59 Triton to a vintage race at Cadwell Park, and that got him interested in racing. It didn't hurt that not only did he have a reputation for looking out for himself, he also had a reputation for riding hard and fast.

By this time, he was married and had his first son, aptly named Joe Norton Mead. A job offer soon allowed him to move his family out of London to Cornwall.

It was there that he bought a '71 Bonneville that was mostly in bits and pieces at the time. He built it up and raced it in pre-'72 classics, finishing as high as second in a couple of races during his novice season. He was also beating modern bikes at the Three Sisters Circuit.

He did more work on the bike, and said he got lots of thirds and fourths, but began to more consistently go up against either bigger Triumph triples or better riders, including a former world and Isle of Man champion.

"Peter Elmore, a former racer from the '50s and '60s, saw me racing my Bonny [sic] and was impressed and offered me a 750 Triumph triple he owned that was built by Ron Barret, an ex Triumph race mechanic. I then started to win more races, eventually taking the championship twice and finishing second another time. Sadly, Ron has since died, but both he and Peter became long-time friends."

At the same time, David was participating in hare and hounds off-road endurance races lasting anywhere from two to five hours, with laps of five to ten miles on all kinds of terrain. He won a twin-shock championship and progressed into modern MXers and moved up to clubman class, typically finishing in the top ten.

From there he went on to compete in three Weston Beach races—a chaotic five-mile course with 1,200 starters. David finished all three. But there were races he still hadn't attempted—the TT and Manx Grand Prix on the Isle of Man being two of them. But to get into the former, he had to compete in the latter as an amateur.

"I entered the Manx Grand Prix races in '91, '93, and '95. The first year, I blew the bike up twice in practice, so I never got to race. In '93, I had the eighth quickest qualifying time on a '92 CBR600 in a newcomers race, but I fell off during the race and broke my ankle. I finally finished the third time on a restored old Manx Norton owned by a Reg Satchwell, a former racer from the '50s and '60s."

David eventually left road racing when he was fifty, but the bug is evidently back. He said he's building a 1931 Rudge to race in future vintage class races.

That absence from racing, however, did not entail any absence from riding or building bikes. David turned his sights to long distance travel and going to rallies in England, Wales, and throughout Europe. Those long trips were mostly done on a trike he built, complete with a VW engine, thanks to his daughter.

"About ten years ago, I took my second son, James Vincent, to see the Isle of Man TT. When I returned, my daughter asked me when she could go. I told her I couldn't take them both. So she said, 'What about the old photos of bikes and sidecars that you had?' So that winter, I built the trike and took them both to the Isle of Man the following year."

By the way, not being content to let anything stay as is, that trike now has a Subaru engine.

Having staked an earlier reputation as what some might consider a hard core biker, then builder and racer, David has some words of advice for people who not only want to build, but who want to be in the world of two wheels.

"If I had to advise, I would say, know what they [motorcycles] do, before what they look like. And learn to ride, not pose."

David's dad, uncles, and other influencers in his life would probably smile and nod at that, too. Their lessons about life and motorcycles came to David at an early age and are likely to stay with him forever.

Some people like to wrench bikes, some like to race, some like to collect—Phil Morris has done all three, and thanks to him, old race bikes live to see another day on the track.

Phil Morris Preserves Motorcycling's Fast Past

The motorcycle world likes categories, which is a bit of a paradox, considering its attraction to free spirits and rule breakers. But look at the different types of bikes, races, parts, and variations of the three and you'll see a tendency to put riders into buckets and silos.

Phil Morris defies most of those categories and, in fact, has probably established his own given his past racing career, his admitted predilection to wrenching, and his world-class museum that is an ode to the history of motorcycle racing. Luckily, he realized early on that, despite his wide-ranging interests, the thing he was best at was working on bikes of any sort.

"I started off-road riding when I was twelve and rode a BSA Bantam. I bought it, stripped and fixed it up myself. Tearing down and repairing bikes was always easy for me. I can pick up any bike, strip it, and put it back together in running condition."

Phil admits his interest in bikes as a kid didn't come from a famous European racer. It was due to Evel Kneivel and the desire to mimic his jumping prowess. He and his friends had access to an empty field and the empty trailer that sat in it, so they tried to jump the trailer.

As Phil got older, he tried racing, including off-road, then when he was nineteen, he got interested in racing cars, so he tried his hand at rally racing and managed to participate in some of the top rallies in Europe, including the RAC and Welsh.

"It finally got too expensive to continue once I got married and my family started to grow. Plus, I continued to be reminded that I was far more comfortable with a wrench than I was racing."

So Phil retired from racing and started a cleaning business—far away from the roar of racing engines and the crowd noise that went with it. But a chance encounter put him down the path he finds himself on to this day.

"In 1988, I happened to be talking to the same guy I'd sold one of my old bikes to years before. It was an Ariel Leader, and he wanted to know if I wanted to buy it back. When I went to take a look at it, it was still parked in the same place it had been the day I wheeled it into the guy's back yard."

The Ariel ended up back with Phil, who spent the next several years restoring it. Once it was back to near-original condition, he showed it in different shows and concours events and started winning awards that went with the effort.

While Phil said he'd always collected tin can bikes, some of which had been his dad's, his growing cleaning business gave him the room he needed to start acquiring more bikes and working on them when he could. So the same year he bought the Ariel, he began collecting other bikes.

"I started buying anything I could get me hands on. Road bikes, off-road bikes, trials bikes, and speedway bikes. Then I branched out to concours and racing bikes. At this point, I'm basically fixing up bikes I'm interested in, then selling them so I could buy others. I finally decided I needed to focus, so I started collecting old problem race bikes. That's what I do now."

To say that Phil Morris collects old racing bikes is a huge understatement. He said he currently has fifty-eight racing bikes on display in a building on his property that he operates as a private museum. But three hundred other bikes sit in storage in various stages of repair, looking forward to the light of day.

But his race collection isn't limited to just bikes. It includes 150 sets of leathers, 280 helmets, 100 sets of racing boots, and a variety of visors, knee sliders, and other racing paraphernalia worn by some of the top names in motorcycle racing.

"At one time, if it had two wheels, I'd buy, it. But I'm very specific what I collect now. It has to have a history to it."

Phil estimates his collection is worth about five million pounds, and that includes over 250 TT trophies formally given to winners who, for whatever reason, gave them away or sold them at some point.

Phil's current focus is on acquiring MotoGP race bikes. It includes Valentino Rossi's number two bike from his early days as the European Champion riding in the 125cc class, Mike Hailwood's first racing bike from 1957, Phil Read's Castrol Yamaha 250 that he won on in the World Championship in 1972 as a privateer, and Kent Andersson's 1972 world championship bike. And, by the way, Rossi's number two bike is worth somewhere around £100,000 (US $135,000).

Today, Phil's son runs the cleaning business, since Phil has turned his love and collection of old bikes into a business of its own. If he's not trading or selling up to add to his collection, he's restoring old race bikes to compete in vintage races. He also has his own modern bike race team with Michelin as a major sponsor, and he conducts an annual vintage bike race event called "Road Racing Legends."

"My brother [Colin] and I had gone to a TT Rider's Association dinner and on the way home started talking about starting our own fund-raising charity, and a vintage race would be the main event. If it flopped, we'd pay for it out of our own pockets. We had our first event in 2006, and it sold out. It's been successful ever since."

Phil's collection has been called one of the finest private collections in the world. World champions like Sheene, Fogarty and Chas Mortimer have visited and placed their autograph on the building's double-door entrance. It's free to enter, but it will cost you five pounds to exit. And you better set aside a Thursday to see it, because that's the only day Phil lets the public inside the large two-story building that essentially sits in his large back yard.

While the idea of putting a building of its size in your back yard shows you some level of Phil's commitment to the history of motorcycle racing, what he went through to complete it puts an exclamation point to it. His property sits in what is known as a conservation area with a view of a nearby castle, which limited both the size and height of the structure in which his collection is now housed. So he had to sink the foundation 1.5 meters and build a massive retaining wall between his property and his neighbors.

"I ended up using over 14,000 bricks to build that retaining wall, but it still cost more money to remove the necessary dirt—260,000 pounds."

Phil says he's pretty content with the size of his museum right now. He said he has a lady who comes in to show people around on the one day a week the museum is open to the public, and he maintains all of the bikes himself. So his costs are minimal, and he is, after all, an admitted gear head.

One would think that with all of the bikes at Phil's disposal he'd be hard pressed to figure out which one to ride on any given day, but Phil doesn't ride any of them. In fact, he quit riding road bikes in 2002.

"I was running the cleaning business. I wasn't enjoying riding as much any more. So I stopped."

While Phil may have long since given up riding, one gets the impression that there's no amount of money that could get him to give up collecting. He readily knows which bike he'd like to get his hands on (Mark Marquez's MotoGP bike). You can hear the excitement pick up in his voice as he talks about a particular helmet he owns, like his latest purchase, a helmet owned by the late Mervin Robinson that still has the technical scrutineering sticker in the back.

"My family thinks I'm crazy and would probably like the whole thing to go to auction, but this is what I like to do, and I have a very patient wife."

Let's hope for the sake of those who don't mind being enthralled with more than one aspect of motorcycling that Phil and his wife stay the way they are a while longer.

ACKNOWLEDGEMENTS

While "this book wouldn't have been possible without..." may be one of the most overused statements in literature, it's also one of the most ignored. I'm hoping that whoever reads this book will make their way to this page because there are people who need to be acknowledged for their role in making this book possible.

First, is Mike Fitterling, publisher of Road Dog Publications, who agreed to edit and publish this book. Had he not agreed to take on this project this would have more than likely been a collection of stories that continued to take up the ether on asphaltanddirt.com. Thanks, Mike, for helping me give these stories and the riders they belong to—including you—the attention they deserve.

Second, I have to acknowledge Zoë Cano, who introduced me to Mike and gave me valuable insight as to how best to market and promote this book. I am also in her debt for her selflessness and willingness to introduce me to a good number of the people whose stories are shared here. Without her help, I would have been about half a dozen or more stories short and would have never met Mike.

Third are all of the people in this book who were willing to share their stories with me and then agreed to have me share them with the world. I set out to show and tell that the biker community was filled with far more good and interesting people than the average non-biker or biker may have thought. Every single one of the people in this book helped me make that point.

Finally, while I've dedicated this book to my wife and daughter, I particularly want to thank my wife, Lisa, for supporting this project and my motorcycle passion, and for being actively involved in helping this book become a reality. She did so despite the fact that the idea of riding on the back of a motorcycle scares the crap out of her!

Appendix

Martin Chirotarrab .... www.spiritmotorcycles.com
Phil Anderson .... www.learndirtbikes.com
Jack Stephenson ...www.facebook.com/TheBistroCannonBeach
Jose Mallabo .... www.vireolabs.co
Sheila McQueen............................ highwaylass.wordpress.com
Zoe Cano .... www.zoecano.com/
Books: *Bonneville Go or Bust* & *Southern Escapades*
Alex Crookes ....eatsleepride.com/
Gary France .... www.garysfrance.com/
Book: *France in America*
Ran Zilca...rideofyourlife.com/
Book: *Ride of Your Life*
Jeff Hesseltine ....www.blacklightningmotorcyclecafe.com
Joe Distefano.............................. www.proridersmarketing.com
UniMotorcycle Racing.................... www.unimotorcycle.com/
Alisa Clickenger...................................motoadventuregal.com/
Peter A. Thomas .... Book: *The Darkness Below*
Sons of Thunder .... sonsofthunder.memberlodge.com
Seth Diamond .... www.foodbiker.com
Foster Kinn...fosterkinn.zenfolio.com
Book: *Freedom's Rush*

Chuck Furey......................www.theoneride.net/OurStory.php
Arlene Battishil.. www.gogogearla.com
Michael Kaiser.. kinderriderinc.com
Kevin Dunworth........................www.loadedguncustoms.com
Eric Hermann .... www.ericherrmannstudios.com
Chris Van Dyke ....www.facebook.com, chris.vandyke.902
Bill Kneigge.......................................www.bluestradatours.com
Michael Fitterling ....www.roaddogpub.com
Books: *Thoughts on the Road* & *Northeast by Northwest*
Ryan Walker/Run Riot.........................//www.facebook.com/
Run-Riot-Motorcycles-149838591841494/
Cari Draft .... www.caridraft.com, www.ecotrekfitness.com
Andrew Pain....................................raveling250.wordpress.com
Books: *Ten Things You Should Know Before Buying an Adventure Motorcycle*, *The Minimal Motorcyclist*, *Going Small 2.0—Lightweight Motorcycles All Over Again*, *Ten Things You Should Know about Motorcycle Packing*, *Going Small—A Guide to Lightweight Motorcycle Touring*, *Going North—Pain, Curiosity and a Bear: Volume 1, 2 and 3*, *The Fall of Awesome—A Tale of Super City*, *Under the Radar— Tale of Super City*, *Sidelines*
Jeff Goorman ....www.rockymountainamca.com/people
Lorne Cheetham...............thecustomshow.com/author/lorne
Ginger Damon ....www.gigimontrose.com
Lee Block .... www.ridergloves.com
Erin Hunter Sills ...... www.facebook.com, HunterSillsRacing
Women Can Ride.............................sistersmotorcycleride.com
Antonia Bolingbroke-Kent ....www.theitinerant.co.uk
Books: *Tuk Tuk to the Road*, *A Short Ride in the Jungle*, *The Next One*
Tony Huegel ....www.backcountrybyways.com
Books/Guides: *California Byways*, *California Desert Byways*, *Colorado Byways*, *Sierra Nevada Byways*, *Utah Byways*, *Washington Byways*
Albie Espinola.................................. www.albieespinola.co.uk
Pat Jacques... advwoman.com

Robert Pandya................ www.facebook.com/robert.pandya
Liz Hardy .... www.pillioness.com
Stilettos on Steel .... www.stilettosonsteel.com
Mark Wilsmore .... www.ace-cafe-london.com
Gard Hollinger................................ www.archmotorcycle.com
Phil Morris.................................. www.philmorrisracing.co.uk

Other Books from Road Dog Publications

Motorcycles, Life, and... — ***by Brent Allen***

Sit down and talk motorcycles, life, and...(fill in the blank) with award winning riding instructor and creator of the popular "Howzit Done?" video series, Brent "Capt. Crash" Allen. Here are his thoughts about riding and life and how they combine told in a lighthearted tone.

The Elemental Motorcyclist — ***by Brent Allen***

Brent's second book offers more insights into life and riding and how they go together. This volume, while still told in the author's typical easy-going tone, gets down to more specifics about being a better rider.

A Tale of Two Dusters & Other Stories — ***by Kirk Swanick***

In this collection of tales, Kirk Swanick tells of growing up a gear head behind both the wheels of muscle cars and the handlebars of motorcycles and describes the joys and trials of riding

Bonneville Go or Bust — ***by Zoë Cano***

Zoë Cano dreamed of riding across the US, so she scrimped and saved, and poured over maps. Finally, she took a leap of faith, flew to the US, and began the adventure of a lifetime—riding solo from Boston to LA on a Triumph Bonneville.

Southern Escapades — ***by Zoë Cano***

Zoë takes in a corner of the US missed on her previous journey. Riding from Florida to Alabama and back through Georgia, she finds her way to Barber Vintage Festival, AIMExpo, and Daytona Bike Week.

Thoughts on the Road — ***by Michael Fitterling***

The founder of Road Dog Publications and Editor of *Vintage Japanese Motorcycle Magazine*, ponders his experience with motorcycles & riding, and how those two things intersect and influence his life.

Northeast by Northwest — ***by Michael Fitterling***

The author finds two motorcycle journeys of immense help staving off depression and the other effects of stress. Along the way, he discovers the beauty of North America and the kindness of its people.

Beads in the Headlight — ***by Isabel Dyson***

A British couple tackle riding from Alaska to Tierra del Fuego two-up on a 31 year-old BMW "airhead." Join them on this epic journey across two continents.

A great blend of travel, motorcycling, determination, and humor. —Dee (★★★★★ Amazon Review)

A Short Ride in the Jungle — ***by Antonia Bolingbroke-Kent***

A young woman tackles the famed Ho Chi Minh Trail alone on a diminutive pink Honda Cub armed only with her love of Southeast Asia and its people, and her wits.

In Search of Greener Grass — ***by Graham Field***

On a used Kawasaki KLR650 and with £5,000 the author sets out from England for Mongolia on a solo ride of 15,000 miles in "Search of Greener Grass." Foreword by Ted Simon.

Eureka

Graham sets out on a journey to Kazahkstan only to realize his contrived goal is not making him happy. He has a "Eureka!" moment, turns around, and begins to enjoy the ride as the ride itself becomes the destination.

Different Natures

The story of two early journeys Graham made while living in the US, one north to Alaska and the other south through Mexico. Follow along as Graham tells the stories in his own unique way.

Distributed by:

NBN
national book network

Road Dog
PUBLICATIONS

www.roaddogpub.com